W9-AYF-237

Fictions of
Feminist
Ethnography

Kamala Visweswaran

Fictions of Feminist Ethnography

University of Minnesota Press

Minneapolis ◆ London

Copyright 1994 by the Regents of the University of Minnesota

The lines from "Cartographies of Silence" are reprinted from *The Dream of a Common Language: Poems 1974–1977,* by Adrienne Rich, by permission of the author and W. W. Norton & Company, Inc. Copyright 1978 by W. W. Norton & Company, Inc. "Night-Scene, the Garden" was originally published by Red Dust Press, 1992. Copyright 1992 Meena Alexander. Used by permission. "Rentike cheddah revadi, Nenu ikkada unnanu" ("Do Not Belong to This or That, but I Am Here") by Kalpana Vrudhula reprinted with permission from the *Committee on South Asian Women Bulletin,* Texas A&M University, 7(3–4): 10, "Between Two Cultures: Emerging Voices."

All rights reserved. No part of this publication may be reproduced, stored in a retrieval system, or transmitted, in any form or by any means, electronic, mechanical, photocopying, recording, or otherwise, without the prior written permission of the publisher.

Published by the University of Minnesota Press
111 Third Avenue South, Suite 290, Minneapolis, MN 55401-2520
Printed in the United States of America on acid-free paper
Second printing, 1995

Library of Congress Cataloging-in-Publication Data
Visweswaran, Kamala.
    Fictions of feminist ethnography / Kamala Visweswaran.
       p.   cm.
    Includes bibliographical references and index.
    ISBN 0-8166-2336-8 (hc : alk. paper). — ISBN 0-8166-2337-6 (pbk. : alk. paper)
    1. Feminist anthropology—India. 2. Women anthropologists—Attitudes. 3. Women—India—Social conditions. I. Title.
GN635.I4V57   1994
305.42'0954—dc20   93-37216

The University of Minnesota is an
equal-opportunity educator and employer.

It was only when I was off in college, away from my native surroundings, that I could see myself like somebody else and stand off.... Then I had to have the spy-glass of Anthropology to look ...

— Zora Neale Hurston, *Mules and Men*

Contents

Acknowledgments

Any piece of writing is always, in some sense, a collective project. I wish here to thank the many people who have succored and sustained me, contributing in innumerable small ways to the work that made this book possible. In India I was welcomed by a vast family that includes Mrs. Padma Ramachandran, Shankar, Krishnan, Subha, Geetha, Giri, Choki and Gayatri Iyer, G. Balachandran, Bala Chitti, Gouri, Pratap, Ramacha, Ramani, Raji, Jaya Periyamma, Lalli, Ramnath Athimber, Avinash, and Girish. My Indian family has always graciously endured my American habits and made Delhi a hospitable place. I must especially thank my cousins Shankar, Geetha, and Krishnan Ramachandran, as well as Pratap Balachandran, who good-naturedly helped me in ways too numerous to recount. I can only express my deep affection in return.

In Madras, I thank Pappi, Visalam Mami, and especially S. Balakrishnan for welcoming me into the family house. Madras would not have been the same without my cousin Radha and Subi, my most usual sari-buying companions, who sometimes also accompanied me on interviews or helped me to transcribe them. My debts to them are as numerous as fond memories of their company are innumerable. Of course, without my grandmother, Mrs. Saraswati Ganesan, Madras would not be home for me at all.

My father reintroduced me to India in 1986, and has always patiently borne the transgressions of a wayward daughter. I know my times in India have often caused him anxiety; I hope this book will not cause him more.

I doubt this book will clarify for my family in California, Illinois, and Indiana what it is that I actually do, but I would like to thank G. Visweswaran, Anita Visweswaran, Rani Visweswaran, Raja Visweswaran, Judy and Becky Lumbert, and Maurine and Lawrence

Pierce for their support, and for asking, "Is the book done yet?" so often that I had no alternative but to finish it. I thank also my parents-in-law, Max and Suzy Prat, for their unfailing words of love and commiseration. I am happy to report that "ce fichu bouquin, ce penible livre," is finally finished.

I must perhaps apologize to friends, relatives, and concerned onlookers who may recognize parts of themselves in the composite individuals described in these essays or, to their dismay, find themselves absent from the description where they should be present. If I can only plead guilty to the excesses of fiction, I cannot express the delight in having certain friends who have lived, or shared in detail, some of the experiences described in this book: Kanchana Natarajan, V. Padma, and Lata Mani.

I would like to thank Max Zutty at Routledge Press for his early interest in this project, and one anonymous reader from Routledge for an instructive (if hostile) review. I thank also reviewers for the book at Minnesota: Deborah Gordon, Caren Kaplan, and especially Dorinne Kondo, without whose vision and supportive interventions this book would not have developed out of its early embryonic stages. The staff at the University of Minnesota Press has been a pleasure to work with, especially Robert Mosimann. Janaki Bakhle's consistent involvement in and advocacy of the project this book undertakes have been a great boon. I thank Pushpamala N. for permission to use an image of *The Voyage* for the cover, and Saloni Mathur for her assistance in providing photos of the image.

The physical and emotional labor that went into the making of this book was shared by Nicolas Prat. This book is stronger for his criticisms and insights; I would not have written it without him.

The work of Renato Rosaldo and Patricia Williams has elegantly posed autobiography as a form of social analysis. My debts to their writings may not always be apparent, but these essays were shaped and enabled by their work in particular ways. The influence of Norma Alarcón, a brilliant epistemologist, is perhaps also not evident, but no less insistent. Finally, I would like to acknowledge four writers I have often turned to when the problems and risks in writing this book overwhelmed me: Ruth Benedict, Ella Deloria, Zora Neale Hurston, and Ruth Landes—women who persevered through their work, and by their examples, shepherded me through a long winter.

A Feminist Fable

It was a hot, stuffy afternoon. I was in the back room of the house transcribing an interview from my battery-operated tape recorder. Another power cut had offed the electric fan. The air was heavy and dense; even the faint breeze from the open door to the backyard did little to unsettle its weight. (Yes, I was there.)

I was hunched over the bench, straining with the effort of deciphering what was on the tape. A swarm of the neighborhood's preschoolers burst into the room and buzzed around me like gnats. They were always excited when the tape recorder came out. "Chitty ennadu?" "Ennadu chitty?" No matter how many times I told them, they asked me the same question with unrelenting fascination. "Tape recorder irukku," I said. Smothered giggles, and then the boldest, usually my niece Swati, would ask, "Tape recorder-a?" adding the elongated vowel that in Tamil automatically signifies a question. After affirming its identity again, I'd give them what I thought was a menacing frown and use one of my favorite Tamil-English phrases, "Disturb-pannadeh" (Don't disturb me).

Minutes later, they were back again, giggling and playing tricks. Suddenly patti's figure loomed in the doorway. Although stooped with the pain of a crippling arthritis, her rangy, broad-shouldered body cut an imposing figure. She was known as a gentle and good-natured person, but when she got angry, people stayed out of her way, even naughty preschoolers.

"Scat!" she bellowed. "Can't you see she's studying?"

Patti sat down on the bench where I worked and handed me a cup of coffee. She watched me quietly for a while, then asked what I was doing. I told her I was transcribing an interview. Sensing her confusion about how this could be History (let alone Anthropology, a word I soon gave up trying to say in Tamil), I tried awkwardly to explain, "Like they do on TV sometimes with famous people." Patti frowned, then shrugged slightly. She didn't understand what this activity was about, or what it had to do with a Ph.D., but she knew I was at a university, and for her, that was enough.

*

Has not my grandmother's voice some powerful relationship to my own? But between the grandmother with a third-grade education and her granddaughter from the United States working on a Ph.D., what kind of communication is possible? We were separated not only by language and generation, but by class and culture. Do not be surprised if the relationship between me and my grandmother informs these essays in specific ways. Misunderstandings, missed understandings—only because there is the search for understanding.

That is my opening fable, told, I hope, with equal degrees of nostalgia and irony. Even if my grandmother could read English, she might not recognize herself in these pages. Nevertheless, this book is dedicated to her.

1

Introduction: Fictions of Feminist Ethnography

One of my favorite sets of images is that of Ruth Benedict reading *The Waves* by Virginia Woolf when she was composing *Patterns of Culture* in 1934, and Virginia Woolf reading *Patterns of Culture* when writing her novel *Between the Acts* in 1940.[1] I believe that these images, as with others I will suggest in the following pages, remind us that writing involves reading, and help us to reexplore the relationship between ethnography and literature. To argue that ethnography is literature is to remind us of our presumptions about literature, to ask again, What is literature? To argue that literature is ethnography is to cause reflection about the functions of ethnography, to ask again, What is ethnography? Clearly, such a juxtaposition provides not a unique but another way of posing questions that have been around at least since the genesis of the academic disciplines that make them their object.

If we agree that one of the traditional ways of thinking about fiction is that it builds a believable world, but one that the reader rejects as factual,[2] then we can say of ethnography that it, too, sets out to build a believable world, but one the reader will accept as factual. Yet even this distinction breaks down if we consider that ethnography, like fiction, constructs existing or possible worlds, all the while retaining the idea of an alternate "made" world. Ethnography, like fiction, no matter its pretense to present a self-contained narrative or cultural whole, remains incomplete and detached from the realms to which it points.

Notwithstanding the riveting (but somehow shameful) novels of Carlos Castaneda,[3] the much debated literary (as opposed to scientific) virtue of M. N. Srinivas's *Remembered Village*,[4] or even the long-awaited reappraisal of Oscar Lewis's life histories,[5] posing "ethnography as fiction" does indeed, as James Clifford foresaw, "raise empiricist hackles"; witness the troubled reception of *Writing Culture*.[6] Yet, as Clifford Geertz tells us, the resistance to acknowledging that the writing of ethnography "involves telling stories, making pictures, concocting symbolisms, and deploying tropes" is symptomatic not only of disciplinary worries but also of more general philosophical confusions "endemic in the West since Plato at least, of the imagined with the imaginary, the fictional with the false, making things out with making things up … lead(ing) to the even stranger idea that, if literalism is lost, so is fact."[7]

Whether the bracketing maneuvers that established anthropology as science in Malinowski's day are still necessary is debatable. Yet in identifying the "literary or rhetorical dimensions of ethnography," the "authorizing fictions" of anthropology, the romanciers manqués, or anthropologists who "write a little too well,"[8] even ethnographers of the experimental kind stop short of considering the novel as anthropology. Perhaps because, in spite of recent proposals for reading autobiography as ethnography,[9] or for an "anthropology of literature,"[10] we have yet to fully understand the relationship of the novel to the practice of anthropology. Just as Marilyn Strathern argues that we pay attention to the "persuasive fictions" of earlier anthropological epochs,[11] so too is the question of fiction and anthropology not merely a question of genre, but one of history as well.

If it has become commonplace to remark upon Edward Sapir's or Ruth Benedict's poetry only to skip too quickly to the textual modes of the present, what are we to make of the fact that in 1922, Elsie Clews Parsons corralled most of her male colleagues into contributing anthropological "vignettes" for a collection titled *American Indian Life,* self-consciously designed for a "popular" audience? Concerned that between the novels of James Fenimore Cooper and "forbidding (anthropological) monographs" there was nothing to read for "anyone who just wants to know about Indians,"[12] Parsons intended her collection to be a "book of pictures."[13] Organized broadly into Native American culture areas (Plains, Middle West, Eastern, Southwestern, Mexican, Pacific Coast, Northern Athabascan, and Eskimo tribes), the collection contains twenty-seven stories authored by university and lay anthropologists, BAE ethnologists, museum curators, and one or two tribal members. (Significantly, if problematically, Parsons's piece on the Zuni of New Mexico identifies her as a "Member of the Hopi Tribe.")

It is Parsons's representational style, however, that establishes her as one of the minority voices in this collection, more than the fact that she is the sole woman contributor. Parsons's generalized life history of a young Zuni girl, "Waiyautitsa"—like that of Edward Sapir's Nootka trader, "Sayach'apis," and Franz Boas's recounting of an Eskimo winter—is a rather sedate biographical mode of presentation. More surprising are the writers like Alfred Kroeber, Robert Lowie, Alexander Goldenweiser, Leslie Spier, Alfred Tozzer, or Pliny Goddard—anthropologists more often recognized by their dry theorizing—who seemingly had few reservations about adopting the fictional mode, alternating between first- and third-person narrative devices for their characters. Indeed, Robert Lowie contributed not one, but four, short stories to this collection.[14]

If *American Indian Life* can be said to represent a first (and possibly final) foray into fiction for a number of Franz Boas's male students, there is also the question of the first generation of Boas's female students and coworkers, women such as Ella Deloria, Zora Neale Hurston, Ruth Landes, or Ruth Underhill, who, like Parsons, wrote feminist tracts or novels and pursued anthropological study. Surely to note only that these women anthropologists also produced novels is to lose sight of the ways in which each came to literature, and the conflicting currents of race and class that marked their textual production. Both Parsons and Underhill, for example, were successful journalists, having written essays or novels before turning to anthropology. Parsons turned out a number of feminist tracts before 1915, which she characterized as "propaganda by the ethnographic method."[15] After that date, she turned to empirical anthropology for the methods of studying the ways that "social forces in society checked expression," and her gesture toward fiction in *American Indian Life* must be located in this context. By contrast, Ruth Underhill's first novel, *White Moth,* was published in 1920 to critical acclaim as a romance that also treated the business rivalry between men and women as an emerging facet of modern life.[16] Underhill went on to produce *The Autobiography of a Papago Woman* (1936), which was praised by Ruth Benedict in terms that recalled "Virginia Woolf's essay on the fact-laden realism of 'modern fiction' through which life escapes,"[17] and dismissed by others such as Clyde Kluckohn because the literary qualities of the text diminished its scientific value.[18]

Neither Hurston nor Deloria had professional degrees in anthropology. Hurston began, but never completed, Ph.D. study with Franz Boas. With Hurston, there is not a clear-cut demarcation of her work into novelistic, autobiographical, or ethnographic genres, or even a clear sense that she worked for a time only in one form to begin with another. Hurston's work represents a concatenation and confounding of genres. For example, Hurston is arguably more autobiographical in her mixed-genre ethnography *Tell My Horse* than in *Dust Tracks on a Road,* which reads less as a straightforward autobiography than as an ethnography of the community of which Hurston was a member, leading at least one critic to call it an "autoethnography."[19]

Ella Deloria, who authored *Dakota Texts* in 1932, a classic for students of Sioux cultures, once wondered in a 1935 letter to Franz Boas whether she should have become an anthropologist. It is not clear that Boas ever encouraged her, as he did Gladys Reichard, for in spite of all her work and expertise, she said, "I certainly do not consider myself one."[20] While Hurston's novels enjoyed some success during her lifetime, Deloria's novel *Waterlily* was not published until after her death. In fact, *Waterlily,* with Ruth Benedict's encouragement, was written at the same time as *Speaking of Indians* (a popular ethnography published in 1944) and was aimed primarily at white audiences. Although the two texts share much of the same factual material, *Waterlily* does not attempt to justify Dakota practices to a potentially hostile audience, but rather assumes the sympathy of the reader, and imbeds Dakota practices in a subtly elucidated cultural logic.[21]

These sketches suffice to say that we have much to learn about the many textual forms produced within the broad rubric of Boasian anthropology. They also point back to the reading practices of anthropologists, both in the field and as they write. The myth of the professional field-worker has it that we all take along a "good" ethnography to turn to when our spirits flag in the field and research seems its most dubious.[22] Does it then matter that Laura Bohannon took along on her first field trip a copy of Shakespeare's *Hamlet?* What are we to make of Ruth Benedict sending Margaret Mead a copy of Nietzsche's *Zarathustra* to read in Samoa? Should it surprise us that Benedict's taste in fiction ran to the "high" modern, and Malinowski's to "low" trash?

If, as James Clifford or Mary Pratt have argued, ethnography sought to establish itself against antecedent (and unprofessionalized) genres of the explorer's tale or travelogue,[23] I want to argue that the emerging discipline also self-consciously marked its narrative production against the novel. Consider the recurrent images of Malinowski admonishing himself for reading novels in his posthumously published *Diary in the Strict Sense of the Term.* He reports being absorbed by novels and idling away time,[24] warning himself,

"Don't read novels unless this is necessary. Try *not* to forget creative ideas."[25] Several more resolutions not to read or "break work with novels" follow.[26] But Malinowski continues to read, "having guilt feelings. It is so easy to read two or three novels a day!"[27]

It is true that early anthropologists, in the process of "disciplinization," had to wrest the field from the hands of "amateurs" (colonial officials, missionaries, traders, explorers, members of learned societies), to place it in the hands of newly created professionals.[28] Yet it is also true that the key tool in differentiating the professional from the amateur practitioner of anthropology was science. Malinowski struggles with his science throughout the diary, pondering the "physics and chemistry of history and ethnography"[29] and the mechanics of scientific temperament. At one point, he even chastises the novelist Chateaubriand for lack of "scientific sense."[30]

And yet, Malinowski appears as a lover of literature. The diary records his ruminations on Charlotte Brontë, Ford Madox Ford, Conrad, *Tess of the D'Urbervilles,* and leafing through Dostoyevski "unable to concentrate."[31] It also reveals an obsession with "trashy novels."[32] At one point Malinowski has to remind himself to read ethnography:

> I ... resolve to shun the line of least resistance in the matter of novels. I am very content that I have not fallen into the habit of smoking. Now I must accomplish the same thing in respect to reading. I may read poems and serious things, but I must absolutely avoid reading trashy novels. And I *should* read ethnographic works.[33]

At various points, Malinowski even thinks of writing a novel — "Excellent setting for a novel" — then wonders, "What about the plot?"[34] only to later rail against his "continual novelistic fantasies."[35] The psychoanalytic metaphors should not be lost here: anthropology appears as conscient science, defined (contrarily) by the act of remembering to do it; the novel as the product of unconscious fantasy that impinges on work to be done.

Malinowski's diary represents an odd triangulation between the novel, the diary, and ethnography. Reading novels prevents him from working on his diary or doing ethnography, yet the diary is where he records his acts of reading: novels as well as ethnography. The diary functions as a kind of self-help book for Malinowski, it is not primarily his device for reading, writing, or doing ethnography. It is ironic that Malinowski's diary of the field does not exactly correspond to the tradition of "field diaries" so associated with his name.

It is not surprising, then, if we view Malinowski's diary as a psychoanalytic rendering not so much of his life at a particular moment, but of the prospects for anthropology, that near the end of his diary Malinowski records a kind of epiphany about his reading of novels. "I must note a certain progress: after reading these things today (Grimshaw and a novel by Locke), when I am still very weak and tired, novels attract me as a 'window open on life.' "[36] Malinowski then (if in his weakness) recognizes that the novel, like ethnography, presents a perspective on life.

Perhaps it is in resuscitating Malinowski's lesser-known heritage, an anthropological self that took pleasure in the plots and twists that structure drama as life, that space for both reading and writing the novel as anthropology is to be found. Notwithstanding one feminist's exorcism of a founding father, the paradox is as potentially empowering as it is profound: Malinowski, wistful, romantic would-be writer of the novel, and its compulsive reader.

Malinowski's diary raises new questions about the relationship of the novel to anthropology. Yet the diary itself has typically been the signpost demarcating the limits of self-revelation in anthropological writing, working to cast sufficient doubt upon the autobiographical as a legitimate source of anthropological knowledge. And yet what we see again is a tangling of genres: autobiography and ethnography. Although historians of anthropology such as George Stocking and Deborah Gordon have revealed much about the imbrication of biography in the intellectual production of ethnography,[37] we have yet to fully understand the relationship between autobiography and ethnography. If it seems that the diaries or autobiographical accounts of a Malinowski, Mead, or Benedict were kept remarkably separate from the field accounts these authors generated, I want to argue that there was also a conflation of these genres at particular junctures.

The most obvious collapsing occurs with the tactics of elicitation practiced by many of Boas's students. Life history narratives were collected from the (often last-) living members of particular tribes or cultural groups to stand as testimonies for lost ways of life. Thus, the life history of an individual came to stand for the life history of a vanishing culture. Ethnography then explored the construction of a culturally constructed self, rather than the individual specificity of that constructed self. This collapsing was in part facilitated because many Native American cultures may not conceive the author function as one of individual creativity or genius but as one of conveying, rather than originating, cultural material.[38] While the notion of a colligative subject or plenary "I" is one that some critics have problematized, others have also suggested that autobiography itself operates as a form of colonial discourse, shunting selves into Western notions of the unique and autonomous subject, noting at the same time the shift of the subject from an individual to a collective one.[39]

Called by some the first "collaborative" texts, for Native American critics they also remain the first evidence of Native American "autobiography."[40] Native American cultures are alive and vibrant today, but contemporary reading of these texts must rest uneasily on the recognition of the practices of the American frontier that obliterated native cultures, and the Boasian liberal ethnography that recorded their passing.

The second collapsing of autobiography and ethnography occurs in what might be termed "ethnographies of race" that emerge between the First World War and the end of the Second.[41] Zora Neale Hurston's *Tell My Horse* and Ruth Landes's *City of Women* are two texts that use the strategy of autobiographical narrative in writing ethnographically about race and gender. It is tempting, in the absence of extensive writing on this subject, to argue that the confluence of race and gender is one juncture at which the boundaries of a newly emergent ethnographic genre are burst by personal narrative; that the rhetorical devices of "objective" ethnography are somehow inadequate to deal with the difficulties and contradictions of writing about race. However, we must await the results of more detailed study.[42] It is important to note that one text written by a black American woman, and another by a white Jewish woman, were both dismissed for not being "proper ethnography." Deborah Gordon's reading of *Tell My Horse* concludes too quickly that written into Hurston's ethnography "are the prejudices, irrationalities and racism that have been relegated to either the ethnographic diary or fieldnotes";[43] Melville Herskovits's objections to Landes were that the research and writing were not done in a "professional" context.[44]

The third moment in articulation between autobiography and ethnography emerges in the sixties and seventies, loosely correlated with a "reflexive turn," and might roughly be termed "experimental ethnography." This moment is examined more explicitly in the following essay, "Defining Feminist Ethnography." What I want to remark upon here is that none of the periodization I have thus far elaborated suggests an easy gendering into "male" or "female" moments of writing. Rather, this periodization asks that we look carefully at the writing strategies adopted by male and female ethnographers at any given historical moment to see how they vary, contest, and inform one another.

The fourth moment, in which this text is located, is for many reasons (with the intrusion of the historical present), less easy to define. It starts with a more elaborate notion of the relationship of autobiography to communities of reception, and a defined politics of location. Nita Kumar's *Friends, Brothers, and Informants* and Margaret Trawick's *Notes on Love in a Tamil Family* are two examples.[45] They navigate the ground between the field diary and the autobiography by terming themselves "field memoirs." Yet reemergence of the field memoir has also ushered in a return to the travel account, or travelogue. Sally and Richard Price's book *Equatoria* is one such memoir, Amitav Ghosh's *In an Antique Land* is another, a novel constructed out of alternating and intertwined sequences of biographical and autobiographical inquiry.[46]

In making the argument that the autobiographical be considered ethnographic knowledge, we must also remember that autobiography has been steadily precipitating toward ethnography. For some of the fundamental premises of autobiography have also broken down. Linking the individual to the universal (especially when the notion of the universal has all but collapsed) is no longer adequate, and in situating an individual within a particular community, the local and specific are broached in ways we might well term ethnographic. Caren Kaplan thus reads ethnography as a means of challenging the genre-structure of autobiography.[47]

Although I am certainly not the first to argue that there is a distinct relationship between autobiography and anthropology, I do want to distance myself from the recuperation of "ethnic autobiography" that would contribute to a generalized "exploration" of pluralist, postindustrial, late-twentieth-century society.[48] Indeed, Michael Fischer argues that the "... process of assuming an ethnic identity is an insistence on the pluralist, multi-dimensional, or multi-faceted concept of self: one that can be many different things, and ... a crucible for the wider social ethos of pluralism."[49] Autobiographies are, of course, fictions of the self, but in my view, this emphasis on pluralism leads to a notion of "trying on identities,"[50] which obscures the fact that identities, no matter how strategically deployed, are not always chosen, but are in fact constituted by relations of power always historically determined.

The essays in this collection transmute and rework the questions of fiction and autobiography presented here. I want to caution, however, that the relationship between fiction and ethnography for marginalized peoples is slightly different from the one I am posing for anthropology. As Talal Asad argues, "Imperializing power has made itself felt in and through many kinds of writing, not least the kind we call 'fiction.'"[51] Still, it is worth remembering that marginalized peoples have often rejected ethnography in favor of other methods of worlding. Albert Wendt, a Samoan writer reviewing the Mead-Freeman controversy, writes pungently about being asked to "examine two contrasting visions of Samoa held by two non-Samoans who claim to know the truth about us,"[52] arguing that in fiction he has built up his own Samoa. There is also the example of Christine Quintasket, who took the pen name Mourning Dove, becoming with the publication in 1927 of *Cogewea: The Half Blood,* the first Native American woman to write a novel. But first Mourning Dove endured the patronage of Lucullus McWhorter, a self-styled ethnographer who charged her with collecting and translating Okanogan texts in exchange for helping her to publish her novel.[53]

There is by now a large literature that proclaims that "natives" are but figments of the anthropological imagination.[54] This assertion, produced just as anthropologists are starting to write about subjects who have now become their audience,[55] needs to be examined more closely. Jorge Luis Borges, for example, asks, "Why does it disquiet us to know that Don Quixote is a reader of Quixote and Hamlet is a spectator of Hamlet?" and then answers, "These inversions suggest that if the characters in a story can be readers or spectators, then we, their readers or spectators, can be fictitious."[56]

With the loss of ethnographic authority, the subjects about whom we write now write back, and in so doing pose us as anthropological fictions. Located in a quest for self-determination, Leslie Marmon Silko's often-contested words mark this fictitiousness as an aspect of "decolonizing the mind":[57] "I tell you, we can deal with white people, with their machines and their beliefs. We can because we invented white people; it was an Indian witchery that made white people in the first place."[58] Finally, in reading through Barbara Pym's wry and elegant ethnographic fictions of the International African Institute in London, where the lives of anthropologists themselves are objects of scrutiny,[59] we must remember that if our subjects write back to contruct us as mere fictions, so, too, do our secretaries.

*

The following essays were written over a ten-year period, from 1984 through 1993, and represent some of my thinking about current quandaries of feminist theory and practice. What I offer is a series of experiments, not programmatic solutions, for the practice of feminist ethnography.

This is a book directed largely (though not exclusively) at North American audiences. This is not to say that I do not anticipate a South Asian readership, but rather to underscore the production of these essays within a series of deconstructive debates specifically located in the North American academy. Many of these debates are hardly the exclusive domain of the American academy. I am, however, painfully aware that discussions about feminist praxis, oral history, and interpretation take radically different forms in South Asian contexts. Apart from the limited discussion in chapter 5, I have not been able to fully address the tenor of those debates here. I do hope to address them extensively in my next project.

Some of the following essays describe events in my doctoral field research in 1987–88 on the participation of Tamil women in the Indian nationalist movement. Initially I was interested in how women in Tamil Nadu dealt with the presence of competing political movements—Dravidian and nationalist—that made different claims on their loyalties. I soon found the interviews with women nationalists more complicated than I had imagined. I discovered that the work I had begun involved not just a simple transcription of their voices, but some kind of analysis of the narratives of nationalism, and the place of the "woman question" in those discourses. The issue of rendering women's subjectivity within the contexts of larger dominant narratives—in this case, Western feminism and Indian nationalism—became of primary importance to me. The question of subject retrieval was not one that could be easily separated from these dominant narratives, and led me to a deconstructive position in regard to both the archival material I had gathered and the interviews I had undertaken. It is partly for these reasons that a deconstructive stance is reflected in chapters 3, 4, and 5. However, the bulk of the interviews and archival materials are dealt with more extensively in the manuscript I am completing, "Family Subjects: An Ethnography of the 'Woman Question' in Indian Nationalism."

I recognize that some readers will feel they need more context to adequately engage the debates about gender and Indian nationalism addressed in these essays. Although I have also wished at times that the "monograph" laying out these arguments had appeared first, I have wanted the dissertation to circulate in India before committing it to book form. As I am still pondering the reactions to the dissertation I have received, "Family Subjects" will take a while longer to complete. I offer this note on the process of production not by way of apology for what some may regard as a fundamental weakness of this text but as a means of underscoring the difficulties and challenges that arise from being accountable to multiple audiences. It has taken me some time to realize that different audiences might require different forms of writing and theorizing.

I am aware that young anthropologists typically produce an ethnographic monograph before they are awarded the essay, a privilege of status normally conferred upon the senior members of the discipline. And yet if I have broken form, surely those same senior writers also recognize that some of the conditions for producing that first monograph have broken down (the tenure system notwithstanding).

George Marcus has recently argued that the essay is a quintessentially modern form, appropriate for the task of experimental ethnography, and "well-suited to a time such as the present, when paradigms are in disarray, problems intractable, and phenomena only partly understood ... a final hedge on the holistic commitments" of anthropology.[60] I regard the essay as a different kind of opportunity for *sustained* systematic analysis that does not attempt the totalizing narrative gestures of the monograph. It can also, as Marcus notes, provide a "metacommentary on the difficulties of doing ethnography in the modern world, while doing it,"[61] enacting, as James Clifford puts it, a "state of being in culture while looking at culture."[62]

In my view, the essay is eminently suited for the converging practices of "conjuncturalism" emerging within feminist theory and ethnographic criticism. With the breakup of discrete cultures, "ethnographic conjuncturalism" as defined by Clifford marks the process of moving between cultures.[63] Moreover, identities, because they cannot be located solely in the continuity of a culture or tradition, are conjunctural and not essential.[64] This conjuncturalist approach to identity, in emphasizing the conditional or contingent, mirrors the insights of recent feminist theory as well. The "feminist conjuncturalist" approach Ruth Frankenberg and Lata Mani describe calls for an understanding of the relationship between subjects and their histories as complex and shifting, yet not "free." They argue that this concept must be carefully specified, used to describe moments, social formations, subject positions and practices which arise out of an unfolding axis of colonization/decolonization, interwoven with the unfolding of other axes, in uneven, unequal relations with one another.[65]

Not so long ago, it was possible to mine the introductory and concluding chapters of an ethnography for its theoretical insights, leaving the "data" of the middle section to the area specialists. In my view, one of the strengths of the essay format is that while it allows for the option of reading the essays out of sequence, it is not possible to read only the initial and final essays for conclusions about the theoretical interventions advanced. If one virtue of the ethnographic essay is that it resists closure, I intend each of the essays below to open out upon adjoining essays as a means of exploring the conjunctures between some arguments and disjunctures among others. I am aware of, and actively embrace, certain contradictions that have marked the exegesis of these essays.

*

Much has changed in anthropological and feminist arenas since 1984, when I first began to think about the possibilities of feminist ethnography. In fact, "feminist ethnography" rapidly developed from an unnamed activity into a full-fledged writing program. Indeed, the same year my essay "Defining Feminist Ethnography" appeared (in 1988),[66] Judith Stacey more hesitantly asked, "Can There Be a Feminist Ethnography?"[67] Lila Abu-Lughod echoed this question two years later with a 1990 essay on the same theme.[68]

The feminist ethnographies that are now appearing are cause both for elation and some concern. If "Defining Feminist Ethnography" has been both read and appropriated in ways I could not have anticipated, I have resisted the impulse to greatly rewrite the essay from hindsight. Instead, I have tried to retain the spirit in which it was originally begun in 1984, which references more the prepublication context of *Writing Culture* than the actual text itself. Thus the essay reads much as it first appeared in the journal *Inscriptions*, although I have changed the conclusion substantially and added material from my 1985 master's thesis, "Reclaiming Subjectivity in Feminist Ethnography," from which the essay was originally derived.

I remain convinced that anthropology must be accountable and responsive to community struggles for self-representation, yet my own thinking on feminist ethnography has certainly changed since 1985, or 1988, when "Defining Feminist Ethnography" appeared in print. Some of the ways in which I now reread this essay and locate it in the context of my current work are addressed in "Feminist Reflections on Deconstructive Ethnography" (chapter 5). For example, if in 1985, I was unable to see why (aside from a conveniently charged "sexism"), the works of women ethnographers were not viewed as textually innovative, I would now argue that this dismissal of feminist ethnography rests in part upon a faulty (albeit gendered) understanding of what constitutes "modernist" anthropology. The question of the "modern" in anthropology is thus a major focus of that chapter.

The essays that follow "Defining Feminist Ethnography"— "Betrayal: An Analysis in Three Acts" and "Refusing the Subject"— reflect radical changes in my thinking and experiment with deconstructive theory, enacting a switch from the "thick" description of an interpretive ethnography to what James Clifford has provocatively called "conjunctural description."[69] "Betrayal" and "Refusing the Subject" rest upon a series of ethnographic and feminist conjunctures. In staging a series of encounters with individual interlocutors, these essays ask what anthropology looks like when the acts of subjects deflecting or refusing our inquiries form a part of the analysis. How does ethnography change when informed by different theories of the subject? Although the intellectual links between the first essay and the two that follow it are perhaps not immediately evident, I do not expound upon them in these two essays, which seek to elaborate deconstructive notions of deferral, displacement, and loss. I ask the reader to bear with me until the fifth essay, "Feminist Reflections on Deconstructive Ethnography," which attempts to address some of the continuities and differences between "Defining Feminist Ethnography" and the essays that follow it. Faced with requests from readers to "explain" "Refusing the Subject" or "Betrayal," my best strategy seemed to be to locate these pieces more explicitly in the interventions I hoped to make with them. In this light I have welcomed the opportunity to clarify certain questions about "postmodern" theory and practice.

Chapter 6, "Feminist Ethnography as Failure" picks up the theme of subject refusal and argues for a feminist practice invested in decolonizing anthropology, and one that rests on the recognition of certain impossibilities, or "failure." The following chapter, "Identifying Ethnography," builds on themes in the first and fifth chapters by exploring the ways in which my own subject positioning is shaped by American identity politics, how identity and community shape anthropological analysis. I review the ways in which ethnography is being reappropriated as "fiction," as autobiography and oral history, by groups previously marginalized by this medium. If chapter 4 plays on the notion of the suspension or disappearance of the subject, "Identifying Ethnography" explores the relationship between claiming an identity or subject-position and particular representational practices. Finally, "Feminist Ethnography as Failure" and "Identifying Ethnography" elaborate on and monitor particular ethnographic conjunctures, the processes of identity formation enacted by shuttling between cultures.

Chapter 8 takes up again the construction of identity by looking at the relationship between the diary, fiction, and ethnography, illustrated in my reading of Malinowski. It is the closest of any of the essays to a "coauthored" text in which multiple readings of a woman's diary are reflected through testimony and experience. "Refusing the Subject" poses a series of unanswerable questions to and about the subject of nationalist historical narrative. "Introductions to a Diary" on the other hand, is founded upon the processes of "being answerable to" the subjects with whom I worked.

The final chapter of this collection, "Sari Stories," completes the move toward fiction by presenting an autobiographical short story as feminist ethnography. This story describes my "home" in India, and the ways in which I am both "at home" and not at home there.

"Sari Stories" enacts an ethnographic description of the ways a gendered body is (ad)dressed intimately by history and culture, age and class. It attempts to make the imaginative leap between what an American woman and a Tamil woman take to be ordinary.[70] In this respect, nothing could be more "ordinary" for many South Indian women than wearing a sari, yet the stories underscore my own confrontations with this most unremarked activity: getting dressed. Of course, the idea of "dressing up" has a history in feminist ethnography, for what we female (as opposed to male) ethnographers wear has some bearing on how we are received as social actors and as anthropologists. There is, for example, the famous scene in *Mules and Men* in which Zora Neale Hurston curses her Macy's-bought $12.74 dress among the $1.98 mail-order dresses at a party,[71] and the well-known photo of Margaret Mead looking less the flapper than a frump in "Samoan dress" next to a local woman in a grass skirt.[72]

This play on the "ordinary" means that numerous Indian and American readers, because they are positioned differently, will respond in different ways to the premises of "Sari Stories." I would only remind readers that the sari is a rhetorical device introducing larger discussions about the social relations between different groups of women.

Throughout this collection I have studiously avoided the heraldic arrival scene. Nevertheless, this collection, and this story, closes with a definite scene of departure and return. Astute readers may notice a potential contradiction between essays such as "Betrayal" and "Refusing the Subject," which offer a critique of realist conventions of ethnography through deconstructive practice, and the final short story, which relies heavily on realist imagery. Although we live in a world of many realisms,[73] this contradiction, if it is that, is common among "hyphenated ethnographers" like me who struggle with the demands of identity and community against the dominant representational practices of social "science," an issue I explore in "Identifying Ethnography." My aim in advancing a variety of narrative forms in these essays is to expose both processes of disaffection and rupture as well as the construction of community and identity.

I can, however, also say that "Sari Stories" is, after all, a strategically posed fiction of selfhood and identity, and that its placement at the end of the collection marks it as critical realist narrative. The autobiographical project is itself a privileged form of impossibility.[74] If I begin with one kind of fable and end with another, I also hope for continual vigilance from readers as they consider both the juxtaposition and progression of these essays: why this particular construction, why this form of deconstruction? If "sisterhood" remains the charter myth of feminism, it is both broken up and reconstituted by contemporary feminist practice in particular ways. It is this very process of sundering and reconstituting, of retraction and assertion that I want to foreground as radical method for feminist ethnography. Of course, I cannot claim total success for this maneuver. Experiments, after all, risk failure.

The essays in this book are focused on the notion that ethnographic accounts are constructed, and tell particular stories — if not always the stories we have come to expect as anthropologists. *Fictions of Feminist Ethnography* clearly calls attention to its own textuality, but it does so in order to better understand the politics of representation, how different narrative strategies may be authorized at specific moments in history by complex negotiations of community, identity, and accountability. Fiction, as we know, is political.

It seems to me that most ethnographic writing, and much recent feminist theory, is founded on the fiction of restoring lost voices. This doubling has led me to address the particular "fictions of feminist ethnography." *Fictions of Feminist Ethnography* plays on the idea that there are demonstrable fictions *of* ethnography in the constitution of knowledge, power, and authority in anthropological texts, and that we may also consider fiction *as* ethnography. This essay has shown that anthropology, from the date of its professionalization in the first part of this century, has always experimented with literary genres of the novel and autobiography. This collection concludes with a short story to show that fiction *is,* indeed, ethnography.

I have often wondered if, in writing "fiction," I would write my way out of anthropology. But by way of an invitation and inaugural prolepsis, I offer words that grace the foreword to M. N. Srinivas's (1976) *Remembered Village*:

> The anthropologist has to be also a novelist able to evoke the life of a whole society.
>
> —Marcel Mauss, *Manuel d'Ethnographie* (1947)

2

Defining Feminist Ethnography

In a recent essay, Renato Rosaldo describes driving through the Santa Cruz mountains, and the following interchange with a physicist who has asked him to define what anthropologists have discovered. As Rosaldo replies in dismay, "You mean something like $E = mc^2$?" it suddenly occurs to him: "There's one thing that we know for sure. We all know a good description when we see one. We haven't discovered any laws of culture, but we do think there are really classic ethnographies, really telling descriptions of other cultures, like the Trobriand islanders, the Tikopika, and the Nuer."[1]

Malinowski, Firth, Evans-Pritchard. This essay is in part a questioning of the discipline's canonization of "classic ethnographies." To ask why it is that the classics most often cited are those written by men, and why it is that what women anthropologists write is so easily dismissed as "subjective," is to invite a mumbled answer of "sexism." Yet, within the latest "experimental" moment of ethnography, ethnographies written by women are again consigned to the margins of what is valorized.[2]

My aim in writing this essay is to describe and suggest possibilities for a "feminist ethnography." Part of this exercise is restitutive, which involves rereading and assigning new value to texts ignored or discarded. In other disciplinary terms—those of literary criticism—this exercise would be called "questioning the canon." Some of the things I will look at are the ways in which female ethnographers confront their biases as Western women, and the processes of identification (or lack thereof) that inform description.

The other part of this exercise is exploratory. So along with the older texts I will reevaluate, I suggest more recent autobiographical and novelistic attempts for consideration. Most of this essay focuses on locating feminist ethnography in the recent challenge mounted by experimental ethnography to ethnographic authority. Anthropology in general can learn from the challenge to ethnographic authority, but this challenge needs to be pushed to its limits. I argue that feminist ethnography can benefit from experimental ethnography's concern for the constitution of subjectivities, but perhaps more important, that experimental ethnography can benefit from a feminist evaluation of some of its assumptions. I will begin by briefly describing competing modes of analysis within feminist anthropology, then consider women's accounts that can be read as feminist or experimental ethnography. In so doing, I level critiques at both the assumptions of feminist anthropology and experimental ethnography.

Competing Approaches in Feminist Anthropology

It is not inaccurate to say that the women's movement in the United States inspired feminist scholarship. But it might be more accurate to say that the women's movement provoked key lines of questioning and demanded answers from academic feminists. The disciplines of anthropology and history were perhaps hardest hit with questions like these: Were women oppressed everywhere, at all historical times, or only in modern capitalist society? Were there female models of power and resistance to "male domination" outside of Western or modern cultures? Infused by feminism's "second wave" and its analysis of patriarchy, this generation of feminist anthropologists tended to cast their arguments against a backdrop of "universal womanhood." For this reason, feminists in the 1970s were sometimes placed in contradictory positions: arguing against essentialism or biological universals on the one hand, but deploying cultural relativism to assert universal sisterhood on the other.

It was in Michelle Rosaldo's work that the tension between relativism and universals was most strikingly evident. In a 1981 article, "The Use and Abuse of Anthropology," she argued for the universal sexual asymmetry of women in relation to men, while taking issue with those feminists who portrayed women of other cultures as "ourselves undressed" — heroines with less sophisticated tools than we, but fighting the same battle against male oppression. In this formula, the oppression of women was the universal product; it was the multiplicands in each society that were relatively different.

It is odd that the study of culture, radical because it emphasizes the nonnatural bases of difference, sparked the opposite effect in feminist anthropology and much feminist theorizing. While women's oppression had different names, it was all part of the same transhistoric phenomenon. For Rosaldo, Mary Daly (the author of *Gyn-Ecology*) probably came to mind as a feminist theorist, who in seeking to prove the commonality of women's oppression wound up with a cross-cultural catalog of women as victims. Audre Lorde's criticism of Daly is by now well known.[3]

Rosaldo opened her essay by arguing that what we now need is not more data (read: fieldwork), but more questions (read: theory). As I see it, this separation of theory from experience loses sight of the fundamentally restitutive value of feminism, and the potential of a feminist ethnography that has yet to be expressed: locating the self in the experience of oppression in order to liberate it. As Susan Griffin says,

> A theory of liberation must be created to articulate the feeling of oppression, to describe this oppression as real, as unjust, and to point to a cause. In this way the idea is liberating. It restores to the oppressed a belief in the self and in the *authority* of the self to determine what is real [emphasis mine].[4]

Rosaldo's separation of experience and theory corresponds to the development of what might be termed "woman-centered" and "decentered" approaches in feminist anthropology. Just as James Clifford noted a late-nineteenth-century division of labor between ethnographers and theorists in anthropology, a similar division exists among feminist anthropologists.[5] The "ethnographers," drawing on the "compensatory scholarship" phase in anthropology ("bringing women back in"), have matured into the chroniclers of women's life history Jane Atkinson and Susan Geiger have so thoroughly documented.[6] The theorists, on the other hand, continue to take a more comparative tack, using field data explicitly to deconstruct Western categories of analysis,[7] or reanalyzing data about women pulled from traditional ethnographies.[8] In contrast to the ethnographer's centering of women in the text, theoretical approaches are becoming increasingly more decentered. That is, if one wants to understand anything about women, don't start with women, but with their relations to men; or analyze relationships among men. This approach is illustrated by Sherry Ortner's analysis of a Sherpa nunnery where women recede from the analysis as the primary analytic category.[9]

It is my contention that a very obvious element has been left out of the above equations for research on women. A woman-centered ethnographic approach need not sacrifice relationality, the virtue of a decentered approach. But rather than foreground men's relationships to one another (which classical ethnography does quite well), or women's relationships to men, perhaps a feminist ethnography could focus on women's relationships to other women, and the power differentials between them. Research on communities of women is a step in this direction,[10] yet relationships between women of the colonizer and women of the colonized also demand systematic attention in the present "postcolonial" world.

There are, however, barriers to this kind of study within the discipline. At birth, feminist anthropology, like her sister subdisciplines, needed to imagine a universal self or "we." The other established was that of "man." Unfortunately, feminist anthropologists have uncritically continued to promulgate this assumption.

Marilyn Strathern's (1987) essay that evaluates feminist anthropology in light of experimental ethnography is a telling example of this assumption.[11] She proposes that feminism and anthropology, instead of being mutually reconcilable, actually work at cross-purposes. She compares the feminist emphasis on experience "as knowledge which cannot be appropriated by others" with experimental ethnography's emphasis on experience, and concludes that while the goal of experimental ethnography is to create a (positive) relation with the other, the goal of feminist anthropology is to attack it. Thus,

> Feminist theory suggests that one can acknowledge the self by
> becoming conscious of oppression from the other. This creates a
> natural kinship between those who are similarly oppressed. Thus one
> may seek to regain a common past which is also one's own.[12]

While Third World women broached the problems of racism, classism, and homophobia that prohibited a universalizing "we" within the American women's movement, it is not a little ironic that feminists in anthropology, versed as they are in the tenets of cultural relativism, maintain an us/them split that does not call into question their own positions as members of dominant Western societies. Insisting on the opposition between a unified female self and male other removes the power categories that exist between all anthropologists and their subjects; the ways in which female anthropologists may pass as honorary males in some societies, or as persons of higher status by virtue of their membership in Western culture.

In experimental ethnography, "pursuit of the other" becomes problematic, not taken for granted. The text is marked by disaffections, ruptures, and incomprehensions. Skepticism, and perhaps a respect for the integrity of difference, replaces the ethnographic goal of total understanding and representation. Feminist anthropology, I would argue, stands to benefit from reevaluating its assumptions about "the other" in terms of experimental ethnography. In the next section, however, I would like to demonstrate how experimental ethnography stands to benefit from a feminist questioning of its assumptions.

"Confessional Field Literature" and Experimental Ethnography

A number of pioneer women anthropologists (continuing through the mid-seventies) portrayed women's lives through the use of third-person objective accounts.[13] Many of the writings I will consider, however, have been dismissed as "popularized accounts," or as "confessional field literature." Often judged as "inadequate science," these first-person narratives have been consigned to the margins of anthropological discourse. In traditional ethnographic practice, if the first-person narrative is allowed to creep into the ethnographic text, it is confined to the introduction or postscript;[14] if a book is devoted to the firsthand experiences of the novice ethnographer, it is after a monograph written in the proper objective manner has been produced.[15]

Proponents of a more experimental mode of writing ethnography[16] have also dismissed such accounts, calling them "fables of rapport," in the end shoring up traditional boundaries of ethnographic authority by showing the process of the ethnographer's "mastery" of culture. George Marcus and Dick Cushman distinguish confessional field literature from experimental ethnography by telling us that

> what is at issue in the self-reflectiveness of recent ethnographies is not merely a methodologically oriented re-telling of field conditions and experiences, such as is to be found in the confessional fieldwork literature which has appeared over the last fifteen years. While such works have certainly helped to stimulate the kind of questioning of the tacit assumptions of research practice that now has led to a more trenchant critical perspective on ethnographic writing itself, their main aim has been to demystify the process of anthropological fieldwork whose veil of public secrecy has been increasingly embarrassing to a "scientific discipline." Such accounts, because they are typically conceived and published as ends in themselves—as separate books or articles—are at best seldom more than tenuously related to their author's ethnographic enterprises. The writers of

experimental ethnographies, in contrast, often represent fieldwork experiences as a vital technique for structuring their narratives of description and analysis.[17]

Thus texts by Paul Rabinow, Jean-Paul Dumont, and Vincent Crapanzano are heralded as exemplars of this new genre,[18] while earlier efforts are treated as so many more throwaway paperback novels. What Clifford and others have missed is that for women writers of this genre, subjective accounts are often first accounts. Moreover, they are as likely to generate tales of distance or alienation as empathic fables of rapport.

The writers I will discuss see the fieldwork experience not only as central to their analyses, but also as definitive of its shaping into first-person narratives. While due respects are paid them for "paving the way" for experimental ethnography, there has been little acknowledgment that these books, radical before their time, had to carve out a space for themselves within a dominant positivist paradigm. Often lumped together with "fieldwork anthologies,"[19] I would argue that anthologies like Saberwal and Henry's (1969) *Stress and Response in Fieldwork* are geared more toward shoring up anthropology as a positive science than are the first-person narratives I review.

These accounts comprise a tradition of women ethnographers, not always professionally trained, often writing in a novelistic or fictive voice about culture. Some of these women were the wives of male anthropologists, men who, upon completion of their fieldwork, continued publishing for a professional audience. Kevin Dwyer[20] has noted that in such cases the male seems to adopt the "objective" explanatory mode, and the female a "subjective, anecdotal" mode.[21] Dwyer suggests comparing the books of Laura Bohannon, Elizabeth Fernea, Margery Wolf (and I would add Marion Benedict) with those of their anthropologist husbands to get some idea of this contrast. This division of labor, for example, is marked in Marion and Burton Benedict's book *Men, Women, and Money in the Seychelles*. The book opens with Marion Benedict's novelized account of her experiences with a Seychelloise fortune-teller, followed by Burton Benedict's account of the Seychelles economy. The preface to the book reads: "Each of us appears to have had a perception of the field which could not include material gathered by the other, yet each of us recognizes the validity of what the other has written."[22]

Other writers, regardless of their marital status, have also been consigned to the genre of confessional or popular literature: Jean Briggs, Hortense Powdermaker, and Elizabeth Marshall Thomas. We might ask why it is that this genre consists largely of women, and why it is that women more frequently adopt first-person narrative as a means to convey their ethnographic experiences.

One cannot convincingly argue that this was a choice circum-scribed by lack of training, since Bohannon, Briggs, and Powder-maker were professional anthropologists. What is it, then, about the power of the fieldwork experience that cannot be contained in the traditional introductory and concluding margins of anthropological discourse? I shall argue that first-person narratives are being selected by women as part of an implicit critique of positivist assumptions and as a strategy of communication and self-discovery. This strategy is evinced in texts that predate second-wave feminism, for example, Zora Neale Hurston's (1938) *Tell My Horse* or Ella Deloria's (1944) *Speaking of Indians* (discussed in the concluding section), and in a host of texts produced at the onset of second-wave American femi-nism: Jean Briggs's (1970) *Never in Anger,* Elizabeth Fernea's (1969) *Guests of the Sheikh,* Hortense Powdermaker's (1966) *Stranger and Friend,* and Laura Bohannon's (1964) *Return to Laughter.* Finally, first-person narratives of communication and self-discovery are pre-sent in texts such as Marjorie Shostak's (1981) *Nisa* and Manda Cesara's (1982) *Reflections of a Woman Anthropologist,* produced at the ebb tide of second-wave feminism.[23]

Reading Confessional Field Literature as Experiments in Feminist Ethnography

During her fieldwork among the Inuit, Briggs finds herself adopted by an Eskimo family as a "Kapluna" (white) daughter, but constantly bridling under male authority. Issues of autonomy are important to her and influence her relationship with Eskimo women. She tells us,

> On one occasion I nonplussed Allaq by asking why it was that men "bossed" women and made all the daily decisions. Allaq, very resourceful when confronted with idiotic Kapluna questions was silent for only a minute, then said: "Because the Bible says that's the way it should be." Wanting to know whether the situation was rationalized in terms of women's inferiority, I prodded her, telling her that some Kapluna men also boss their women because they believe that women have less *ihuna* (judgement or mind) than men. She assured me this was not the case among Eskimos.[24]

Briggs continues to question Inuit sex roles and rebels against what she comes to see as repressive igloo life, affirming her need for self-expression. The Eskimo with whom she lives see her as angry and irritable. Finally, one day she loses her temper and is ostracized by the community. Briggs is never able to fully comprehend her ostracism, and the dispute evolves into a permanent misunderstanding that she can never repair. The last pages of her book call into question the very nature of ethnographic understanding.

Briggs's difficulties sprang in part from her positionality in Eskimo culture. Questions of positionality more often confront female than male fieldworkers, and the female ethnographer is more likely to be faced with a decision over which world she enters.[25] I will discuss three examples among many.

Elizabeth Fernea's book, *Guests of the Sheikh,* like Briggs's account, marks points of rupture and acts of transgression, underscoring the problems of identification. Living in what is typically described as a "sex-segregated society," Fernea is consigned to the women's world with sometimes disastrous consequences. Although Fernea's identification with Iraqi women is such that she grows used to wearing a veil, and worries about being caught without it, she is unable to entirely accept the restrictions placed on her freedom of movement. When other women of the village ask her out, they insist she first get permission from her husband, "Mr. Bob." No amount of explaining will convince the women that she does not need to get permission from her husband to move freely.

One day Fernea accepts an invitation to go driving in the country with the (female) schoolteacher, and her somewhat disreputable (male) cousin. Fernea's best friend, Laila, wants to accompany them, so Fernea asks Laila if she should first get permission from her father. Laila says no, and Fernea does not pursue the matter.

Upon return to the village, however, Laila's friends are furious with Fernea for having placed their reputations in jeopardy. For an unmarried woman to be seen with an unmarried man, especially one as unsavory as the schoolteacher's cousin, was to risk extreme censure and possibly death, as a father would be forced to act to protect the reputations of other women in the family. Soon the issue is a village matter. If the schoolteacher's cousin were to gossip about the two women in the coffee shops, then the good names of the women and the honor of the entire tribe would be at stake.

Although she and Laila were close in age, Laila's family held Fernea, married and therefore more mature, responsible for Laila's conduct. Fernea's husband is also lectured for "letting his wife go out alone." The incident eventually blows over, but Fernea is either unwilling or unable to describe fully what happens to Laila, alluding only to the likelihood that she was beaten for her disobedience.

I pull my second example from Hortense Powdermaker's book *Stranger and Friend,* the title of which astutely suggests the intrinsic duality of the anthropologist. Observing Lesu women practicing ritual dances, Powdermaker sought a way to stay awake during the long evening sessions. She soon began to practice with the women as a means of relieving the tedium of observation. When she is asked to participate in the upcoming festivities, however, Powdermaker is taken by surprise. Fearing a refusal would be seen by the women as a rejection, she self-consciously agrees, and recounts:

> There I was in my proper place in the circle; the drums began; I danced. Something happened. I forgot myself and was one with the dancers. Under the full moon and for the brief time of the dance, I ceased to be an anthropologist from a modern society. I danced. When it was over I realized that for this short period, I had been emotionally a part of the rite. Then out came my notebook.[26]

Later, being invited to watch ceremonial circumcision of the village boys, Powdermaker decides,

> since I had been identified with the women, even to the extent of dancing with them, it seemed unwise in the hostile atmosphere between the sexes to swerve suddenly from the women's group to the men's. Or perhaps I was unable to switch my identifications so quickly.
>
> From then on the quality of my relationships with the women was different. I had their confidence as I had not had it before. They came of their own accord to visit me and talked intimately about their lives.[27]

It is with the illness of Powdermaker's friend and "best informant" that she feels her uselessness and the tribe's withdrawing into itself. Then she realizes that "no matter how intimate and friendly I was with the natives, I was never truly a part of their lives."[28]

My third example is drawn from Laura Bohannon's "anthropological novel," *Return to Laughter.* Bohannon was perhaps even more acutely aware than were her contemporaries of the disciplinary boundaries surrounding truth and fiction, hence the nom de plume Elenore Smith Bowen. Profound crises of identity mark Bohannon's account, initiated by a confusion over which role, as a woman, she should assume:

> We reached Udama's hut. There the bride was handed to her mother-in-law. The women scrambled in the hut after them. I tried to follow. Udama herself stopped me. "You must make up your mind," she announced loudly so all could hear, "whether you wish to be an important guest or one of the senior women of the homestead. If you are an important guest we will again lead out the bride so you may see her. If you are one of us, you may come inside, but you must dance with us."[29]

Bohannon says that without stopping to consider the ramifications, she went inside. But it is her refusal to remain in the women's world, and her determination to enter the men's world, that eventually earns her the title "witch." Caught in a battle between two powerful village elders, Bohannon, almost against her will, is forced to play out her role as witch.

Bohannon is confronted throughout her fieldwork experience with a number of moral dilemmas, some of which involve decisions to dispense medication or aid those afflicted with smallpox banished from the Tiv homestead. But perhaps the moral problem that upsets Bohannon the most involves what she regards as callous jokes villagers play on the helpless. One in particular haunts Bohannon and recurs as a motif signifying the limitations of cultural understanding: the villagers tell an old blind man a snake is in front of him on the path, then laugh watching him try to run. In the end, Bohannon feels she can come to terms with the villagers' sense of humor because she comprehends the tragedies of Tiv everyday life, in particular the effects of a devastating smallpox epidemic on the village. Finally, there is a "return to laughter."

> Many of my moral dilemmas had sprung from the very nature of my work, which had made me a trickster: one who seems to be what he is not and who professes faith in what he does not believe. But this realization is of little help. It is not enough to be true to one's self. The self may be bad and need to be changed, or it may change unawares into something strange and new. I had changed....
>
> I had held that knowledge is worth the acquisition. I had willingly accepted the supposition that one cannot learn save by suppressing one's prejudices, or, at the very least, holding them morally in abeyance. The trouble lay in my careless assumption that it would be only my "prejudices" that were to be involved, and never my "principles" — it had not occurred to me that the distinction between "prejudice" and "principle" is itself a matter of prejudice.

> It is an error to assume that to know is to understand and that to understand is to like. The greater the extent to which one has lived and participated in a genuinely foreign culture and understood it, the greater the extent to which one realizes that one could not, without violence to one's personal integrity, be of it.[30]

Bohannon's closing words are marked by an awareness of the integrity and ineffability of difference. Recognizing that her "principles" (her use of quotation marks around the word is quite deliberate)— those of positivist science—are a matter of prejudice, Bohannon is a long way from shoring up the boundaries of positivist science. Her questioning does not stop with the distinction between prejudice and principle but extends to the very nature of self.

More recent works by women anthropologists have also been excluded from consideration as experimental ethnography. Marjorie Shostak's book *Nisa,* for example, reveals a complex negotiation of positionality within a single gender domain. Shostak is puzzled by !Kung women's insistence on talking to her about sex. Thinking that the fault must lie with her questions (their misunderstanding what she wanted to talk about), she says,

> All Kung women it seemed, loved to talk and joke about sex. I was still willing to talk about it, but I was not quite as interested as I had been four years earlier. I now wanted to focus on less romantic matters: on friendship, on women as providers, on childcare, and on avenues for self expression and creativity—issues that had also become more relevant to my own life.
>
> Although I made it quite explicit that *my* work involved a broader scope than it had years before, I found conversations drifting, if not being totally diverted, toward sexual topics. Also, the women usually reported on their daily activities in a dutiful manner, but when they discussed their relationships with men—either fanciful or factual— they often expressed delight in *our* work.[31]

Shostak finally decides that talking about sex "may have been easier than talking about more troublesome matters," and concludes that while her "prior reputation may have magnified their tendency to make sex a prime topic of conversation ... certainly it did not create that tendency."[32] Shostak's attempt to balance the !Kungs' agenda with her own is expressed in her equivocation between "my work" and "our work" in the passage cited above.

Such speculation, however, shows the extent to which full comprehension of a cultural other may be blocked by the ethnographer's own conceptual categories. !Kung women may in fact be talking about what is most important to them. Shostak's insistence that sex talk is the fluff before getting down to the brass tacks of emotional relationships is, I think, belied by her own narrative. !Kung women may not articulate "emotional relationships," or, more important, sex is perhaps the idiom through which they describe emotional relationships between men and women. The fact that Nisa alone is able to describe emotional relationships in ways that approximate Western terms is accounted for by her continual contact with anthropologists. Still, Shostak recounts Nisa's own resistance to speak of emotional affairs:

> During our first interview, I asked about the years I had been away. She asked, "You mean about men?" I explained that I hoped we would review everything that had happened to her, men included, but that I now wanted to hear about the truly important things. For the next hour, she talked about lovers, mostly those of the past. No matter how I tried to lead the discussion elsewhere, I met with little success. It was only during later interviews that she seemed to feel comfortable enough with me to discuss some of the more "personal" issues in her life.[33]

The conclusion to this compelling book indicates another ruptured understanding. Nisa has adopted Shostak as a niece, relationships between aunts and uncles with their nieces and nephews being emotionally charged among the !Kung, and particularly significant in Nisa's own life as well.[34] When a girl did not get along with her parents, she simply went off to live with grandparents or aunts and uncles who succored and cared for the wayward child. On the last page of the book, Nisa's words to Shostak are, "My niece, my niece ... you are someone who truly thinks of me." Shostak's reply represents her failure to either accept or understand Nisa's meaning: "Almost every experience I have in life is colored and enriched by the !Kung world and the way Nisa looked at it. I will always think of her and hope she will think of me, as a distant sister."[35] Is Shostak's denial of the kinship Nisa constructs for them due to her feminist bias toward the category "sister" and its positive emotional connotations, or is it perhaps a more subtle repudiation of their unequal child-teacher relationship, with an assertion of one in which they are "equal"?

Unlike Shostak, Manda Cesara, an economic anthropologist, did not set out to study women. During the course of her fieldwork, however, her perspective shifts. She tells us,

> My outburst of anger against the condition of Western women or that of oppressed women generally surprised even me. I was not the least

bit interested in the study of women as a graduate student. I came to Lenda to study the broad problem of the interaction between religion, kinship, and economic activities.[36]

Cesara's identity as a Western woman is confronted in the field by her failing marriage. Changing notions of her own sexuality are shaped by how she comes to understand "Lenda" sexuality and marriage. She recounts a discussion with a Lenda man on the nature of Western marriage:

"Would you like to take your wife to friends, beer drinks, dances, and hold her hand and show the world you love her?"
"That's what you do really?" he asked. I nodded affirmatively.
"No," he said. "If I took my wife, I could not talk to other women. I could not explore what others are like."
I looked at him with as much gravity as I could muster.
"Would you like to be ostracized from couples when you are single? Would you accept, upon meeting a nice married woman, that you should not be attracted to her and could not marry? Would you like to feel alone? Would you like to feel there are few women, or that you may never find one because most are married?" He looked at me with great fright. "No," he said. I took a deep long, satisfying breath. "Then don't complain about your women," I said.[37]

Despite Cesara's feeling of affinity for Lenda women, she is unable to establish relationships with them. She reports:

I seem to be misreading women somehow. Anyway it is a darned lot easier and more pleasant to work with Lenda men than with Lenda women. It's the men who are the talkers here. Women are taciturn, proud, and I would say managerial. Sometimes I have the impression that women see me as foolish for talking to men.[38]

Cesara's book is decidedly experimental. She pastes together, montagelike, field notes, diary pages, letters, and analytic streams of consciousness. Like Elenore Smith Bowen, Manda Cesara is a pen name. And like many a male experimental ethnographer, *Reflections of a Woman Anthropologist* follows the author's first published traditional ethnography.

It is not difficult to read the works discussed above as "accounts which deal with fieldwork as an intellectual odyssey," qualifying them as a kind of experimental ethnography.[39] It is more difficult to read them as "fables of rapport." More precisely, they can be read as the fables of "imperfect rapport" Rabinow's and Dumont's books exhibit. The women ethnographers I have discussed glossed the fieldwork experience in terms of its disjunctions and gendered misunderstandings long before "experimental ethnography" appeared as a historical moment in anthropological practice. Briggs and Bohannon, in particular, question anthropology as a positivist endeavor. Giving these women the credit they deserve is one way experimental ethnography can incorporate a feminist critique of its assumptions. A second criticism of experimental ethnography's assumptions follows.

Women and Natives: Recalcitrant Subjects?

Focus on women's lives has been made an epistemological problem by male ethnographers such as Edwin Ardener and, more recently, Roger Keesing.[40] Ardener attempted to explain men's willingness to provide cultural models for the anthropologist and women's reluctance to do so with the idea of "muted discourse." While Ardener was criticized for biologism and essentialism,[41] the boldest argument of his paper—that men and women in different cultures might have separate realities—has been ignored.

In Keesing's reassessment of Ardener's theory, he attempts to analyze historic and structural reasons for his previous failures to elicit detailed information about women from women. While Keesing's sex was a large barrier, so was the fact that he was commissioned by Kwaio men to record the *kastom* of their society. Women, not initially seeing their activities as a part of this endeavor, saw no point in talking to Keesing. Keesing concludes that "what women can and will say about themselves and their society can never ... be taken as direct evidence of what they know and don't know, or of women's status."[42] Of course, we might consider whether "what men can and will say about themselves and their society is direct evidence of what they know"; however, I choose to see Keesing's report as a welcome rejoinder to feminist anthropologists who returned from fieldwork claiming they could not study gender because it was not "at issue" in that society. Indeed, the fact that it was not at issue may have been the issue. Perhaps women chose not to discuss gender issues with an outsider. I would argue that a feminist anthropology cannot assume the willingness of women to talk, and that one avenue open to it is an investigation of when and why women do talk—assessing what strictures are placed on their speech, what avenues of creativity they have appropriated, what degrees of freedom they possess. Thus far epistemological problems about women as subjects have been framed in terms of anthropological models (like Ardener's), when much feminist theo-

ry outside the discipline takes the problematic of voicing as its starting point. Yet feminist theories of language have not informed
ethnography. In fact, I would argue that feminist anthropologists
stand to learn not only from women's speech, but women's silences
as well. Like Adrienne Rich, we might learn how to plot those
silences, very possibly strategies of resistance, in the text.

> Silence can be a plan
> rigorously executed
>
> the blueprint to a life
>
> It is a presence
> it has a history   a form
>
> Do not confuse it
> with any kind of absence.[43]

According to James Clifford, it is the intercultural dialogic production of texts that constitutes one of the key moments in experimental ethnography: "With expanded communication and intercultural influence, people interpret others, and themselves, in a
bewildering diversity of idioms—a global condition of what Bakhtin
called 'heteroglossia.' "[44] Yet heteroglossia is not a ready-made solution. It assumes voices, most likely male ones, and does not confront problems of coming to voice. Experimental ethnography's critique of anthropology's scientific ethos should also explicitly name
patriarchy, and examine the way in which the scientific voice is at
once patriarchal. This voice, Griffin says,

> rarely uses a personal pronoun, never speaks as "I" or "we," and
> almost always implies that it has found absolute truth, or at least has
> the authority to do so. In writing ... this paternal voice became quite
> real to me, and I was afraid of it.... You will recognize this voice
> from its use of such phrases as "it is decided" or "the discovery was
> made."[45]

This is my second feminist critique of experimental ethnography's
assumptions.

Clifford's analysis of the prospects for experimental ethnography
envisions coauthored, joint texts. As Rabinow points out, proponents of experimental ethnography go only so far in their critique of
anthropological representation; they stop just short of calling themselves into question.[46] Marcus and Cushman note that experiments
with dispersed authority risk "giving up the game."[47] On the con-

trary, I argue that dispersed authority represents anthropology's last grasp of the "other." I am not surprised that no inclusion of work done in ethnic studies or so-called indigenous anthropology is made in experimental ethnography, but I am dismayed. This, despite the fact these writings explicitly challenge the authority of representations ... of themselves. Self writing about like selves has thus far not been on the agenda of experimental ethnography. To accept "native" authority *is* to give up the game.

If we have learned anything about anthropology's encounter with colonialism, the question is not really whether anthropologists can represent people better, but whether we can be accountable to people's own struggles for self-representation and self-determination. Paula Gunn Allen, a teacher and critic of Native American literature, argues that

> when a people has no control over public perceptions of it, when its sense of self is denied at every turn in the books, films, television, and radio shows it is forced to imbibe, it cannot help but falter. But when its image is shaped by its own people, the hope for survival can be turned into a much greater hope: it can become a hope for life, for vitality, for affirmation. [48]

Thus when the "other" drops out of anthropology, becomes subject, participant, and *sole* author, not "object" then, in Kevin Dwyer's words, we will have established a "hermeneutics of vulnerability" and an "anthropology which calls itself into question."[49] Another way in which feminist theory can make a contribution to the study of colonialism is through a critique of the politics of representation itself.

This is my point, alluded to at the outset of this essay, about experimental ethnography not pushing the challenge to traditional anthropology far enough. What would our alternate ethnographic canon look like if it included books like John Langston Gwaltney's *Drylongso,* Maxine Hong Kingston's *Woman Warrior,* or essays like Renato Rosaldo's "When Natives Talk Back"?[50] This is not a uniquely feminist criticism, but it can be expressed in feminist ways.

What would experimental ethnography's concern with the constitution of subjectivities, the politics of *identity,* look like if it addressed a politics of *identification?* If it addressed the dynamics of autobiography and community, rather than authority and disaffection? For a movement that claims interest in experimenting with how selves are constituted or represented, experimental ethnography has been strangely reluctant to embrace other forms of writing, such as the novel, short story, diary, or autobiography.[51] At a time when literary critics read such texts as expressive of culture, why can't anthropologists? Novels, much less novels by Zora Neale Hurston or Ella Deloria, would never be considered anthropology in the old canon, but perhaps they can be in the new one.

Zora Neale Hurston was trained by Franz Boas as an anthropologist, yet she is known more for her contributions to the Harlem Renaissance than for her contributions to anthropology. In part this is because Hurston chose not to objectify African-American cultures using normative anthropological approaches, but to imbed them in the logic of a storytelling tradition. Hurston captures lyrically the idiom and tenor of speech of African-American and Afro-Caribbean communities at particular moments in time, accomplishing what few of her contemporaries in anthropology were able to achieve. My purpose here is not to include an exhaustive survey of her work, since by now the literature on Hurston is exhaustive. I want, rather, to read her tendency to blur genres and to rely on first-person narration both as "experimental" and as an early example of feminist ethnographic work.

In Hurston's ethnography, community is seen not merely as an object to be externally described, but as a realm intimately inhabited. Thus, Eatonville is a community Hurston returns to again and again in her writing. The first half of her 1935 "ethnography," *Mules and Men,* is set there. Her first novel, *Jonah's Gourd Vine* (1934), takes place in Eatonville, and the central characters are modeled after the lives of her own parents, a thread picked up again in her 1942 "autobiography," *Dust Tracks on a Road.* Hurston uses her parents' relationship to explore the construction of gender (and its limits) in the community in which she was raised. The theme of gender relations is one she explores again in *Their Eyes Were Watching God.*[52] Hurston's quest to portray black women as speaking subjects is the underlying thread of this novel, as the protagonist, Janie Crawford, sets out to fight the bonds of silence her first two husbands have placed on her:

> Janie did what she had never done before, that is thrust herself into the conversation.
>
> Sometimes God gits familiar wid us womenfolks too and talks His inside business. He told me how surprised he was 'bout y'all turning out so smart after him makin' yuh different; and how surprised y'all is going to be if yuh ever find out yuh don't know half as much as you think you do. It's so easy to make yo' self out God Almighty when yuh ain't got nothin' tuh strain against but women and chickens.[53]

Some critics, notably Mary Helen Washington,[54] have expressed disappointment in Janie's inability to claim full voice and autonomy. Yet I feel this text can be read as an extended negotiation of gender roles and patriarchy. It is important to realize, however, that Hurston's analysis of patriarchy is often shifting and strategic. For example, *Tell My Horse: Voodoo and Life in Haiti and Jamaica* is a work that mixes the conventions of the novel with those of the travelogue.[55] It is also a text where Eatonville emerges in the pages of a Caribbean ethnography. *Tell My Horse* reveals Hurston's own processes of self-fashioning and her attempts to redefine the terms of her womanhood in different cultural contexts. Gwendolyn Mikell observes that Hurston's feminist perspectives emerge most clearly in the section on Jamaica in *Tell My Horse*.[56] Yet it is perhaps the juxtaposition of *Their Eyes Were Watching God* and *Tell My Horse* that reveals most clearly Hurston's cross-cultural reflections on gender roles and patriarchy. In fact, *Their Eyes Were Watching God* was written while Hurston was still in Haiti conducting the fieldwork that would become *Tell My Horse,* revealing an entirely different relationship between the novel and ethnography than that evoked by Malinowski. Hurston composed *Their Eyes Were Watching God* in seven weeks, during the period of September 1936 to March 1937 when she was in Haiti. It was published when she returned to the United States in September 1937. During the months of February and March 1938, Hurston completed *Tell My Horse,* and it was published later that same year.

Hurston's opening foray on gender roles with a Jamaican man in *Tell My Horse* occurs the day following a wedding both had attended. Hurston tells her readers, "I do not remember how we got around to it, but the subject of love came up somehow."

> He let it be known that he thought women who went in for careers were just so much wasted material. American women, he contended, were destroyed by their brains.... He felt it was a great tragedy to look at American women, whom he thought the most beautiful and vivacious women on earth, and then to think what little use they were as women. I had been reclining on my shoulderblades in a deck chair, but this statement brought me up straight. I assured him that he was talking about what he didn't know.[57]

What follows is a spirited but heated exchange between Hurston and her Jamaican visitor, punctuated by "scornful snorts" and "aggravated grunts" on both sides. At one point Hurston chases her interlocutor to the running board of his car when he exhibits an inclination to end the conversation. As Hurston recounts, "When I showed a disposition to listen instead of scoffing, we had a very long talk. That is, he talked and I listened most respectfully."[58] Hurston's use of humor and sarcasm to chip away at patriarchal attitudes here is instructive. And it is worth noting that Hurston concludes this chapter with an account of female ritual specialists preparing young girls for "love," which is as eroticized as it is a tongue-in-cheek rendering of her interlocutor's notion of the ideal woman: "The whole duty of a woman is love and comfort.... She must accept her role gladly ... not make war on her destiny and creation."[59]

The fifth chapter of *Tell My Horse,* titled "Women in the Caribbean," however, offers a more sustained reflection on her own positioning:

> It is a curious thing to be a woman in the Caribbean after you have been a woman in these United States. It has been said that the United States is a large collection of little nations, each having its own ways, and that is right. But the thing that binds them all together is the way they look at women, and that is right too. The majority of men in all the States are pretty much agreed that just for being born a girl-baby you ought to have laws and privileges and pay and perquisites. And so far as being allowed to voice opinions is concerned, why, they consider that you are born with the law in your mouth, and that is not a bad arrangement either. The majority of the solid citizens strain their ears trying to find out what it is that their womenfolk want so they can strain around and try to get it for them, and that is a *very* good idea and the right way to look at things.[60]

Hurston's move here to posit a strategically unified American womanhood, without invoking the power differentials between different groups of American women, is an important, if problematic one. Notwithstanding Hurston's many controversial positions on race, her intervention here can be read as an attempt to assert an idealized Eatonville to stand for the whole, bypassing a mode of comparison that continually takes white society as the standard of measurement. I believe this interpretation is supported by Hurston's varying descriptions of gender relations in Eatonville, where women are portrayed as powerful (if also victimized), and in Hurston's opening chapter for *Tell My Horse,* in which Jamaican race distinctions are interrogated gently but firmly in her position as an "American Negro." She records with humor the attempt of the president of Atlanta University to establish solidarity with his upper-class mulatto audience in Jamaica by beginning his speech with "We negroes ..."

and the panic and consternation this provoked in his audience, noting,

> When a Jamaican is born of a black woman and some English or Scotsman, the black mother is literally and figuratively kept out of sight as far as possible, but no one is allowed to forget that white father, however questionable the circumstances of birth. You hear about "My father this and my father that" and "My father who was English you know," until you get the impression that he or she had no mother. Black skin is so utterly condemned that the black mother is not going to be mentioned or exhibited.[61]

In speaking for the black mother, a recurrent theme in *Jonah's Gourd Vine* and *Dust Tracks on a Road,* Hurston effectively utilizes a critique of patriarchy to simultaneously criticize a racial hierarchy. It is an attempt to reach across cultural boundaries to establish solidarity with women, to make the transition from the observation "This is how women are treated" to the moral statement "This is how women should be treated." If at times Hurston's generalizations seem to claim too much ground, she is also careful to assert difference and specificity just at the moment she seems to posit an essentialized identity. She portrays at first a bleak picture of Caribbean womanhood:

> Women get no bonus just for being female down there. She can do the same labors as a man or a mule and nobody thinks anything about it. In Jamaica it is a common sight to see a skinny-looking but muscular black woman sitting on top of a pile of rocks with a hammer making little ones out of big ones. They look so wretched with their bare black feet all gnarled and distorted from walking barefooted over rocks.[62]

Yet Hurston as quickly breaks down the picture of "woman as victim" by asserting class as an analytical category, reminding her readers that "upper class women in the Caribbean have an assurance that no woman in the Unites States possesses."[63]

Like Zora Neale Hurston, Ella Deloria worked with Franz Boas and, like Hurston, never attained recognized professional status in anthropology.[64] While her *Dakota Texts* (1932) is a classic for those working on Sioux tribal cultures, her more popularly written ethnography *Speaking of Indians* (1944) is out of print, and her novel *Waterlily,*[65] while written at the same time, was not published until 1988. With Ruth Benedict's help, Deloria cut and revised *Waterlily* in 1947, but Benedict's untimely death in 1948 deprived Deloria of the professional assistance that would have enabled publication of the book.[66] The dedication to the book forty years later still reads, "In Memory of Ruth Fulton Benedict, Who Believed in Waterlily."

In many ways, Ella Deloria's work presents a contrast to Hurston's. *Speaking of Indians* was explicitly written to persuade a potentially hostile white audience of the value and worth of Indian lifeways, and attempted to speak frankly about some of the difficulties of reservation life. In 1945, Deloria remarked to a friend that World War II "had ushered in an era of practical social science, and American Indian Ethnology was no longer perceived as an endeavor with high priority."[67] It is perhaps the wartime context that explains why so much of *Speaking of Indians* is dedicated to Native American contributions to the "war effort." Although Deloria's tone is often conciliatory, she does criticize patriarchal white society. She reasons, for example, that Dakotas fail in business because they sacrifice financial interests for the sake of kin obligations. In recounting the story of a once-successful Dakota rancher, Deloria observes,

> Just when he has some fine sleek steers ready for market, his mother-in-law dies. What does he do? He neglects his shipping program to attend to her funeral. He kills a beef and gives a big feast. The white neighbors are amazed. "Why the man has gone crazy, stark crazy," they say. "What's the matter with him anyway? See? That's the way of the Indian. He can't stand up long."
>
> They cannot possibly know that Dakota kinship requires the utmost in mutual courtesy between a man and his mother-in-law. His mother-in-law had always treated him well as he had her. This that he was doing was an indispensable part of the pattern of mutual respect. This has always been so, between son-in-law and mother-in-law. The white man, with his rude, and sometimes cruel mother-in-law jokes, cannot understand that.[68]

Speaking of Indians and *Waterlily* both emphasize the integrative theme of kinship in traditional Dakota life, and they share some of the same ethnographic anecdotes. Agnes Picotte calls *Waterlily* a "narrative fiction, a plot invented to provide a possible range of situations that reveal how cultural ideals shaped behavior of individual Sioux in social interaction."[69] More specifically, *Waterlily* carves out a space for the analysis of gender by emphasizing again and again the range of women's roles among the Dakota.

Deloria's novel traces the life of the central character, Waterlily, through the lives of her mother and grandmother. Both Waterlily and her mother are married twice (remarriage is permitted after a death or divorce), exemplifying three types of marriage practiced by the Dakota. Waterlily's mother, Blue Bird, foolishly elopes with a man who later abuses her and finally divorces her by "throwing her away" publicly. Waterlily's first marriage is contracted through a form of bride-price paid for her, but when her husband dies from smallpox, her second marriage, like that of her mother, is arranged by mutual consent. "Waterlily had been elaborately bought once; this time she married in the other sanctioned way, the way most women married who had the good sense not to elope—the way of mutual agreement, openly declared."[70] Similarly, when Waterlily joins her husband's kin upon marriage, the differences in her positioning with affinal as opposed to consanguineal kin are demonstrated again, as they were earlier in the narrative of her mother, Blue Bird's, life:

> She was sure of Rainbow's mother. It was her kinship duty to devote herself to a son's wife. She would even scold her own son if she thought him remiss in his care of his wife—no matter who that wife was, no matter how inadequate she might be. That was the role cut out for mothers-in-law, and few women would neglect it, at least in the open, for fear of censure. But as it happened, Gloku was truly fond of Blue Bird.
>
> It was Rainbow's sisters Blue Bird must be cautious with. She watched herself very carefully, knowing she could irritate them unless she conducted herself with extreme tact. If she should be so stupid as to mistake their tenderness as a personal tribute to herself rather than for what it was—their way of honoring their brother and his coming child—and if she should overstep her bounds by making absurd demands on their brother, they would instinctively shift their loyalty from her to him.[71]

Waterlily is a historical novel that attempts to reconstruct nineteenth-century Dakota life before the tribes were forced onto reservations. It is a richly worked tapestry of relations among women located in a community's pride and struggle to survive not only the conditions of nature, but also smallpox infestations and other portents of the arrival of white society.

Texts such as Hurston's and Deloria's speak to the ways in which an analysis of positioning is key to understanding how feminist ethnographers theorize. If in the first group of texts reviewed in this chapter gender appeared as the primary means of negotiating position, Hurston and Deloria's writings expose how race and gender intertwine to establish a feminist ethnographer's positionality. These "anthropological novels" address relationships of power not only within culture, but also between cultures, something the bulk of ethnography, experimental or otherwise, has been slow to undertake.

Barbara Herrnstein Smith, in her seminal essay "Contingencies of Value," reminds us that "the entry of marginal texts into the modern curriculum not only 'opens up' the canon but opens to question the idea of a canon."[72] For what is at stake, as Cornel West reminds us, is not simply the canon, but a cultural and historical crisis, namely, "the decolonization of the Third World associated with the historical agency of those ... exploited, devalued and degraded by European civilization" that renders a radical reordering of the canon necessary.[73] If this essay has questioned the place of confessional ethnography, "anthropological novels," and writings by people of color in the alternative canon of experimental ethnography, perhaps we too can consider the project of feminist ethnography as one that continually challenges the very notion of a canon.

3

Betrayal: An Analysis in Three Acts

Instead of interrogating a category, we will interrogate a woman. It will at least be more agreeable.[1]

In this essay, I attempt to confront some of the dilemmas within recent contemporary feminist theorizing of difference by reading a series of specific social relations ("betrayals") as allegory for the practice of feminist ethnography.

Such a theme is poignantly suggested by Judith Stacey's (1988) article "Can There Be a Feminist Ethnography?" Here Stacey argues that "feminist researchers are apt to suffer the delusion of alliance more than the delusion of separateness,"[2] and that such a delusion may lead to what she calls "the feminist ethnographer's dilemma," in which the ethnographer inevitably betrays (or, I might add, is betrayed by) a feminist principle. Stacey concludes by asserting that there can be no fully feminist ethnography.

In Stacey's narrative, the paired terms *betrayal* and *innocence* metonymically recall one another. Feminist innocence is betrayed by relations of power; betrayal signals the loss of innocence. The terms recur as place markers for the loss of an earlier moment in feminist thinking that theorized a sisterhood without attending to the divides that separated women. Donna Haraway has recently noted that the costs for feminist theory of maintaining such moments of innocence are great,[3] especially in the questioning of what is meant by feminism. If, for example, one exchanged Stacey's definition of feminism based on assumed affinity and identity for a contested field of meanings around issues of specificity and difference, how would a feminist ethnography be reconstituted?

I suggest that "betrayal," rather than signaling the impossibility of a feminist ethnography, can more appropriately be read as allegory for its practice at a moment when feminist theory is repositioning itself along the lines of difference.[4] Allegory, as James Clifford has reminded us, "draws special attention to the narrative character of cultural representations, to the stories built into the representational process itself."[5] It generates multiple levels of meanings, and further allows us to say that "this is a story about that."

If this is a story about "betrayal," then the central, unspoken betrayal here is of course my own assumption of a universal sister-hood between women. At crucial junctures, this assumption both informs and is interrupted by the analysis that follows, forestalling, I hope, any reading of this piece as redemptive allegory. There are places where this analysis is deliberately uneven, points at which I stray from definitive reportage, moments when I undercut my own authority, moments when readers will inevitably challenge my authority. The response of many a disciplinary practitioner confront-ed with questions of authority posed by experimental ethnography has been to attempt a more authoritative account. My response has been the contrary, to offer a decidedly less authoritative account so that readers continually question it as ethnography.

This analysis takes a dramaturgical form. Allegorical in the Shake-spearean sense, it opens with a betrayal and ends with a death.[6] As such it is a story about loss and transgression, violation and disap-pointment. The three acts outlined here are themselves social per-formances, which, as Turner has argued, "enact powerful stories pro-viding social process with a rhetoric and mode of emplotment and meaning." This analysis is framed as theater, not only to emphasize agency as performance, but also to underscore the constructedness and staging of identity.[7] Identities are constituted by context and are themselves asserted as partial accounts.

Agreeing with Marilyn Strathern's analysis of the differences between feminist anthropology and experimental ethnography,[8] Stacey herself posits a certain rapprochement between feminist ethnography and experimental ethnography on the notion of "par-tial accounts." In this essay, however, there is a deliberate concate-nation of the partial account with the partial(ly revealed) identity. For this reason, I attempt a move from the history of the fragment (or partial account) to its epistemology.

Let me then indicate the shape of this analysis in three acts. The key characters are two women, Janaki and Uma, who met when they were imprisoned together in the days of the Indian nationalist movement for committing acts of individual satyagraha. The first act of analysis attempts an "accountable positioning," an effort to situate a series of "betrayals" within an organization of knowledge in order to recuperate it within the parameters of a feminist epistemology that describes the production of knowledge as situated and relational.

Act 2 attempts to work this feminist epistemology into a feminist ethnography by stressing temporality, silence, and the multiple identities set into play by silence. Here my reading shifts to a reading of betrayal as symptomatic of an inequality and power differential between women, as also a marker for women's agency. I examine how Janaki's identity in particular is partial, contradictory, and strategic: how her silences can be read as both resistance and capitulation.

Act 3 of the analysis situates this emergent feminist ethnography in the specific ideological context of its production. It traces the influence of the master narrative of Indian nationalism upon individual narratives as an attempt to locate other sources of ideological subject positioning. I emphasize the importance of Janaki's and Uma's silences, their refusals to speak, by situating them in a larger arena of nationalist silence: the family. Finally, I demonstrate the potential of women's agency to defy the containments of Indian nationalist discourse.

Act 1, Scene 1

First Interview with Uma

Q: At what age were you married?
A: At age sixteen.
Q: That's late for those days?
A: Yes, but my mother married young and she was determined I should marry later.

Second Interview with Uma

Q: What are your ideas about child marriage and widow remarriage?
A: There should be no child marriages. My mother's mother was married when she was one. My mother's sister was married when she was five. That is wrong. At that age what do they know about marriage? These people would act as if marriage was doll's play. Then after ten or twelve years, they would make the marriage legal. After marriage they would put the couple together. This is wrong. It can't be done like that. So a law brought the age of marriage to

fourteen. But that was also wrong, so a new law brought the age of marriage to eighteen.

Q: Have you seen any widow remarriages?

A: I have seen. It was very good, but we should not force them. We can do it only if it's their choice. It's a good thing.

Act 1, Scene 2

A few days later I met Janaki. A friend of Uma's from her jail days, Janaki and I had first met in Uma's home. This time I was meeting Janaki in the cramped quarters of the CPI-M (Communist Party of India-Marxist) office in Washermanpet, a congested area of North Madras, several miles from the orthodox Triplicane neighborhood where Uma lived.

It was now the end of a long (three-hour) interview. I had run out of tape and was getting ready to leave.

"By the way," asked Janaki with a twinkle in her eye, "did Uma tell you she was a child widow?"

I was stunned and shook my head in confusion. At first I thought I'd misheard her. Janaki gave me a triumphant grin. "Yes, that Subramanian is her second husband, the one she married when she was sixteen."

"No," I said slowly, "she didn't tell me that. I always assumed Subramanian was her first husband."

"Well, she was married when she was five or six, then that man died. This Subramanian was very progressive — a Congressman — he didn't mind marrying a child widow. That's why he married Uma."

"Don't tell her I told you so," warned Janaki as she sent me out the door. I could only nod my head in mute agreement.

Act 2, Scene 1

First Interview with Janaki

Q: When you were selling khadi in Madras, did people say anything about your being unmarried?

A: I left that work when the Congress Socialist party came; no one knew I was unmarried. At first there was talk. There were problems when I stayed with my brother and his family. He had three girls. He used to ask, "Why are these girls still unmarried?"

Q: Did your family ask you to leave for the sake of the three girls' marriages?

A: Nobody said anything. I left the house on my own.

Second Interview with Janaki

Janaki speaking:

> Didn't they think that all women who lived in the city were
> prostitutes? Even if there is a party, there are obstacles to joining
> politics. We changed that today. The reason is I myself have stood for
> election. I told my sister that after making a chain I am going to wear
> it. Seeing it, people thought it was the "tali" (marriage necklace), and
> I stood for election.

Act 2, Scene 2

I was sitting in the Egmore Archives looking at Janaki's jail file. Getting the record itself had been quite an achievement. Files were
often misplaced, or the harried and overworked staff often simply
said that the file didn't exist. That was what they had told me the
first time I requisitioned the file. The second time I requested it, I
received it along with nine other files. So now I was looking
through it and trying to make sense of the information it held.
There was the report from the Inspector of Police, Intelligence Section, on the occasion of Janaki's sentencing on January 1, 1941. It
said:

> Mrs. P. R. Janaki is the wife of a Brahmin priest but has not been
> living with him.

But the text of the judgment given a day earlier read:

> Accused is Mrs. P. R. Janaki, wife of one Mr. Ramachandran Iyer, who
> is reported to be employed in a film company at Calcutta and who is
> a four anna Congress member.

To confuse matters more, there was an appeal to the Chief Secretary of the Government of Madras from one T. N. Ramachandran,
"playwright and film director," protesting the sentencing of his wife
P. R. Janaki to C class, the lowest designation in the British prison
classification scheme.

The final document in the file was a letter addressed to a T. N.
Ramachandran Pillai from the General Secretary of the Madras All
India Hindu Mahasabha stating his inability to make inquiries into
Janaki's sentencing.

I was left to wonder, Who was the Brahmin priest? Could it have
been the Ramachandran Iyer referred to in the judgment? But two
documents said that Ramachandran Iyer was involved in films—a
strange occupation for a priest if that was really what he was. Or

perhaps the British officials had just confused the caste name with occupation (a common enough occurrence). "Iyer" was a Brahmin name and Brahmins were the priestly caste.

But then the letter from the Hindu Mahasabha addressed Janaki's husband as "Pillai," a different caste altogether, and a non-Brahmin one at that. There was something disturbing about the way the records almost, but not quite, meshed.

Then I remembered that Janaki had not told me she was married at all.

Act 3, Scene 1

The next time I met Janaki was in Tangam's house. Tangam was a friend who also worked in the women's wing of the CPI-M and who knew Janaki well. In fact, Janaki frequently came over to play with Tangam's two children (they called Janaki "patti," or grandmother). Tangam said she often grew impatient with Janaki's stories, but Tangam's husband liked to listen to her, and so she would seek him out in particular.

I had told Tangam about the record I'd discovered in the archives. Tangam knew the whole story. "We'll ask her about it," she said. "But I don't know if she'll be frank with you."

"That's all right," I said. "If she doesn't want to talk about it, I have to respect her decision."

Act 3, Scene 2

Tangam nudged me. "So tell her about the record you found." Already uncomfortable about the interview, I hesitated before I began.

"Janaki, I found a record at the archives that said 'Mrs. P. R. Janaki. . . .' What does that mean? Why does it say Mrs.?"

"Oh," said Janaki blithely, "we often told the jail authorities we were married so that they would give us more respect and not harass us."

I should have stopped there. But I didn't and I couldn't. "The record says you were married to a Brahmin priest—who was it?"

"No one."

Tangam looked at Janaki. "Why don't you tell her about it?"

Janaki tried another tack. "Oh, yes, as a child I was married to an old man, but we were poor and my family could not pay the groom's family the dowry we promised. As I myself was against getting married, we left it."

"Really?" I asked.

Tangam said to me in English, "She is not going to be frank. I don't know why, but she is not telling you the truth."

"Leave it," I said. But Tangam had grown impatient with the old lady. "Tell her about Ramachandran," she insisted.

Betrayal flickered in Janaki's eyes; they seemed to plead with Tangam not to expose her. Instead, Tangam turned to me and said, "Tell her about the letters Ramachandran wrote."

Janaki's eyes sparked and then her face deflated. Her secret was out.

*

Some things, of course, were clearer, but a high price had been paid for that clarity. The Brahmin priest referred to in the records was Janaki's first husband-to-be. As an arranged marriage it would have been an in-caste affair. Ramachandran, on the other hand, had been the partner of her choice and was not necessarily a Brahmin. As one document suggested, he could have been a Pillai (a prominent non-Brahmin regional caste).

I had wanted to stop, but now I could only see what I had started to its painful conclusion. I did not know the exact nature of Janaki's relationship to Ramachandran, whether they had actually been married or not. I knew only from Tangam that at a certain point Janaki left him to live alone again. Yet it was possible that Janaki had never known of Ramachandran's efforts to get her status reclassified in jail, and perhaps that knowledge would be of some small consolation.

"Did you know," I began, "that someone named Ramachandran had been very concerned about you when you were in jail in 1941? He wrote a lot of letters to people trying to get you into B class."

"No," said Janaki, sulking. But I noticed her face had brightened a little. Then she abruptly turned to Tangam and asked, "Why does she want to know these things?"

Tangam told her: "Only if she knows what it was like for women of that time can she write about it accurately. What were the problems women faced? What were their difficulties? Kamala is very sympathetic; she is not going to blame you. She only wants to understand."

Janaki stared briefly at the wall, then changed the subject.

*

I thought of the foreword to Le Roy Laudurie's book *Montaillou: From Inquisition to Ethnography*. Was I, to use his terms, "ethnographe et policier"? "A kind of obsessive and compulsive Maigret"?[9]

46

What kind of knowledge was I policing, anyway? And what kind of confession did I hope to produce?

In playing detective, I searched for hidden facts, hoping to fit together different pieces of a puzzle. Then followed the interrogation in which I sought confirmation of facts uncovered. "Facts," as we know, are compelling. And facts were compelling me. A will to knowledge had been set into play, but whose will was it? It was a will that was at once alien to me, and one in which, with some shock, I felt myself sentient.

I could not help wondering, Had I been "simply" a cultural anthropologist, would I have gone to the archives to detect the record that gave me conflicting information about Janaki? And had I been "only" a historian, would I have imagined that the women I encountered in the archives might choose to tell me a story at odds with documented "facts"?

Of course, these were ruminations as confused as they were reductive. Anthropologists have been struggling with the interpretation of history, as well as social life, for many years. And oral historians, in particular, have had to address issues of the construction of evidence and narrative veracity from the beginning. No, what happened was not the result of an unforeseen confluence of the methods of history and anthropology, of reading narratives and hearing them.

An inquisition had been set in motion, and I was its naive if unwilling architect. The questions were not merely "Why did Janaki betray Uma, and Tangam betray Janaki?" or even "Why was Tangam's help enlisted in confronting Janaki?" for would anyone have betrayed anyone else had the anthropologist not provided the opportunity? For a year or longer I was paralyzed by this set of incidents. The horror of my trespass lingered. I did not know how I could, or should, write about it. Indeed, I thought more that I could not, and should not.

I recognize that the issue extends beyond my own agency and culpability; it has to do with the very organization of knowledge and structure of inquiry. Still, I want to imply neither a kind of complete, self-willed agency (I only am responsible) nor a kind of total overdetermined agency (what happened was solely the product of my training). The answer, I think, lies somewhere between the two extremes. I had witnessed one betrayal and staged another, but it was equally clear that I was a secondary character in a drama that existed before my arrival, and that would continue after my departure.

*

The three ethnographic acts I have described—Janaki's revelation of Uma's secret and Janaki's story about pretending to be married; my consequent discovery of Janaki's marriage in the archives; and my confrontation of Janaki with Tangam—converge to produce a questioning of the interlocutor. Yet I narrate these events of "betrayal" not with the aim of producing a more vivid confessional ethnography nor with the object of rehearsing the timeworn ethnographic formula that it is only after talking to our informants over a period of time that we eventually learn the "truth." My concern is rather one of epistemology. How do we arrive at what we call the "truth"? And conversely, what is the truth produced by a specific kind of epistemology?

This analysis of betrayal is not a philosophical point about the perversity of information retrieval, nor is it intended as a fable about my loss of innocence as a feminist researcher.[10] It is an attempt to locate myself in a field of power (the West) and in the production of a particular knowledge (about the East). It is an effort at "accountable positioning" (to use Donna Haraway's term), an endeavor to be answerable for what I have learned to see, and for what I have learned to do. Here I want to advance the case for a critical feminist epistemology that finds its stakes, as with other interested and subversive epistemologies, in limited location and, as Haraway puts it, "situated knowledge." This feminist way of knowing sees the process of positioning itself as an epistemological act.

Situated accounts by definition exclude some analytic elements from their purview while focusing intensely on others. Acts of omission are as important to read as the acts of commission constructing the analysis. A partial account also locates one of the ideological processes of subject positioning within the production of knowledge itself: both for the "I" who investigates and the "I" who is investigated. It assumes that the relationship of knower to known is constituted by the process of knowing.[11] Conversely, the process of knowing is itself determined by the relationship of knower to known. Such a focus leads us to ask how the terms of our current discussion, betrayer and betrayed, are implicated in the relationship between some women's refusal to be subject(ed) and my own subject position. Indeed, this essay is perhaps more about the proliferation of a certain kind of subject position that enables me to write than it is about the subject positions of the Tamil women about whom I write.

And what of this subject position, my own location, intellectually and otherwise? It has become almost commonplace to rehearse inventories that begin with middle-class and end with Western or Western-educated.[12] Nor can I better specify the peculiarities of my own positioning (more "second generation" than "postcolonial") by characterizing the contours of my audience. Although the questioning shifts from "who speaks" to "who listens,"[13] such a maneuver has become increasingly sterile, for it is clear that I write for an audience narrowly constituted by the academy, be they feminists, anthropologists, or postmodern critics.

Then there are the expectations and demands of this Western, if not largely American, audience, its hunger for news of the "Third World Woman," which, as Trinh Minh-ha has noted, "came to listen to that voice of difference." Gayatri Spivak has likewise dubbed this the (Third World) "information retrieval system."[14] My admittedly limited strategy as a member of this system is to resist at the junctures I am able, even as I knowingly (if not always willingly) perpetuate it.

Although one of my identities was that of anthropologist, such a term had no currency among the people with whom I spoke. Janaki perceived me as historian, and as such a writer of "official history" — an official history of which she was aware, and in which she wanted to be included. As I argue later, her choice to stage for me only certain aspects of her life has as much to do with the censoring power of official history and nationalist ideology as with her "own reasons." Perhaps along with the situated knowledges Donna Haraway advocates, we can also speak of "situational knowledges" — knowledges produced both in and for a specific context. That is, these acts of "betrayal" can also be read as a series of moments of self-staging and fashioning: Uma's, Janaki's, and my own. Thus I am not concerned with whether Janaki lied to me; I want more to understand why she told me what she did. For Janaki tells me not about being married, but about *pretending* to be married, and it is this staging I want to apprehend.

It is important to recognize that confronted with facts at odds with her story, Janaki does not "confess." For her the secret closest to her heart was not that she was married, but that she was married to Ramachandran. She reveals the facts about her marriage strategically, and in the end when she sees I know of Ramachandran, refuses to either confirm or deny that knowledge. It is also significant that what I learned about Janaki outside of what she herself told me in no way altered the substance of her self-representation as a courageous and independent woman. If anything it deepened and enriched it.

In the end I can only speculate on certain aspects of Janaki's life. That moment of shock when I saw myself reflected in the panopticon has become the space in which Janaki has reclaimed the integrity of her secrets. She is no longer a puzzle for me to solve, but a woman with her reasons, not so unlike me. Finally there is a complicity between different kinds of refusals: Janaki's in refusing to tell me what I wanted to know, and my own as ethnographer, in refusing to tell my audience all it wants to know about Janaki. This strategized complicity between unequal subjects in power unfolds into a peculiar form of knowing, one in which the confounding yet tactical junction of disclosure and exposure is dramatized. In interrupting a Western (sometime feminist) project of subject retrieval, recognition of the partially understood is not simply strategy but accountability to my subjects; partial knowledge is not so much choice as necessity.

*

My first act of analysis has been to suggest that a set of betrayals is emblematic of the unequal power relations involved in the production of ethnographic knowledge. Now let me shift gears and move to another level of analysis. Consider the question: What are the tactics a feminist epistemology can deploy to develop a different kind of ethnography? I want to claim shifting identities, temporality, and silence as tools of a feminist ethnography.

First, a feminist ethnography can consider how identities are multiple, contradictory, partial, and strategic. The underlying assumption is, of course, that the subject herself represents a constellation of conflicting social, linguistic, and political forces.[15] Individual narratives can be seen as both expressive and ideological in nature. However, the category "experience" is utilized not to pin down the truth of any individual subject, but as a means of reading ideological contradictions.[16] It could gauge the processes of subject constitution in the articulation of individual with master narratives.

Experimental ethnography has argued that we play with voicing, but let me suggest that we look not only at language, or how things are said, but also at when and where things are said. The partiality of identity is seen to be inextricable from the contingency of speech. In locating the temporality of speech, we gain another lens on the constitution of subjectivity. Further, understanding gender as a temporal construction underscores what it means to be "at times a woman."[17]

But who said what to whom is equally important, for knowledge is also relational. Here the "truth" is refracted through a series of unequal relationships of power: that between me and Uma, me and Janaki; between Uma and Janaki, Janaki and Tangam. Janaki's reluctance to speak is framed by Tangam's betrayal of her and her own betrayal of Uma. Interpretation was now seriated through a chain of relationships, although one of those relationships—that between Janaki and Tangam—remains outside the purview of this analysis.

In the previous essay, I indicated some of the difficulties of merging feminist theorizing too quickly with strategies of experimental voicing. I suggested that polyphony and multiple voicings are not a solution to the vexed problems of power and authority, and that we should be attentive to silence as a marker of women's agency. I argued that a feminist ethnography cannot assume the willingness of women to talk and maintained that "one avenue open to it is to investigate when and why women do talk; to assess the strictures placed on their speech; the avenues of creativity they have appropriated; the degrees of freedom they possess."[18] Perhaps then, a feminist ethnography can take the silences among women as the central site for the analysis of power between them. We can begin to shape a notion of agency that, while it privileges speaking, is not reducible to it. My aim is to theorize a kind of agency in which resistance can be framed by silence, a refusal to speak.[19] In this my task is partly, as one critic has suggested, one of "measuring silences."[20]

Often our theorization is limited in its formulation of resistance as speech. Bourdieu's notion of heterodoxic discourse is a good example:

> Private experiences undergo nothing less than a change of state when they recognize themselves in the public objectivity of an already constituted discourse, the objective sign of recognition of their right to be spoken and spoken publicly.... This is true not only of establishment language, but also of the heretical discourses.[21]

But Bourdieu has failed to theorize the third term between the "what goes without saying" and the "what cannot be said." This is the "refusal to say," that which is willfully not spoken. Indeed, it is this third term that interests me the most.

Acts 1 and 2 reveal decisive silences in Uma and Janaki's narratives of their marriages. I have dramatized these silences, but this does not mean that listening is not a part of the process of speaking. If we do not know how to "hear" silence, we cannot apprehend what is being spoken, how speech is framed.

It is possible that both Uma and Janaki did not experience their child marriages as something "real" and therefore do not remember them. In this sense, Uma's words, "At that age, what do they know of marriage?" can be taken to be somewhat self-referential. But we cannot rule out the force of social opinion and nationalist ideology—the former, which regarded child widows as objects of fear and disgust, and the latter, which depicted child brides as objects of pity and reform. Uma's and Janaki's refusals to speak of their child marriages reflect the stigmatized nature of this category, and, perhaps, considerable affective distress.

In speaking of her grandmother's child marriage, Uma avoids speaking of her own. Just as in "betraying" Uma's child marriage, Janaki avoids speaking of her own. Here women's silences about their early marriages are bordered by their descriptions of other child marriages. It is almost as if they are unable to think of the fate so narrowly escaped, and this kind of nonremembrance is coupled with a sublated reference to specific women—child widows—with whom they disavow any identification. This disavowed identification, however, is also the means through which they are able to articulate some agency. For a child widow is not in control of her own destiny. She is incapable of acting to change her fate. Indeed, the very source of her widowhood is the sin she has committed in another lifetime, for which she is now paying with the death of her husband. Janaki, for example, talked scornfully of her older sister, widowed at age eleven, who refused to try to change her fate by going to the widow's home:

> She was shaved. After she was shaved, she was given a white sari to wear and could not eat in the evening. She must only sleep on a grass mat, she could not eat hot food. Like this, everything was so strict then.
>
> The family was very orthodox. I ignored the old ways. I joined the women's organization. And my sister, I also opposed her. Always the hypocrisy, if you touched like that she would wash, so orthodox. So I joined. I wanted to do something besides sitting in the house like her.

Of course, Uma avoids the fate of the child widow only because she is remarried to a man who is willing to marry a widow. Janaki, on the other hand, avoids her fate first because of her family's poverty, and second because of her own insistence that the marriage not be finalized. This is the factor that I think triggers Janaki's "betrayal" of Uma.

Yet was Janaki's betrayal of her friend Uma really a betrayal? It was no accident, I think, that the tape recorder was off, or that I was on my way out the door before Janaki made her revelations. In a sense, Janaki had preserved her friend's secret in the moment of its utterance. Was Janaki not, after all, playing by the rules of official history? The tape recorder was off, and the notebook was closed. Therefore, what she told me could not be recorded as "fact." And, as I was on my way out the door, I had no further opportunities to question her about what she had told me.

I read Janaki's exposure of her friend, then, as a partial exposition of her own agency. It is in laying bare the aspects of Uma's life to which I did not have access that the contrast to Janaki's own life is heightened.

During the course of the second interview, Janaki parodies married women like her friend Uma. In asking her about the difficulties married women encountered in jail, Janaki had replied, "Once the husband was arrested, he became so concerned about his wife's chastity that he sent her to jail too so he didn't have to worry that she would run off with another man!" Weeks earlier I'd asked the same question of Uma and she'd commented that "husbands and wives both used to go to jail so they didn't have any problems." Thus Janaki's response to this question reveals a critical deconstruction of nationalist ideology even as Uma's recapitulates it. Gandhi, for example, always emphasized the importance of women securing permission from their father or husband before going to jail. Janaki's betrayal of Uma, then, is a way of emphasizing her own agency at the same time she undercuts Uma's, who, she insinuates, went to jail because her husband sent her there.

In this way, Janaki again constructs her own agency through the projected nonagency of another woman, her friend Uma. In Janaki's eyes, Uma was what she was because of her husband. Had Subramanian not married Uma, Janaki implies, Uma would have lived the rest of her life as a child widow and would not have joined the nationalist movement. Janaki, on the other hand, is presented as a woman of her own self-fashioning.

[Is my audience disturbed at the claim that a woman's agency is constructed in reference to other women, but at the same time resists that reference? Uneasy that I see a contrast not between active men and inactive women but between active women and inactive women? Concerned that a woman's own volition could be contrasted with the lesser, or lack of, volition of other women?]

What I describe now is a specific relationship of power between two women that hinges in part on class difference. For although Uma and Janaki are friends, and both are Brahmin women, their friendship is not immune to the effects of class that radically alter their life experiences. Both women begin their lives as the subjects of child marriages and end their lives alone, though it is not clear whether Janaki can exactly be called a widow. But there the similarity ends. Uma has lived a life of comfort, in a nice house, surrounded by family. Janaki, however, has lived much of her life as an activist alone, in a shifting hand-to-mouth existence. Her narratives are scattered with references to hunger.

The class-differentiated nature of these women's experiences is suggested by Janaki's account of her first political demonstration:

> I was on a march with Ambujammal, Manjubashini, and others that happened to pass by my street. I felt very proud to be marching with them. Then I saw my brother and tears on his face. He was crying, "If women start participating in the Freedom Struggle, where will the country go?" When I saw the tears on his face, I thought the reverse — that they were tears of happiness. But when I came home, he threw me inside a room and slammed the door. He shouted, "Pavi! [Sinner!] We are only poor Brahmins. They are all rich people educated abroad. What does it matter if they are arrested — they will get A class. You will get a warrant in your name and you'll get C class along with the prostitutes." So saying he bolted the door.

In the prison classification scheme of that time, A class was reserved strictly for the nationalist elite, those who could prove they had great wealth or status. B class was more subject to negotiation. One had to have some means, but often one's status was enough to be granted B class, particularly if one was English-educated. Class C was for those with neither means nor status, and it included the category "common criminal." Much energy was expended by nationalists on getting the British to accept the category "political prisoner" in order to be granted minimum B class status. Thus when Uma goes to jail, she has both class and gender privilege. The first because she receives B class, and the second because she is a married respectable woman who has her husband's support. It is this differential that is underscored by Janaki's narrative.

For Uma, marriage is a proudly acknowledged aspect of her identity. But marriage for Janaki is something that she is continually playing with, repudiating one moment and appropriating the next. At times she is the married woman when she is not: as when she buys a gold chain she knows will be taken for a tali while campaigning for election. She is the city woman who is bold enough (and here again the reference to prostitutes) to run for election. Yet she gains respect while campaigning by wearing a gold chain that implies she is married. At other times she is married, but keeps this a secret, possibly because of Ramachandran's occupation, acting, which was not then considered respectable.

In disavowing her status as wife, however, Janaki forfeits the only identity available to her through nationalist ideology. If it is true that the multidimensional nature of Janaki's subjectivity is clearer seen in relief to that of other women, it is equally true that Janaki is ineligible for many of the identities claimed by women that are posited by nationalist ideology: that of mother, daughter, and sister. Janaki has no children, so she is denied the status of mother. She loses both of her parents in early childhood, so she is not the "dutiful daughter." She loses contact with her three brothers after the oldest one disowns her for moving too freely in nationalist circles, so she is no more a sister.

Although Gandhi attempted to open up the subject position of "wife" by arguing that the terms of the marriage contract be changed and women allowed to choose their own husbands, such a move can still be seen as a strategy of containment, an attempt to keep women within defined roles. Janaki's rejection of the only remaining term in this gendered sign-chain—that of "wife"—is perhaps her attempt to forge a different identity for herself as a single woman outside of known familial relationships; thus her appropriation of "unmarried" status through a kind of silence or refusal to speak about her marriage(s).

Nationalist ideology, of course, translates the status of "unmarried woman" into "spinster" or "widow"—both of which are defined by their failure at marriage: the former through a failure to achieve it, and the latter through a failure to maintain it. Janaki avoids both of these identifications, even though Gandhi himself tried to carve out a space for the spinster as celibate, unmarried woman. But in Janaki's self-representation she has never desired marriage and therefore cannot be called a spinster. She has never been married and therefore cannot be called a widow. Janaki, then, resists with her silences and refusals to speak the negative subject positions nationalist ideology would slot her into, widow or spinster, even as she plays with the only positive subject position accorded to her, that of wife. Janaki's experimentation with the role of wife reveals the strategic construction of her subjectivity and the partiality of her identity.

Yet Janaki's resistance is not unproblematic. At times she is trapped by the oppositional subject position she occupies. Uma has lived her life with all the privileges and security of a married woman. Uma's chastity was never in doubt. By virtue of this recognized status she earned the title "chaste woman." The status conferred on Janaki as an unmarried woman is quite different. She struggles to achieve recognition as a chaste woman; her narratives are marked by references to prostitutes and threats to her sexual integrity. Class and status are collapsed in Janaki's narratives to identify her as a lower-class, unmarried woman. Consider, for example, the end of Janaki's second interview:

> Q: Is there any memorable incident in your life during the freedom struggle?
> A: There are so many. I can't say which one in particular ... Well, in Congress there was one Baliah. He was from Trichy. He would come to my house often. But since I was alone he thought he could do whatever with me. I would do stitching. When he came he would give fives and tens (rupee notes). From 1935 to '36 I did needlework. Afterward, when party work came I left it. I am not worried about money. He would come at night to talk about politics. He was a Congress MLA [Member of the Legislative Assembly]. He thought I should go with him when he went to meetings. One day as soon as I saw him, I knew there was something strange. "Sir, please go to my brother's house," I said just like that. They called me to a meeting in Rajapalayam. He insisted I must not go. I gave him the keys and sent him outside.
>   At my brother's house they had gone to a movie. "I'll stay here," he said. "I am stubborn." "You are a pervert," I said, and locked the door and left. When I returned from the cinema he asked why I was not coming to my room. "I am going to my brother's house; I'll stay there only," I said. "I'll come along," he said. I saw the broom and gave him a lot of whacks. An MLA, but then how awful he should be! It happened then, when I was seventeen or eighteen years old. When I lived on Govinda Naickka Street.

It is quite significant that Janaki narrates this episode at the end of the interview. Janaki's response to a question about the memorable incident in her life during the Freedom Struggle is unusual. Most respond with a description of their first meeting with Gandhi or of various other freedom fighters encountered. The fact that Janaki closes this narrative with an episode that marks her vulnerability as a young woman is particularly striking.

The silences irrupted by the betrayals I have described tell us much about the expressive and ideological lived experiences of these two women. The "betrayals" themselves define the parameters of women's agency and identity. They reveal how women who fell outside the sign chain of possible nationalist subject positions could be compelled to construct themselves as lone individuals, even in relationship to their friends. I have discussed the exposition of Janaki's agency in relation to Uma, as well as the relationship of Janaki's agency to the gendered ideological subject positions of nationalism. For the third act of analysis, I will examine in more detail how women's narratives are produced both through and against the master narrative of Indian nationalism. Here I will move from an analysis of women's silences to a discussion, however limited, of their speech.

*

One of Gandhi's interventions in nationalist discourse was to gender it by inscribing the rule of the family into politics; the family is written again as metaphor for the nation. He says, for example, that the "doctrine of satyagraha is not new: it is merely an extension of the rule of domestic life to the political."[22] Yet with "family" now metaphor for the nation, the term becomes discursively fixed, leaving relations within the family pointedly undiscussed.

Even such a schematic understanding allows us to reply more clearly to the historians of India who are puzzled by why the family does not appear to change under nationalism. They are concerned with "the absence in every phase of any significant struggle by women themselves to change relations within or outside the family."[23] Yet the family does not appear to change, because, seen discursively, it is the point of nationalist silence. As Partha Chatterjee has suggested, it cannot change precisely because the Home is the realm of nationalist victory over colonialism when the World has been lost to the West.

But there is no simple reproduction of the family and nation through marriage. Ideological discourses can be interrupted, if only briefly, by individual agency. For marriage is a term negotiated by women in different ways. It is by being married *differently* that women displace the family-nation metonymy and assert their own agency.

This, then, is the ideological context for understanding Uma's and Janaki's agency. Their refusal to speak of their marriages must be measured against this larger silence. Uma, for example is eclipsed in its shadow; she capitulates. She reproduces the nationalist silence on the "woman question" (read: the family) when she is questioned about whether she was able to take up issues of widow remarriage while doing District Congress Committee work:

> There was no time to take them up. Then in our Congress Committee, we discussed what we would do and how we would act after freedom came. In that time, how to get freedom, how to send the Raj out of the country; how to win rule of our country. For us this was the main point. Dr. Muthulakshmi Reddy, Subbalakshmi, women like this only did these things. In the party there was no time to think of this. Then it was, "In which village should we have a meeting? What to say, what to do? In which village should we make propaganda?" Those kinds of things we were doing.

Whereas issues concerning women and the family disappear in Uma's account, Janaki's foregrounds and questions the nature of the family. Here, Janaki's speech confronts discursive hegemony. She describes her sentencing by the district magistrate upon her first arrest:

> Then the question of my caste arose. I said I couldn't say. "Well then, what is your parents' caste?" they asked. I said my mother is of the woman caste and my father of the man caste. "No, no. A family has to have a caste," they insisted. "Is that so?" I said. "In my family there are two castes: a man caste and a woman caste. Nothing else." I was sentenced to three more months in prison because I would not tell my caste. They said they would give me A class just for telling them. If I refused I would get C class. "You can put me in a class even lower than C class," I said. "I am here for my country's freedom, and not for my personal convenience."

Janaki's account is radical. Yet even as it breaks boundaries it is at the same time constrained by them. She questions the caste system by insisting on her gendered status, appropriating a popular saying of the Tamil woman saint Avvaiyar,[24] itself instructive. Avvaiyar, known for her teachings emphasizing wifely duty, was herself unable to square a wifely role with that of the wandering teacher, and failed to reconcile devotion to a cause with service to the husband.[25] Janaki, however, uses Avvaiyar to problematize the family by marking it as a site of power. While families contain both men and women, it is the male that rules the family. Thus gender is like caste, which exists in a state of relational inequality. (Indeed, even the counterhegemonic moments in Gandhi's own thinking often collapsed the status of women with that of the most deprived caste, Harijans, in order to show the baseness of their oppression.) On the other hand, as Janaki's own brother implies, she was likely to get C class along with the prostitutes in any case. But Janaki's refusal to reveal her caste is still a way to assert her agency, even if it is to choose what would necessarily be given to her. There can be no total resistance, but neither is there total capitulation.

I want to emphasize, finally, that Janaki's speech with me, her interlocutor, was as strategic as her silences. She told me the story of her first sentencing on three different occasions, each time with relish and humor. She was disappointed with me the first time, my Tamil was not good enough, I was listening too closely and I missed the punch line. The second time she was impatient with me; I had heard the story before and had laughed without fully appreciating her skill as an orator. But for her third performance I caught all her rhetorical flourishes, the significant pauses, her powerful gestures, and we laughed together for what seemed like a long time.

Close Curtain

Uma died unexpectedly just before I left Madras in September 1988. Unexpectedly because she was a full ten or twelve years younger than Janaki and she had been in good health. Her death was a shock to everyone.

It was the thirteenth day after her death, and this Brahmin family was marking the end of a formal period of mourning by inviting friends to join them for a ritual meal. This was the Subha Sveekaram, the day for the family to push aside sorrow and disbelief with acceptance of the death of their loved one.

Mountains of food were piled on our plantain leaves, and though I did not feel much like eating, I did my best to conform to the idea of the day. Uma's brother was entreating the guests to eat more food, and his wife hovered nearby with an ever-ready platter of rice.

True to the spirit of the occasion, none of Uma's family showed anything but positive emotions, except her young niece, who was openly crying (and later gently reproached for it). The other guests were chatting and sharing pleasantries, except for Janaki, who sat a little way off from the rest.

Janaki watched the others eating, then stared at the food on her leaf. She took a few bites, then pushed the plate away from her in disgust. It was the day of acceptance, but as usual, Janaki was not going to accept anything. "I'm not hungry," she said. And for me those simple words expressed how much she missed her friend.

4

Refusing the Subject

This is the story of a woman who would not talk to me—who refused, in short, to be my subject. It is also the story of how I make her subject refusal itself a subject; of asking what new forms of subject constitution are forced upon her by now inscribing her silence in speech.

"Lies, secrets, and silence" are frequently strategies of resistance. Yet the ethnographer's task is often to break such resistance. Normative ethnographic description itself is rife with the language of conquest: we extort tales and confessions from reluctant informants (or shall I say informers?); we overcome the resistance of recalcitrant subjects when we "master" their language or "subdue" their insistent questioning. The ethnographer finally arrives when she renders a people or person "subject." Even if this text is marked by an absence of trials or triumphant language, does not my puncturing of a carefully maintained silence replicate the same moves of a colonial anthropology? Or does the very shape of this analysis perhaps signal a small victory for the refusing subject? For the story I give you is not exactly about this woman (who even categorically refuses the term);[1] it is rather more about how I negotiate and understand the construction of a silence, how I seek to be accountable to it.

Subjecthood requires a category or name. Yet Denise Riley in asking "Am I That Name?"[2] warns us of the "dangerous intimacy between subjectification and subjection."[3] The naming process itself suggests a juridical or inquisitorial model of history, one that interrogates the subject beginning with the first question, "What is your name?"[4] What, then, if this subject refuses a name, refuses also to be named—as freedom fighter, famous woman, noteworthy newspaper item? What is the relationship between naming and identity, between not naming and subjectification, between speaking "as" and not speaking at all? How should I name this woman who wishes to be anonymous? And what identity do I construct for her?

It is at this juncture that I would argue we pay more attention to our own naming practices in anthropology. Naming, even in the choice of a pseudonym, produces authenticity. The pseudonym is a false name that stands for a "real" person. As such it marks a key site between the real and fictitious in anthropological writing. Yet some fictions are expected, indeed required, to figure both ethnography and authority. Is it not, then, the moment to probe further the relationship between authoring and authorizing fiction?

What if I were to call this resisting subject Françoise or Ghislaine? Surely my audience, anticipating the story of an Indian woman, would object, knowing that the anthropological pseudonym connotes place-name if not ethnic identity. What if I were to give her a typically English or American name—Mary or Susan—and then pronounced those names differently to show the cadence of an English appropriated by another land? Or, what if I were simply to call her Revathi? Surely the easiest choice, since it is unmistakably an Indian name.

That, however, would make my readers entirely too comfortable. I have toyed with the idea of calling my subject Jennifer. Yet that name I doubt you would have accepted. A name conjuring up Western images of fresh youth would hardly have done for an old South Asian woman in her eighties.

So instead I have adopted a tactic from the clandestine correspondence of forbidden love affairs (another dangerous intimacy) and the cheap detective novel. I have decided to call her by an initial, "M." As we all know, the use of a first initial signifies an enigma, a mystery to be solved, an identity to be exposed or unmasked; it is the sign of a linear movement from unknown to known via the process of detection, the end result being discovery and denouement. Of course, my use of the first initial departs radically from the trajectory of the typical detective novel, for here M stands for a person who shall not be exposed, an identity that will not be elaborated on. A noninnocent subject is not, after all, guilty. (Here, perhaps, I commit an epistemic trespass? What are the consequences of theorizing what is hidden and unknown into a feminist way of knowing?)

My objective is to move away from a declarative or official historiography founded on transparent "realist" narrative. For, as Catherine Belsey reminds us, the classical realist text is itself constructed around an enigma:

> Information is initially withheld on condition of a "promise" to the reader that it will finally be revealed. The disclosure of this "truth" brings the story to an end. The movement of narrative is thus both towards disclosure—the end of the story—and towards concealment—prolonging itself by delaying the end of the story through a series of reticences ... snares for the reader, partial answers to the questions raised, equivocations.[5]

Belsey suggests that disclosure is a form of closure.[6] To suspend disclosure, then, is also to forestall closure. This analysis thus will shroud itself in a series of delaying tactics, reticences, equivocations: questions posed, left unanswered, hinging on the practices of deferral. In so doing, I hope to construct what Belsey describes as an "interrogative" text, one that emphasizes the subject split into both subject and object, as continually in the process of construction: a "subject in process."[7] This interrogative text discourages identification of the reader with a unified subject of enunciation. "The position of the author inscribed in the text if it can be located at all, is seen as questioning or as literally contradictory."[8] My authority rests not on positing facts; rather, it risks forfeiture by posing more and more questions. In so doing, my role as an unreliable narrator is activated.

Is it possible to produce an interrogative text without interrogating a subject? In selecting an initial for the woman about whom I will speak, I identify the suspect (pardon me, the *subject*) without naming, without having recourse to the pseudonym. The pseudonym, we remember, stands for a "real" person. Yet this subject neither authored nor authorized her own representation. She did not wish to be "real" for people outside her own history and daily life. Therefore I have written her as a fiction, knowing all the while that you will never accept her as such. For you understand that this story was based on "fieldwork," something recognized as "real" experience. Here I will issue no disclaimers: any resemblance of the following to fictional narrative is intended and purely noncoincidental.[9]

Well, on with the story. . . .

One day I had been visiting my friend's aunt when I mentioned to her that I'd like to meet a close relative of hers, M, a woman who was one of the well-known leaders of the nationalist movement in Madras. My friend's aunt immediately offered to call M. "She is very busy, you know, even at her age she rises by four in the morning! Can you believe it? She's more than eighty! But if I call her I think she'll agree to see you."

My friend Mala had warned me that her great-aunt M had an acute disdain for journalists and had stubbornly refused to grant even one interview over the last thiry or forty years. So I listened with hesitant hopes as Mala's aunt made the call and arranged for me to see M the following afternoon.

The next day I arrived at M's house promptly at 4 P.M. One of her helpers, a woman of perhaps fifty or sixty, whom I took for another relative, opened the gate and gave me a puzzled glance. "I'm here to see M," I said, hoping to clarify matters.

"Yes, well, she's just gone down for her nap," the old woman told me.

"Oh dear," I exclaimed. "Perhaps there's been some mistake. I thought she'd asked me to come at four o'clock."

"Do come in," said the woman, giving me a warm smile, and quite gratefully I followed her inside.

As I recall, I was given some very good South Indian coffee and the usual biscuits. It was a few minutes before M emerged from another wing of the house. She ignored me at first, moving quickly from one corner of the large room to another, shuffling through neat piles of papers and sending out quick orders to a servant. I think I found her presence slightly intimidating. Finally, her helper, standing anxiously nearby, endeavored to introduce me. "Ma, this is Kamala, Mala's friend from the States."

"Oh yes, how is Mala? In the States, is she? A while since I've seen her," said M. We talked briefly about Mala's brilliant academic career, and then M asked me what I was doing in Madras and where I was staying. I told her that I'd come in part to stay with my grandmother, but also that I planned to do research for my Ph.D. "What kind of research?" asked M. I told her I hoped to interview women from Tamil Nadu who had participated in the Freedom Movement.

It seems to me that M, who was anyway not a woman to sit still for long, shot up from her chair to search again through more papers on a desk nearby. Or perhaps she excused herself and went out of the room for a brief moment, I can't say for sure. In any case, I used that moment, discreetly I thought, to pull out my tape recorder and lay it on the chair next to me.

"I'm sorry," said M, turning back to me. "I haven't any more time to talk to you today. I'm very busy."

"I suppose I've come at a bad time," I stammered. "I thought you had time to talk to me today."

"You said you wanted to *meet* me," said M sharply. "Now you've met me." Stunned by the exactitude with which she interpreted the word *meet,* I suggested that we could talk at another time about her experiences in the nationalist movement.

"Yes, yes," she said testily, "but I'm very busy for the next two weeks." M then thrust a paper in my hand as I was shown to the door. It was an invitation to a fund-raiser for the orphanage she ran, to be held in two weeks or so. "If you want, you can come to this," she said.

*

Well, I myself left for Delhi by train the next day, and was not to return for another month. Once back in Madras I was immediately engrossed in a series of interviews with people who seemingly couldn't wait to talk to me. Over time I managed to forget the sting of M's forthright rejection.

I did, however, try to contact M again some months later. After leaving a couple of messages that were unreturned, I once managed to get around M's helpers and actually got M herself on the phone. After I identified myself, she shouted "Who?!" deafly into the phone, and then, "I'm very busy," and hung up.

It was after this second rejection that I became determined to talk to this cranky and energetic old lady. I resolved again to enlist the aid of Mala's aunt.

When I next met Mala's aunt, I explained to her that I thought M had simply forgotten who I was after so many months. Could she possibly call M again? I was leaving for the States soon and I felt it was imperative to talk with her. In fact, everyone I met in Madras repeatedly told me to talk to M. Her name was beginning to follow me around. The more old newspapers I pored over, the more I ran across her name; the more jail files I looked at, the more M's name appeared.

Mala's aunt was, I think, a bit surprised at my request, but generously made the call. Of course, she understood fully what had transpired. "This time," she said, "you must talk to her about the orphanage; it's the one thing she really cares about these days. In fact," she continued, "this time you'll have to meet her at the orphanage — she says that's when she's free during the day."

Two days later I took the bus into T-Nagar, and after quite a walk in the shimmering heat, I reached the orphanage. It was now August, and the year had changed numbers since I'd first met M December last of the winter monsoon.

I was ushered into M's office at the orphanage with great ceremony and told that "Amma" was expecting me. This time M greeted me with a sunny smile. "Yes, I remember you, you're Mala's friend. So you've come to see the orphanage, how nice. We need more young people like you. Here, this is Dipti, Mala's cousin. She'll take you around."

For the next hour and a half, I had the full tour of the orphanage. I visited the work station where teenage girls were printing gift cards, the woodshop where the older boys were making furniture and small knickknacks. Then I saw the nursery, the dormitories, the classrooms, and a puja room.

At the end of the tour I was both impressed and fatigued by the display of well-intentioned hegemony in yet one more social welfare institution. Dipti told me that the older children often did not want to leave once they had reached age eighteen, or that they complained about being schooled only for crafts or trades, and not for an education that would prepare them for a white-collar job. I was also quite frankly distressed to learn that one of M's policies was not to adopt children from her orphanage out to Muslim or Christian families. Only Hindu families were eligible. It seemed to me an oddly communal practice for a confirmed Gandhian like M.

But when I returned to the office, there was M, bright as ever. "How did you like my orphanage?" she queried. I managed, I think, a fairly sincere smile. "I'm very impressed with how well ordered and organized things are," I said. "I see that your care really makes the orphanage work." I think I might have also told her that both of my parents were social workers, which pleased her greatly, though it was more an attempt to avoid speaking of my own conflicting feelings about social work.

M beamed at me, and in a most genial manner delivered the Gandhian lecture to which I was now quite accustomed: how it was the task of my generation to return to India to run institutions like these, to carry out the task of social uplift left uncompleted at Independence, to fight against the graft and corruption that characterized modern India. Almost imperceptibly, she began to tell of her life and times during the nationalist movement, to narrate something of the vision of India for which she had fought. Her words were nostalgic and seductive. I must have perked up noticeably, because her eyes then took on a mischievous glint as she rattled off stories and anecdotes about all the marches she and her girlfriends led, their numerous arrests; about the printing press she set up in her friend's attic to print illegal leaflets during the Quit India movement of 1942.

I sat in front of M's desk, willing myself to accept her narrative

on the terms she had set. I tried not to think of my absent tape recorder, or even the lack of pencil and paper to jot down notes.
Wasn't M herself all too aware that the tape recorder wasn't there to
catch her words? Wasn't that, indeed, part of her play?

I vaguely remember the end of our conversation, but I do recall
M reaffirming her Gandhianness by commenting on her avoidance
of the journalists. "You see," she said, "this work is not about any
one individual or personality. So many people come and want to
give this award or that award, but Gandhiji said that the work itself
is its own reward."

*

I pondered her words as I rode the bus back to Mylapore. In a
sense, M had been saying that what had not been achieved was not
worth the telling. I'd met a subject who refused to historicize herself, who repudiated not only the telling of her own history, but
that of the nation's as well. I felt again, as I had so often after an
interview, the deep anguish of that generation, the form of a question that itself remained unresolved: Had they somehow failed the
nation, or had the nation failed them?

Ironically, in almost a year of not talking to M I had suddenly, it
seemed, learned something of what the young owe the old. I realized
that my grandmother's generation looked at our parents' flight from
India with something more than alarm. And it was true, the "Quit
India Movement," a term used with cynical humor by Delhi intellectuals to refer to colleagues departing west in search of lucrative
jobs, did not mean the same thing it had in 1942. Nevertheless,
those of us reared in the West, bearers of foreign accents and
strange habits, born to a generation exercising and fleeing its own
Independence, signaled the hope of a return.

I understood that to M I represented the promise of a new generation that was somehow not implicated in the history of a "failed"
nation, a generation that would remold the country from the ashes
of a forsaken vision. In visiting the orphanage, I had somehow, if
belatedly, paid my respects to that originary dream. It seemed no
accident that M would finish out her days dedicated to instilling this
vision in caring for the young.

Gandhi had seen social reform as political program, yet when the
two were cleaved into distinct, competitive elements by the nationalist movement, many Congress workers followed Gandhi into the
villages to continue the "constructive program." Thus M had
renounced her considerable stature as a political leader and devoted herself to social work. In so doing, even M the woman disap-

pears into a subject position as readily occupied by men as women, for the true social worker had no gender. In fact, not marking one's gender could be seen as a further sign of great humility. This, too, was quite common among Gandhians.

It seems to me that M, in refusing the subject, enacts a particular critique of the nation. For like many "freedom fighters," she is keenly aware of the uses to which her subjectivity may be put.

First, there is the material gain of a pension awarded by the Indian government to its most dedicated freedom fighters, those who had served time in jail. Of course, M, as an upper-class Brahmin woman, with considerable family resources and prestige, can afford to snub a state-sponsored pension; her refusal, read as a rejection of the nation, underscores her own class privilege. Janaki, the subject of the preceding essay, could not. I first came to know of Janaki, also Brahmin, but lower class, through a local historian who, when compiling the *Who's Who of Freedom Fighters* for the state of Tamil Nadu, had helped to document her claim for a pension by tracking down and certifying her jail records. Thus there are very real material processes at work that allow one subject to avoid the historian, and force another subject to search her out.

Second, there is the fame and glory of continual press coverage when old freedom fighters are honored by being asked to inaugurate or preside over various state functions, perhaps legitimating, in M's eyes, a vision struggled for and not won. For to participate in the nation's newly won status was to confirm that the nation had already arrived and was not still in the process of arrival. It was the means of nationhood, not the end of nation, that was important. If "Hind Swaraj" meant there could be no self-rule without self-respect, then until true self-respect had been won, one could not speak of a real Independence.

I had come to greatly respect and admire this woman who had made, indeed changed, the history of India but who would not, by her own design, make the pages of its history books. M's refusal to participate in the recording of her past problematizes our own assumptions about the relationships between memory, experience, historical record, and written testimony. I want to argue that it is in rethinking such relationships that refusing the subject becomes indeed the ground of a feminist ethnography.

*

How might a feminist ethnography pose the question of memory and identity? The form this question takes is deliberate, for I do not intend this essay to be an exercise in Benedictine "memory ethnography,"[10] or even the remembered ethnography of M. N. Srinivas. I raise the issues of memory and historical identity because they have consequences for imagining another form of ethnography. How are the identities of self related to the mechanics of memory, and the relevance of the past? Or, more specifically, what are the identity-defining functions of memory?

Memory, as we know, is not to be relied upon; memory always indexes a loss.[11] It is not uncommon for the experienced oral historian to caution, "All memories are subject not only to simple, gradual erosion over time, but also to conscious or unconscious repression, distortion, mistakes, and even to a limited extent, outright lies."[12] There are also the assumptions of the historians of popular movements who tell us that "loss of memory is equivalent to the loss of historiography, of a usable past, indeed of historical agency."[13] No memory, no history. No history, no agency. The historian, then, must adjudicate between loss of memory and memory itself as a site of loss; between the failure of memory and failed memory.

Yet memory is what establishes the relationship of the individual to history. "The commonplace elements in self-representations are taken to reveal cultural attitudes, visions of the world and interpretations of history, including the role of the individual in historical process."[14]

That historical process, we know, is inescapably bound up in the teleology of the nation. If we consider that one of the functions of nationalism is to constitute subjects (citizenship again), then refusing the subject is implicitly to refuse the nation. As Homi Bhabha puts it, "People are the historical 'objects' of a nationalist pedagogy," contributing to the authority of nationalist discourse; they can only be the subjects of a process of nationalist signification.[15] Bhabha reminds us, too, that the telling of an individual story necessitates the whole laborious telling of the collective itself.[16] The work of the subject is inevitably the work of the collectivity. Notwithstanding an ideal of citizenship that founders along lines of gender, there is the sense of certain women being elected to stand for the nation, and a sense of proprietorship: one can speak, for example, of Jeanne d'Arc being the creation of Michelet, even as the Rani of Jhansi symbolizes, for many historians, the Indian "mutiny" of 1857.[17]

Gayatri Spivak has asked the question "Can the Subaltern Speak?" and answered with an unequivocal no. Speech has, of course, been seen as the privileged catalyst of agency; lack of speech as the absence of agency. How then might we destabilize the equation of speech with agency by staging one woman's subject refusal as a refusal to speak?

M's subject refusal, deployed in full irony, must be located at the juncture of (at least) two competing processes of identity formation—the feminist one, which would retrieve her voice to fulfill certain subject functions in the West, and the nationalist one. Judith Butler urges us to examine institutional histories of subjection and subjectification, to comprehend the "grammar of the subject."[18] She asks, "Is it not always true that power operates in advance, in the very procedures that establish who will be a subject who speaks in the name of feminism, and to whom? And is it not always clear that a process of subjection is presupposed in the subjugating process that produces before you one speaking subject of feminist debate?"[19]

M's refusing the subject of the feminist historian may look like an all-too-common gendering—an inability to see the value of her own contribution within larger social or historical narratives that would work to deny it. For M's narrative does not take the "I am my own heroine" form much feminist oral historiography uncovers.[20] Rather, M is poised at the edge of history, neither its victim nor its heroine, forcing the feminist historian to hesitate between subject bestowal and subject suspension. Of course, the feminist historian herself is no longer hero of her own story, for she, too, has come to doubt the university rescue missions in search of the voiceless.

If Susan Sontag has written suggestively of "the anthropologist as hero," Pierre Nora has written more resignedly about the losses of the historian. In lamenting that "the historian's is a strange fate; his role and place in society were once simple and clearly defined: to be the spokesman of the past and the herald of the future,"[21] Nora suggests the passing of the time of historian as hero.

When the historian can depict neither past nor future, chronologies are destabilized, and temporality itself is subject to suspension. That is to say that the subject of such a history is itself one in suspension, signaling a suspended temporality, a repudiated nation. The subject speaks betwixt and between time and places.[22] "The subject is graspable only in the passage between telling/told, between 'here' and somewhere else,"[23] delinking memory from place, what Nora has called "les lieux de mémoire."

If history is ultimately the telling of a nation, what, then, are the mnemonics of history? Pierre Nora's recent analysis delineates a fundamental antagonism between memory and history:

Memory and history, far from being synonymous, appear now to be in a fundamental opposition. Memory is life, borne by living societies founded in its name. It remains in permanent evolution, open to the dialectic of remembering and forgetting, unconscious of successive deformations, vulnerable to manipulation and appropriation, susceptible to being long dormant and periodically revived. History, on the other hand, is the reconstruction, always problematic and incomplete, of what is no longer. Memory is a perpetually active phenomenon, a bond tying us to the eternal present; history is a representation of the past.[24]

Nora goes on to say that "memory is by nature multiple and yet specific; collective, plural, and yet individual. History, on the other hand, belongs to everyone, and no one, hence its claim to universal authority."[25] This process is elaborated most clearly in the concept of the nation. "Relationships between history, memory, and the nation were characterized as more than natural currency: they were shown to involve a reciprocal circularity, a symbiosis at every level": [26]

No longer a cause, the nation has become a given; history is now a social science, memory a purely private phenomenon. The memory-nation was thus the last incarnation of the unification of memory and history.[27]

This splitting apart of memory and history, then, is perhaps the place of articulation for critical subjects of the nation. The question is *how*, if M presents herself as a subject not of history but of memory, *my* memory.

With the breakdown of universal History, there is a lapse into a kind of individual pluralism rather than a necessary restitution of the collective. As Nora puts it, there is a multiplication of private memories demanding individual histories. "The transformation of memory implies a decisive shift from the historical to the psychological, from the social to the individual. . . . In the last analysis it is upon the individual alone that the constraint of memory weighs insistently as well as imperceptibly."[28] Nora warns that the less memory is experienced collectively, the more it will require individuals to become "memory individuals."[29] Nora's notion of "duty memory" suggests more than the obligation to remember; rather it is a discursive will operating to force the individual to remember. Yet the process of remembering implies that one must *speak* of memories. If one does not speak is memory lost?

While Nora speaks of the will to remember, Bhabha speaks of a necessary forgetting of the nation's past: "the violence involved in establishing the nation's writ."[30] It is this forgetting that constitutes the beginnings of the nation's narrative. Bhabha argues that it is in this "syntax of forgetting"—being obliged to forget—that the problematic identification of a national people becomes visible.[31] The confession is a kind of speaking in order to forget.[32] The mechanics of nationalist thought, then, must rest on confessional history. Is this the juncture at which to locate M's refusal to speak? How do we locate Butler's proposed grammar of the subject in the nationalist syntax of forgetting and the individual duty to remember?

The processes of breakdown and reconstitution that have marked the disciplinary formation of anthropology in the past two decades have also affected history. That is to say that history, too (via Collingwood), sought to differentiate itself from science and art. "What distinguished history from science ... was the operation of an 'a priori imagination' that governed the activity of historical construction; what distinguished historical imagination from the artistic imagination was its respect for evidence."[33] There was, too, an equal conflation of genres. In French historiography, for example, contes, nouvelles, and mémoires judiciaires, all quasi-fictional modes, while recognized as means of telling stories, counted as marks of reality, and therefore evidence,[34] even if Jules Michelet's *Sorcières* was read as a novel, and not as history when it first appeared.[35]

Finally, if official history formerly dealt with states, its turn to the individual, that is, the biographical, was not without questions of proof. This led to the identification of "world-historical individuals" who could be seen as the exemplars of a universal history.[36] Any other kind of biography (that dealing with lower classes, for example) was relegated to the status of "imaginary biography"—heightening the gap between history and fiction.[37] Carl Ginzburg makes the case for a "conjectural historiography," one that relies on the conditional mood "perhaps," or "might have been," raising the possibility of changing the past in the future simply by making it the past of a different present."[38]

Such a historiography works in ways contrary to the judicial form of official history that regards history as a trial to establish veracity. Here, Victor Turner's analysis of Max Gluckman's work on legal discourse may yield some useful insights. Turner tells us that "the judicial process seeks to establish the facts by means of cross-examination of witnesses and the assessment of conflicting evidence in terms of 'as-if' models" and that "narratives are placed in such 'as if' frames in order to move from the subjunctive mood of 'it may have happened like this or that' to the quasi-indicative mood of 'these would appear to be the facts.' "[39]

The shift from judicial (or indicative) history to subjunctive or conjectural history then parallels the shift we have argued for from declarative (or realist) to interrogative texts. Here we must speak of an imagined history, rather than one that proceeds from the compilation of facts.[40] This should not surprise us given that history remains a tale of the nation, and that we are now accustomed to speaking of the nation as an "imagined" community.

Ginzburg argues that the subjunctive analyses of historians like Natalie Davis[41] speaks to the difficulties of historical reconstruction. To my mind, however, conjectural historiography speaks equally to the realm of deconstruction. In fact, it mediates between the two: the one indicating the realm of possibility, the other, the realm of impossibility. M's subject refusal has been located in a conjectural, as well as conjunctural, history. It is a conjectural history because I have indeed speculated on her reasons for refusing to speak. It is a conjunctural history because I have located the impossibility of her speaking in the conjuncture between memory and history, between nationalist and Western feminist processes of subject retrieval.

Like an unreliable narrator, the fidelity of the conjectural historian, confronted with the choices if——, then? and if not——, then? cannot be assumed. Subjunctive historians are then faced with their own apologies. Perhaps this is why, like Natalie Davis, in her analysis of the sixteenth-century French pardon tale,[42] I, too, will also ask my subject(s) to pardon me . . .

5

Feminist Reflections on Deconstructive Ethnography

"It still strikes me as strange that the case histories I write
should read like short stories."[1]

— Sigmund Freud

"Betrayal" began in a flush of catharsis; of bitterness melting into
something like acceptance. In retrospect, I can see how the apostasy
of a friend I had counted on was necessarily entangled in my
understanding of other friendships, leading to a telescoping of the
relations between telling a story, being told on, and telling on
someone. The psychoanalytic, as we know, foments a certain critical perspective through the engagement of analysis. Yet if psychoanalysis rescripts the anthropologist-"informant" relationship into a
doctor-patient scenario,[2] something rather different is being said
about the nature of confidences and intimacy in the field. Here,
however, I invoke the psychoanalytic frame to underscore a particular moment where power cannot be denied, and must be assumed.
Thus while the origins of "Betrayal" can be (too) quickly located in
a form of fieldwork catharsis, its sustained critical energy is drawn
from deconstruction.

Gayatri Spivak warns that the deployment of psychoanalytic categories is the sign of foreclosure, and while I will not here follow
her into "psychobiography,"[3] I have found the form of deconstruction she practices to be the most useful for my project. Spivak once
summarized the deconstructive position as saying an impossible no
to a structure that one critiques, yet inhabits intimately,[4] a theme to
which I will return shortly.

In what follows, I locate "Betrayal" first in the context of "Defining Feminist Ethnography" as a means of anchoring discussion of
the continuities and differences between the feminist ethnography I

now write and the feminist ethnography originally outlined in that essay; second, in the context of debates about postmodernism in anthropology; and third, in the context of debates about postmodernism's relevance to the "Third World." As a means of entering the discussion of postmodernism, I will address two of the most important critiques leveled at "Betrayal," the accusation that deconstructive theory somehow enacts a more violent form of subject constitution than normalizing ethnography, and the argument that theories of multiple positioning only allow liberal, pluralist notions of difference to emerge.

Distinctions between the terms *postmodern, poststructuralist,* and *deconstruction* are often elided in popular academic usage, and it is important to recognize that they can be conceived as connoting different theoretical positions arising out of overlapping, but isolable trajectories. I understand deconstruction as one of a set of theories emerging within a general poststructuralist framework, and postmodernism (following Jameson) as a historical moment expressed as the "cultural logic of late capitalism." While I use the term *deconstruction* somewhat interchangeably with *postmodernism,* I also distinguish between the two by discussing deconstruction in terms of its techniques and practices, and postmodernism more as a question of place and periodization.

Defining (Discontinuities in) Feminist Ethnography

"Defining Feminist Ethnography" was written during a period when the optimism of writing about "other" women was beginning to break down, and although I myself tried to locate the essay in this context, I believe its reception in the larger community of feminist scholarship has augured ill for the full implications of my argument. One recuperation of my argument has been a (not unwarranted) return to the canon, to search out ignored classics of anthropology written by women, but at the expense of vexed questions of power and representation I tried to foreground in that piece. Thus, while some feminist colleagues have noted the apparent discontinuities between that 1988 article and my more recent experiment with deconstructive ethnography, I myself note some continuities.

First, I argued that the relationship between women of the colonizer and women of the colonized (however variously that might be defined), could ground feminist ethnography in the analysis of power. Second, I argued that while the newly emergent experimental ethnography had sadly enough not been informed by feminist theories of language and subjectivity, feminist ethnography itself could benefit from utilizing such theory. I called for an understanding of the "disaffections, ruptures, and incomprehensions" that mark fieldwork, but warned that polyphony and heteroglossia were inadequate solutions to the vexed problems of voicing. Thus, while some programs for postmodern ethnography call for dialogical or multiply voiced texts,[5] I have opted to see the text as overdetermined, becoming something like an omniscient narrator. Finally, I argued that we could consider literature by feminists in marginalized communities as part of a new anthropological canon.

However, if then I thought that by simply adding the works by Third World writers or women of color to the anthropological canon, a substantial shift in anthropological practice would occur, I am no longer as optimistic. In that essay, I relied on a rather undifferentiated notion of gender. Although my attempt was to show how, with an analysis of power, the category of "women" breaks down along the lines of class or race, I assumed a notion of gender based on a simplistic male-female dichotomy, without clearly locating gender in relation to sexuality.[6] In addition, a number of my readings of feminist ethnographic texts assume that gender is the central term for determining other axes of oppression. If "Defining Feminist Ethnography" was inspired by a particular misreading of *This Bridge Called My Back,* my current understanding of gender is heavily indebted to Norma Alarcón's essay "The Theoretical Subjects of *This Bridge Called My Back.*"[7] Here, Alarcón has argued that in spite of the added attention given to women writers of color, the epistemological categories of feminism have not changed, permitting a logic of identification that proceeds with gender at its center. Thus it is not enough to consider race, class, and sexuality as additive categories to a central concept. What Alarcón is suggesting, I think, is unsettling this logic of identification (which also permits all kinds of appropriations), by displacing gender from the center of feminist theory, and starting from a consideration of how race, class, or sexuality determines the positioning of a subject—not with being "women," but how women are different. What Alarcón proposes is a critical reworking of Simone de Beauvoir's phrase "One is not born, one becomes a woman."

This is in part what I attempted with "Betrayal"—to break down any easy identification between women, to mark that process of dissembling (via an analysis of class and gender positionings in nationalist thought) as an epistemological moment. Suspicious of feminist and ethnographic desires to "know" the other, I rendered a subject who resists any single positioning for very long. My attempt was to describe how *a* woman emerged out of a series of performances and positionings, and not to render the category "Woman" intelligible through recourse to sociological variables as abstract descriptions of reality.[8]

Reading "Betrayal"

Spivak's notion of intimate habitation—in my case, simultaneous levels of anthropological knowing, teaching, and writing in the American academy—accounts for what some readers have called the "curious embeddedness" of "Betrayal." "Betrayal" allegorizes three distinct but interlocking sets of problems that impinge on the exercise of feminist ethnography, though it foregrounds only one, the moment of feminist innocence where sisterhood or solidarity prevails automatically, in spite of the vicissitudes of difference. The second is the moment where nation betrays feminist promises, and postpones the "woman question" indefinitely. The third is the notion of faithfully brokering a culture, the humanist project to know a culture "on its own terms" and render those terms responsibly and intelligibly. Betrayal is what locks these themes together: the recognition that cultural interpretation is power-laden and involves more than translation or brokering, that sisterhood cannot be assumed but must be fought for, that national interests were not necessarily women's interests. Deconstruction intensifies these moments, enacting simultaneous anthropological, feminist, and nationalist betrayals. The ethnography of "Betrayal" stages multiple allegories of betrayal: nationalism betrays feminist hopes of full citizenship, feminism interrogates and betrays anthropology's staging of the "other," and Western anthropology betrays national sovereignty by searching out the gendered differential of nationalist ideology.

The narrative structure of "Betrayal" rests less on the fragment, or technique of pastiche, than on the irruptive act of telling a story, and interrupting it with others. As in a play, there are multiple shifts of scene and setting for the narrative. Although each break in the narrative represents a moment where the analysis of power escalates, its fabulistic ending is meant not to suggest closure, but to underscore a central irony in much feminist writing: How is it after such an analysis of power, complicity, violation of boundaries, and betrayal that I return again to a master narrative of sisterhood, even if in mourning its loss, and not its celebration? Do the final words of the analysis suggest the return to a humanist impulse in a largely antihumanist exercise?

Betrayal does not end with the premise that we can never know anything. It does presume that to confront the subaltern is not to represent them, but to learn to represent ourselves[9] and that such a project takes us into a critique of disciplinary anthropology, showing how baldly what we come to know is engendered by relations of power. "Betrayal" seeks (if unsuccessfully) to subvert those relations of power by exposing their unfolding in the telling.

My use of the dramatic metaphor is meant to highlight interpretation as an act, that is, to show not only how interpretation is deeply and interestedly constructed, but also how knowledge and understanding are contingent on performance. It has become commonplace to note that social theory in the past twenty years has more and more assumed the dramatic metaphor. Yet Victor Turner is surely one of the first to bring the analysis of drama and literature to anthropology. As he puts it,

> The dramaturgical phase begins when crises arise in the daily flow of interaction. Thus if daily living is a kind of theatre, social drama is a kind of meta-theatre, that is a dramaturgical language about the language of ordinary role-playing and status-maintenance which constitutes communication in the quotidian social process. In other words, when actors in a social drama ... "try to show others what they are doing or what they have done," they are acting consciously, expressing ... the ability to communicate about the communication system itself.[10]

My invocation of Turner here is deliberate. As one of the founders of symbolic analysis in anthropology, he is one of the significant few who have attempted to navigate the turn from reflexive to postmodern analysis.[11] While I am interested in reading Turner's notion of performance away from the sociological realm and into the epistemological, I believe such a move is not foreign to Turner's own understanding of and engagement with theory. For Turner, especially in his later writings, anticipated many of the moves postmodern theories were to advocate. Indeed, Turner as a theorist showed much more openness and interest in understanding what has come to be called the "postmodern turn" than many of the anthropologists Turner trained as students, welcoming the "contaminated," "promiscuous," and "impure."[12] Thus, I find myself in agreement with Turner when he proclaims,

> Postmodern theory would see in the very flaws, hesitations, personal
> factors, incomplete, elliptical, context-dependent, situational
> components of performance, clues to the very nature of human
> process itself, and would also perceive genuine novelty, creativeness
> as able to emerge from the performance situation.[13]

Where I depart from Turner's analysis is in his assumption of the "freedom of the performance situation." While Turner draws upon Dilthey's notion of "the idealism of freedom," my view of the performance situation is that it is simultaneously a focus and site for the enactment of various conjunctural relations of power. It is interesting to note that Turner's work stands at an important junction between symbolic anthropological analyses and postmodern theories. In fact, the same criticism that is made about both is often made about either one separately: that they fail to consider relations of power.

The proximity of an interpretive anthropologist like Turner to certain forms of postmodern theory, I believe, has encouraged an undue categorization of deconstructive ethnography as but another form of reflexive ethnography. In fact, while both share the objective of laying bare the process of how the ethnographer comes to know what she knows, I would argue that there are significant differences that separate the two. Perhaps the major distinction to be made between reflexive and deconstructive ethnography is that reflexive ethnography, like normative ethnography, rests on what Belsey terms the "declarative mode," while deconstructive ethnography enacts the interrogative mode through the practice of deferral, a refusal to explain. Belsey's terms are drawn from the linguist Emile Benveniste, who argues that the declarative mode is one of imparting knowledge to a reader whose position is stabilized by invisible claims to a shared discourse. The interrogative mode, by contrast, disrupts the identity of the reader with a unified subject of enunciation by discouraging identification.[14] Thus, while reflexive ethnography jettisons the idea that the observing subject is separate from the object of investigation, hermeneutic comprehension is enacted through a unified subject of knowledge working to establish identification. Deconstructive ethnography attempts to disrupt that process of identification, often through recourse to a fractured, multiply positioned subject.

While it is true that some of the more sophisticated interpretive ethnography calls into question the limits of cross-cultural understanding, it cannot directly embrace epistemological failure because that would be to forfeit an authority that has already been placed in jeopardy by a subjective, self-reflexive mode. Self-reflexive anthropology questions its own authority; deconstructive anthropology attempts to abandon or forfeit its authority, knowing that it is impossible to do so. It is this level of the negotiation of impossibility that deconstructive ethnography adopts as method.

In his later work, Turner worked to extend his original notion of social drama arising in conflict situations, or out of disharmonic social processes, to the notion of "performance," while continuing to draw heavily on Gregory Bateson's and Erving Goffman's differently elaborated ideas of "staging" and "framing":

> With the postmodern dislodgement of spatialized thinking and ideal models of cognitive and social structures from their position of exegetical preeminence, there is occurring a major move toward the study of processes, not as exemplifying compliance with, or deviation from normative models, both emic and etic, but as performances.[15]

Thus Turner is concerned to read postmodern theory as another form of processual analysis. Marilyn Strathern agrees, arguing that postmodernism is a kind of method embodied in its own enactment or performance,[16] which results in being "out of context."

*

Laura Bohannon's classic essay "Shakespeare in the Bush"[17] reads as an early interpretive exercise on the limits of cross-cultural understanding, turning a Western tragedy into a comedy of errors about ancestors and ghosts. However, my invocation of a Shakespearean kind of framing for this analysis is less a reflexive than an epistemological exercise. According to Phyllis Gorfain, a drama such as *Hamlet,* for example, might mirror for anthropologists their own processes in studying others—depicting an unremitting series of inquiries and representations; attempts to close epistemic gaps between past, present, and future to secure the truth and authority of experience.[18] Gorfain argues that a text such as *Hamlet* serves as an allegory for the inability to push knowledge beyond a series of performances; it is a "master text" of the anthropologist's desire to know what she also learns will always elude her.[19]

"Betrayal," however, attempts to move past the assumptions of a Geertz or Turner that cultures can be read as straightforward texts or performances. For if, pushing Gorfain's terms a bit, the reflexive mode says that we must confront our own processes of interpretation,[20] I would argue that the deconstructive mode says we must confront the plays of power in our processes of interpretation. If the reflexive mode emphasizes not what we know, but how we think we know, the deconstructive mode again emphasizes how we think we know what we know is neither transparent nor innocent. Self-reflexive ethnography is imbedded in humanist principles of representation, deconstructive ethnography in particular antihumanist practices.

"Betrayal" is the site of multiple and simultaneous confessional modes, for in emphasizing processes of suspicion and self-delusion, in highlighting the fabrication of events in a kind of fictional time and place through use of the dramatic frame, "Betrayal" as an analysis also confesses to its own feigning, underscoring the analogy between fiction and deception.[21] "Betrayal" attempts to reflect back at its readers the problems of inquiry, at the same moment an inquiry is conducted, striking the epistemological paradox of knowing through not knowing.[22] The last issue raised is, of course, the problem of knowledge and responsibility:[23] how does one act knowing what one does? This is the point in "Betrayal" at which I turn to Donna Haraway's notion of accountable and situated positioning.

Critiques of Deconstructive Ethnography

It is increasingly remarked that postmodern theory indexes how interpretation has become its own object, ushering in a "crisis of representation."[24] For this reason, few and scattered are the calls for a "postmodern ethnography" stressing the importance of the fragment, allegory, or performance. Stephen Tyler's postmodern framework for an "evocation" based in "cooperatively evolved texts" that emphasizes ethnography as a "mutual dialogical production" in the creation of a "participatory reality"[25] is probably the most interrogated. Criticisms of this form of postmodern ethnography often focus on the naive dialogical faith advanced by its advocates.[26] While I, too, am wary of dialogical solutions to the unequal power relations that obtain in most anthropology, it is only reasonable to note that several of the critics pronouncing on the inadequacy of the dialogical never get around to examining the power differentials inherent in their own ethnographic enterprises.

What is also striking is that related critiques of deconstructive ethnography converge, and are not bound by disciplinary configurations. For example, Steven Sangren in his review of *Writing Culture* objects that "the rhetoric of the textually oriented anthropological theorist reproduces in forms more opaque and mystifying than do many of the older forms it delegitimates, the same strivings for hegemony, power and authority that it attributes to the older forms."[27] Literary critic Radhakrishnan also agrees that

> if canonical anthropology made an informant of the native, this new form of self-reflexive ethnography achieves an even more subtle effect. Thanks to poststructuralism, these discourses have found a way to de-politicize, de-realize, and de-ontologize "non- western" realities in the very act of talking about them. These "other" realities become mere fictions in the autocritical/self-reflexive gaze of western feminism. The highly valuable and necessary project of knowing the other as both different and related degenerates into an act of complex narcissism. The deconstructive dominant Self overlooks the historical asymmetry that underlies the relationship between the First and Third Worlds and prescribes its particular form of autocritique.[28]

Such an analysis, while collapsing deconstructive into self-reflexive ethnography, is reminiscent of the admonishment one anonymous reviewer has made about "Betrayal":

> The author needs to understand that the kind of paper she has written reads as a violent appropriation of certain ethnographic moments to Western discourses of gender, agency and subject-constitution. Beneath its apparent celebration of the situated and situational context of the production of knowledge is a more naked exercise in discursive hijacking than of most normalizing ethnographies I have read.

These statements all rest on a hegemonic humanism, but the first and last statements in particular seem to call again for faithful (as opposed to faithless) brokering, the unspoken assumption being that the transparent qualities of normalizing ethnography somehow mean a less violent appropriation of the Third World subject by "Western discourse of gender, agency, and subject-constitution." Need I underscore the fact that the call for transparency "marks the place of interest"?[29] Humanist holism is the essential fiction of ethnography. We would do well to remember Jean-Paul Dumont's declamation that "nothing seems more fictitious ... than the classic monograph in which a human group is drawn and quartered along the traditional categories of social, economic, religious, and other so-called organizations, and everything holds together."[30] In my view, the violence of Dumont's metaphors seems to do rather more justice to the everyday "discursive hijacking" entailed by normalizing ethnography.

Critiques of anthropological and feminist representation emerged, after all, precisely because of the power moves they concealed. I am in agreement with Gayatri Spivak when she says that one responsibility of the critic is to write (and read) so that the impossibility of "interested individualistic refusals of the institutional privileges of powers bestowed on the subject" is taken seriously.[31] This is what "Betrayal" reveals, the impossibility of saying no to the power that inheres in the anthropologist's own subject formation. Deconstructive ethnography allows one to view the process of asserting facts, to question at every moment what is being asserted as "fact," bringing a different epistemological process to bear on "facticity." It is not that facts disappear, but that their limits are exposed. Those concerned with the reliability of "data" need to first address the purposes for which reliability is being marshalled. Of course, such analyses *are* naked, discursive exercises in power, but then *all* social analysis is ultimately, no matter how transparent or unremarked its claims to authority. Might showing some of the junctures where power operates in an analysis open up new ways of accountable seeing? Indeed, I find Judith Butler's recent argument about deconstruction a very helpful one:

> To deconstruct the subject is not to negate or throw away the concept; on the contrary, deconstruction implies only that we suspend all commitments to that which the term "the Subject" refers, and that we consider the linguistic functions it seeks in the consolidation and concealment of authority. To deconstruct is not to negate or dismiss, but to call into question and, perhaps most importantly, to open up a term like the subject, to a reusage or redeployment that has previously not been authorized.[32]

It is thus possible to see the agency of Janaki (the central subject of "Betrayal") as reauthorization of particular subject positions within feminist and Indian nationalist discourses.

Postmodern Turns

The literature on postmodernism in the past two decades has provoked an excessive outpouring of positions, counterpositions, attacks, counterattacks, allegations, and denials, with the result that little clarity, and less levelheadedness, prevails in these debates than among others. In feminist theory, for example, heavy-handed treatises about the opposition between "feminism" and "postmodernism" want reminding that there are as many postmodernisms as feminisms.[33]

I do not want to attempt in this essay to resolve a set of debates that to my mind are best left contentious in order to remain productive. Rather, as I wend my way through these debates, I want to argue that the question of the postmodern begs immediately the question, Which modern? And then, turning the question around again, I want to contend that if there are multiple moderns, surely also there are multiple "postmoderns"; not one postmodern turn, but many. Let me, then, begin by mapping some of the moderns that impinge on the question of feminist ethnography.

Anthony Appiah in an important essay has noted that postmodernism properly follows *from* modernism rather than after it, suggesting that postmodernism completes an incomplete modernist project. More significant perhaps is the contestatory aspect of postmodernism that implies a rejection of things modern. Appiah argues, however, that what constitutes the modern for any given disciplinary or aesthetic formation is likely to differ. Thus, in philosophy, postmodernism signals the rejection of modernity in a metaphysical realism underwritten by a unitary notion of reason: Cartesian or Kantian logics (in France or Germany), or logical positivism (in America). In architecture, postmodernism represents the rejection of the modernist ideal of exclusive function or monumentalist structure. In political theory, the rejection of modernism signals the repudiation of master narratives like Marxism, and in literature, postmodernism reacts to the high seriousness and irony of modernism appreciable only by a cultural elite.[34]

If it is true that "modernism derives its energy from a steady opposition to realism,"[35] then the question of modernism in anthropology must tackle the question of ethnographic realism. In what follows, I argue that the "modern" period in anthropology is most productively associated with various forms of "interpretive" or "reflexive" ethnography, allowing a more careful comparison between forms of modern and postmodern ethnography, or between interpretive and deconstructive ethnography.

In 1959, Oscar Lewis, introducing his *Five Families,* described the family portraits in the book as neither "fiction nor conventional ethnography." For lack of a better term, Lewis termed his method of exposition *ethnographic realism,* in contrast to *literary realism.*[36] To my knowledge, Lewis was the first anthropologist to self-consciously employ this term.

More than two decades later, George Marcus and Dick Cushman in their review of "Ethnographies as Texts" define ethnographic realism as a "mode of writing that seeks to represent the reality of a whole world or form of life."[37] This formulation, however (like Lewis's earlier assertion), bypasses more instructive definitions of literary realism, and it may be useful to compare the two more systematically.

In her succinct study *Critical Practice,* Catherine Belsey argues that "what is intelligible as realism is the conventional, and therefore familiar 'recognizable' articulation and distribution of concepts. It is intelligible as 'realistic' precisely because it reproduces what we already seem to know."[38] Belsey goes on to say that whatever the events of a story, the experience of reading a realist text is reassuring because "the world evoked in the fiction, its patterns of cause and effect, of social relationships and moral values, largely confirm the pattern of the world we seem to know."[39] Ethnographic realism then aims to reveal and confirm patterns of a knowable world. An apparent jump must be made from the extraordinary to the ordinary; the project becomes one of making the strange familiar, establishing order and function out of apparent disorder and disharmony. Belsey tells us, however, that classical realist texts also hinge on the creation of enigma or disorder, resolved only with the reestablishment of order. Both literary and ethnographic forms of realist narrative, then, appear to rest on the inscription of disorder into order.

Marcus and Cushman identify nine different conventions that work to establish the transparency of the normative ethnographic text, among them the nonintrusive presence of the ethnographer, statements of typicality and generalization, and a focus on everyday life situations. As Marcus and Cushman explain, the transparency of the realist ethnography is produced by "severing relations between what the ethnographer knows, and how (s)he came to know it."[40] Again following Belsey's discussion, the direct intrusion of the author into the realist text is seen as an impropriety. The technique of impersonal narration relies on "showing" the truth, rather than "telling" the truth.[41] Self-reflexive or modernist texts, then, seek to "tell" how the ethnographer comes to know what she knows, departing from realist conventions.

Recently, theorists have begun to distinguish between modernism as "theoretical determinant" and modernism as "social effect";[42] between modernism as a mode of aesthetic cognition or type of subjectivity, and modernism as a historic moment. I want to argue that the question of technique cannot be so easily divorced from the question of periodization, and that the task is one of historicizing any given set of aesthetic interventions at a given moment. The question of the "modern" in anthropology is in fact a crucial one, and I will argue that a particular misunderstanding of modernism is partly responsible for experimental ethnography's sidelining of the feminist ethnographic texts discussed in chapter 2. Since George Marcus argues with Dick Cushman in 1982 that ethnographic realism has been the dominant textual mode of anthropology for the past sixty years,[43] it is not surprising that he should later argue (with Michael Fischer) that anthropology never had a modernist moment until present-day readings of literary and classical modernism were brought to bear on ethnography by writers such as James Clifford, Paul Rabinow, or Vincent Crapanzano.[44] In my view this is a fundamentally gendered and mistaken reading of modernism and anthropological analysis.

Marc Manganaro has recently attempted to characterize the modern period in anthropology as that between 1900 and 1945, but this periodization quickly breaks down when he considers conflicting reviews of the field.[45] Edwin Ardener, for example, marks the questioning of the authorial status of the anthropologist (with which some of the above-mentioned authors are associated) as the end of the modernist period in anthropology.[46] For Ardener, this modern period is characterized by rejection of historicism in favor of holism and synchrony, and enabled by Malinowskian notions of "fieldwork." Marilyn Strathern extends Ardener's notion of ethnographic modernism by identifying the implicit reflexivity of the anthropological enterprise in the self-conscious division between observer and observed typified by the exercise of fieldwork.[47] Following George Stocking, she notes the establishment of the monograph (based on holist premises) as a totalizing form of ethnographic explanation.[48] Finally, there is the "realization that frames are only frames, that concepts are culture based, that analytical terms are themselves buried in premises and assumptions," and a "discovery of the ordinary in the bizarre, civilization under savagery."[49]

In this sense, the modernism of a Malinowski, "while comparable to that of the fieldworker who strives to render the unfamiliar comprehensible," must be contrasted to his surrealist contemporaries in France who "tended to work in the reverse sense, making the familiar strange."[50] Both strands of ethnography exorcised notions of the familiar, albeit from opposite ends.

In fact, I would argue for a rather more consolidated view of "ethnographic modernism" than has previously been advanced, located in the contemporaneous production of three distinct but interlocking manifestos of the 1920s: the Malinowskian manifesto based on the technique of fieldwork,[51] the (first) Surrealist mani-festo implicating ethnology in avant-garde projects,[52] and a latent Boasian manifesto, voiced by Edward Sapir, and based on the dis-crimination between "Culture, Genuine and Spurious."[53] Thus what might be termed "ethnographic modernism" arose in France as a critique of the First World War and decadent bourgeois society, and in the United States as a critique of "American civilization" and industrial society. In each instance, the result was the same—a kind of unrelenting "primitivism" or search for the "genuine culture."

Strathern argues that the modernist transition Malinowski made from Frazier's historicism articulated a new version of primitiveness. "The difference between 'us' and 'them' was conceived not as a dif-ferent stage in evolutionary progression but as a difference of per-spective. 'They' did not use the same frames as 'we' do through which to visualize the world." Strathern marks this as a moment where "ethnocentrism was invented both as a theoretical principle and as an organizing framework for writing ... displayed in the arrangement ... of ideas internal to the monograph."[54]

James Clifford has argued that modernism ushered in a new "ethnographic subjectivity."[55] If the surrealists experimented with the methods of fragment or montage, Malinowski and some of the Boasians seem to have been driven by what Richard Handler has termed "a fully secularized individualism."[56] In this sense, the diaries of Malinowski or writings of Benedict feverishly pursue "self-real-ization to the fullest possible development of one's personality." For Malinowski and several of his contemporaries, this meant "placing oneself in a situation where one might have a certain kind of ex-perience."[57] Yet the questing self of the ethnographer is formed by an anthropology born to the parents of Western imperialism and the Enlightenment, which comes of age precisely at this moment in the early twentieth century.[58] Much remains to be learned of the col-lapsing between modern ethnographic and imperialist techniques of self.

My point, in this brief discussion of ethnographic modernism, has not been so much to dispute as to refine Marcus and Cushman's assertion that ethnographic realism has been the dominant textual mode of anthropology for the past sixty years. For if, as Belsey argues, expressive realism originates in the period of industrial capi-talism in the West, it also seems to me that the origins of ethno-graphic realism are roughly coterminous with the last phase of colo-nial expansion, spurred by industrial capital. Thus, it is not surprising that ethnographic realism throws up at its moment of origin the seeds of its own modernist critique, revealing not a clear periodization but rather an overlap between ethnographic realist and modern reflexive modes. That Malinowski or Benedict should stand both for the standard normative ethnography *and* its modernist critique is not surprising. Nor is it surprising that an author such as Ruth Landes or Gladys Reichard should produce within a few years ethnographies in a normative realist mode (*Ojibwa Woman, Social Life of the Navajo Indians*) and still others (*City of Women, Spider Woman*) in a first-person, self-reflexive "modern" narrative mode. The writing of Zora Neale Hurston also contains recognizable critiques of objective description in addition to numerous and contesting self-reflexive poses. To argue, however, that writers such as James Clifford, Paul Rabinow, or Vincent Crapanzano usher in the modern moment in anthropology (notwithstanding their powerful reformulations of modernist critique) can only rest on a faulty understanding of what the modern connotes in anthropology. The question of the modern in anthropology is an important one, for the thrust of what I am arguing is that self-reflexive anthropology needs to be placed in clear proximity to the modernist critique of the realist ethnographic text, in order to distinguish it more clearly from forms of deconstructive ethnography.

*

If there are difficulties in periodizing the modern for any given disciplinary formation, the question of modernity in the Third World is no less vexed, and extends the formulation to which modernity, where? The point here is not to announce, as have some, that modernity is everywhere,[59] but to ask, as does Geetha Kapur, "How are we placed?"[60]

Like Dipesh Chakrabarty, who argues that nationalism is the modernizing ideology par excellence in the Third World,[61] Kapur agrees that nationalism and modernism are historically consonant, manifested in the Nehruvian modernizing paradigm for India, but insists on a mutually critical relationship between nationalism and the modern.[62] Thus "nationalism ... is at the very least a foil to the universal modern. It helps resist imperialist hegemony up to a point."[63] Yet as Fredric Jameson has recently reaffirmed, "the traces of imperialism can be found in Western modernism, and are indeed constitutive of it."[64] Put less equivocally, "Europe's acquisition of the adjective modern for itself is a piece of global history of which an integral part is the story of European Imperialism."[65] Modernism, then, is engendered by imperialism, and generates in turn the sites of resistance to it in nationalism, producing what Kapur calls the "paradox of nationalism," or what Chatterjee has termed its thematics and problematics.[66] Rey Chow reminds us, too, that modernism "needs to be bracketed within an understanding of modernity as a force of cultural expansionism whose foundations are not only emancipatory but also Eurocentric or patriarchial."[67]

"Modernity" has most frequently been discussed in the sociological literature on India as the question of "modernizing a Great Tradition." (The "great tradition" is, of course, that of Hinduism, and points to a certain complicity of modernization theory in the construction of a nationalism that is also communal.) The "Sociology for India" debates waged in the pages of *Contributions to Indian Sociology* throughout the sixties and seventies bear testimony to the hegemony of these debates.[68]

Kapur, in seeking to locate herself "in maps of the world's modernisms," calls for a reperiodization of the modern, a recognition that modernism is contingent on the diachronics of modernization, giving modernity itself an expressly historical rather than a mainly ontological mission.[69] And yet that ontology has particular consequences for what modernism means in India:

> Instead of internationalism, there is in India the double discourse of
> nationalism and modernism. It is, however, a generative discourse.
> When projected outward, it becomes a four-part equation:
> nationalism recalls the category of tradition; modernism always
> implies internationalism. The four-part equation further enables one
> to confront the question of tradition (or "invented tradition") that
> ensues during nationalism with a current internationalism (or
> globalism) and its appropriative techniques.[70]

Here, Kapur broaches the question of the postmodern, which, in its hostility to the sovereign subject, can be seen as an attack on sovereignty itself, in particular the nationalist self as collective identity.[71] Kapur contends that as national formations are broken up by social movements, the regional privileges ethnic over political definitions, leading at once to multiplying nationalisms and a minutely differentiated global multiculturalism.[72] The demise of nation-states around the world is an urgent issue, and not one that can be served any justice in this short essay. I do, however, want to note that if it is true that postmodernism may work to break apart certain collective identities, it is not also true that we are left only with an individualizing pluralism. The breakup of certain sovereign subjectivities may make way for the formation of new, coalitional subjects.

While Kapur's attention is drawn primarily to the "when" and "where" of postmodernism, KumKum Sangari, in her essay "Politics of the Possible," is drawn to the "where" and "how" of postmodernism. She begins by noting that the epistemological problem of postmodernism is a historical one, located largely in the West.[73] She calls the "self-conscious dissolution of the bourgeois subject" a universalizing move that "may well turn out to be in some respects, another internationalization of the role of the West."[74] In this context, I agree with Sangari that the question of the "present locales of undecidability" is a crucial one.[75]

Sangari continues that while "postmodernism both privileges the present and valorizes indeterminacy as a cognitive mode, it also deflates social contradiction into forms of ambiguity or deferral, instates arbitrary juxtaposition or collage as historical 'method,' preempts change by fragmenting the ground of praxis."[76] Writing against a kind of epistemological despair, Sangari asserts that "the difficulty of arriving at fact ... tends to assert another level of factuality, to cast and resolve the issues of meaning on another more dialectical plane, a plane on which the notion of knowledge can be made to work from positions of engagement within the local and contemporary."[77]

Here I find myself in agreement with Sangari, even if, for me, resolutely or otherwise located in the West, the drive toward the local and contemporary will signify a different problematic. The strength of Sangari's analysis is that it posits a historical and methodological analysis of postmodernism, attentive to the specifics of geographical location and intellectual formation.

Anthony Appiah focuses not on postmodernism, but on postmodernization, forms of writing that "seek to delegitimize not only the form of realism, but the content of nationalism." Appiah says we would be mistaken to read a novel such as Yambo Ouologuem's *Le Devoir de Violence* as a postmodern text. Rather, this novel engages "postmodern*ization,*" as a politics, rather than aesthetics. According to Appiah, this novel rules out the possibility that, as the modernizers said, after colonialism comes rationality. Ouologuem's novel is then typical of others written during the postcolonial period that reject both Western imperialism and the nationalist projects of the postcolonial bourgeoisie.[78]

Appiah argues that this claim to delegitimization is based not on postmodern precepts but on the assertion of humanist "ethical universals." What postcolonial writers choose is not the nation, "but

Africa—its continent and people."[79] This is the basis for a transnational, rather than a national, solidarity[80] that might take a regional Pan-African form rather than the form of transcendent transnationalism advocated by some (see chapter 6).

Appiah concludes that postcolonialism, like postmodernism, contains a post that challenges legitimating narratives. On those grounds it is not an ally for Western postmodernism, but rather an agonist, from which postmodernism may have something to learn.[81] Appiah argues that we take care to distinguish between determining the "role that Africa, like the rest of the Third World, plays for Euro-American postmodernism" from the "role postmodernism might play in the Third World."[82] Indeed, it is the second half of this equation that I want to examine now.

In arguing that we "reperiodize the modern," Geetha Kapur has not considered the idea that postmodern theory might aid in this endeavor. Nellie Richard, while agreeing that postmodernism seems to reformulate the old dependencies of the center/periphery model, does argue that postmodernism offers "the possibility of a critical rereading of modernism."[83] Linda Nicholson concurs that "postmodernism urges us to recognize the highest ideals of modernity in the West as immanent to a specific historical time and geographical region, and also associated with certain political baggage."[84]

Kapur argues that modernity and modernization are discontinuous, that modernity is inevitably superseded by postmodernism to complete the process of modernization.[85] In this sense, the "post" in postmodern is the same as the "post" in postcolonial, for modernization continues as a postcolonial practice built on colonial dependency. Rey Chow also speaks of modernism in the Third World as a displacement that exceeds the binary logic of modernism/postmodernism that attempts to contain it. Or, as Norma Alarcón explains, the modern and postmodern are not sequential but rather interreferential.[86] That is to say that the attempt to periodize modernism to establish when the postmodern begins is inadequate, because in some sense, "postmodernism is only a belated articulation of what the West's others have lived all along."[87] Richard describes Latin American "discontinuities of history marked by a multiplicity of pasts laid down like sediments in hybrid and fragmented memories," producing the experience of "continuous dissociation."[88] This notion of living the fragment parallels what Chela Sandoval describes as a differential oppositional consciousness arising among subjects forced to experience the aesthetics of postmodernism for survival.[89]

We are still, however, faced with the critique that as postmodernism breaks down all master, legitimating narratives, "we are left only with local legitimations," "immanent in our own practices" in which "justice turns out to reside ... in the institutionalization of pluralism."[90] Kapur is quite clear that the regional (read: local) is but another way of legitimating the Western universal:

> A revamping of the older term, regional diversity, into cultural difference, does not entirely take away its subordinate status. One way or another, internationalism is the norm of the 20th century. Regionalism implies territorial-cultural integrity preserved in the peripheral zones. But this too is a viewpoint from the cosmopolitan center, as is the notion of multicultural difference.[91]

In other words, "the regional provides the resources that make up the universal." And it is the regional specification of local knowledges that authorizes anthropological intervention.[92]

Yet as Rey Chow reminds us, instead of the local, accounts of postmodernism usually yield lists demonstrating Lyotard's notion that "not only can one speak of everything, one must": "The impossibility of dealing with the local except by letting everyone speak/ everything be spoken at the same time leads to a situation in which hegemony in the Gramscian sense is always a danger."[93] To this danger, Chow poses as remedy the notion of a "critical regionalism"[94] that would resist the recuperation of the regional as an instance of the everywhere (universal) by posing the notion of the coalitional subject:

> Pressing the claims of the local ... does not mean essentializing one position; instead it means using that position as a parallel for allying with others. For the Third World feminist especially, the local is never "one." Rather, her own locality, as construct ... means that pressing its claims is always pressing the claims of a form of existence which is by origin, coalitional. [95]

Similarly, Norma Alarcón, in dismantling the unified, autonomous, self-making, self-determining subject of Anglo-American feminism, posits a plurality of selves enacted by women of color. In speaking of the "woman of color" as a coalitional subject, she argues that "multiple positions may arise from a series of multiple displacements, feminist/lesbian, nationalist, racial, socioeconomic, historical etc."[96] For the writers of *This Bridge Called My Back,* "the peculiarity of their displacement implies a multiplicity of positions from which they are driven to grasp or understand themselves and their relations with the real."[97] "Multiple-voiced subjectivity is lived in the resistance to competing notions for one's allegiance or self-identification."[98]

Increasingly, however, what might be termed "feminist location theory"—attempts to situate the subject in shifting axes of power and knowledge—has come under attack for its apparent invocation of pluralist difference. For example, historian Gyan Prakash says,

> The issue of the heterogeneity of social identities and cultural forms raised by the relationship of colonialism to capitalism is not one that can be resolved easily by the extension of the race-class-gender formula; the question of colonial difference is not one of the adequacy of a single (class) versus multiple factors, nor are we constrained to choose forms of sociality other than class. What is at issue in the articulation of class with race, caste, gender, nation, ethnicity, and religion is that these categories were not equal, woman as a category was not equal to worker; being an upper-caste Hindu was not a form of sociality equal with citizenship in the nation-state that the nationalists struggled to achieve. *Thus, the concept of multiple-selves, incorporating a variety of social identities and so popular with the contemporary liberal multiculturalists, cannot be adequate for conceiving colonial difference.* Instead we have to think of the specificity of colonial difference as class overwriting race and gender.[99] (my emphasis)

Prakash is, of course, perfectly right to insist that the issue is not one of single as opposed to multiple determinants of oppression. Nor is he making the usual additive argument about class *and* race *and* gender. Prakash is, however, saying that race or gender must be apprehended through particular class formations, ignoring the insights of feminist historians such as KumKum Sangari and Sudesh Vaid, who have argued not that caste or class determines patriarchy, but rather that patriarchy is intrinsic to the formation and transformation of categories such as caste or class.[100] Insisting on the primacy of class puts us back at the elementary critique of what maintaining class at the center of materialist analysis *excludes* when other categories are subordinated to it. The same can be said for feminist theory attempting to hold gender at its center subordinating the experiences of race, class, and sexuality.

The issue, again, is not whether to examine such categories, but *how* to do so. "Betrayal" does lay claim to notions of multiple positioning, but it does so in order to undertake a form of "relational" analysis by reading the ways Janaki's gender and class identities are activated by or staged through nationalist ideology, then strategized as possible sites of resistance by the feminist historian. Janaki's positioning arises out of the originary displacements of gender by Indian nationalist ideology. The analysis does not assert that "woman" is equal to "worker," or that an "upper-caste Hindu" is immediately subaltern. It does assert that a *poor,* Brahmin woman may be subaltern with respect to the gendering of nationalist ideology, and in so doing insists on the *relationality* of subalternity. This is where I find Chandra Mohanty's elaboration of Dorothy Smith's notion "relations of ruling" as the interpenetration of multiple sites of power, useful for locating specific experiences of sexual politics in concrete historical forms of colonialism, imperialism, racism, or capitalism.[101]

Prakash does what many do too often—collapse examples of multiple positioning into liberal multiculturalism and pluralism, without being attentive to the specific questions or resolutions posed by analyses of multiple positioning. For much of this theory is not produced out of the idea of reconciling "to each her own (difference)," but rather highlights how such multiple positions are strategic precisely because they are contestatory, combative, and competitive.

Conclusion

As a means of closing this essay, I sign my agreement with Rey Chow when she observes that "the postmodern cultural situation in which non-western feminists now find themselves is a difficult and cynical one."[102] Thus,

> The task that faces Third World feminists is not simply that of animating the oppressed woman of their cultures, but of making the automatized and animated condition of their own voices the conscious point of departure in their interventions. This does not simply mean they are, as they must be, speaking across cultures and boundaries; it also means that they speak of the awareness of "cross-cultural" speech as a limit, and that their very own use of the victimhood of women and third world cultures is both symptomatic of and inevitably complicitous with the First World.[103]

Chow's words bring us full circle to the practice of deconstruction as intimate habitation. If the limits of an analysis like "Betrayal" are clearer, I hope that its interventions are as well. I have located "Betrayal" in a series of debates about postmodernism and interpretive analysis in the discipline of anthropology, and as it is deliberated by Third World critics. The questions surrounding the application of postmodern theory cannot be engaged apart from their audiences of reception. In addressing the concerns of some Third World critics, I have argued for a postmodern practice consolidated by its attention to the local and coalitional. That is to say that while I agree some forms of postmodernism may reinaugurate a universal subject through its appropriation of the regional, or of difference in general, I do find theories of multiple positioning enabling forms of postmodern engagement with particular histories and particular locales. It will not do, in my view, to dismiss postmodern theories out of hand without attention to the specificities of how they are deployed.

My own method of deconstruction has hinged on the practice of deferral in "Refusing the Subject," wielding what Butler has called the "fearful conditional." "Betrayal," on the other hand, has played on notions of displacement and loss. Both essays underlined the representational difficulties of subject retrieval. If practices of deferral, displacement, and loss broach questions of failure, the next essay theorizes the epistemological thrust of deconstruction as failure, catalyzing further reconceptualizations of the local. In what follows, I argue that theorizing the local calls our attention not to the processes of deterritorialization, but to reterritorialization. With the loss of geographically bounded notions of culture, I contend that anthropology, if it is truly to enact a form of "critical regionalism," must turn now toward the proxemics of home.

6

Feminist Ethnography as Failure

"What happens to the recorder of failed texts?"[1]

The dusk of Madras often drops upon the city like a sari of pink gauze, and it is on one such evening that my friend Geetha and I thread ourselves through a narrow lane in search of a woman I was told had been jailed during the Indian nationalist movement. After several queries—Which granny? That one who lives across the street from so-and-so's uncle, or the granny who stays with her daughters at the end of the lane?—we arrive at a tiny house with a picket fence wistfully erected against the usual small children, kittens, goats, and chickens, running in, out, or between houses and street.

Inside the house was a quiet, stout woman and a younger woman introduced as her daughter. We explained that my cousin at the magazine *Ananda Vikatan* had told us that Mrs. Ramaswami had been involved in the Freedom Movement and might agree to be interviewed. Mrs. Ramaswami, after recovering from her initial surprise, smiled sweetly and said that although she didn't understand why we were interested, she would be happy to talk to us. She started to settle in comfortably among some cushions along a low-lying bench, and I explained hastily that I didn't want to impose on her without notice. I asked whether we could possibly talk to her the next evening. The woman's puzzlement returned. All manner of people routinely show up on the doorsteps of Indian households, and no matter how bizarre the story (in fact, the more bizarre the better), the mention of a familiar name is usually enough to warrant a patient hearing, and if one was lucky enough, the discovery of shared relatives, or long-lost friends. It thus made no sense to Mrs. Ramaswami that after an involved introduction indicating that we wanted to talk, we would then leave, refusing, in effect, to talk. Geetha also found it extremely odd, but I kept thinking that if someone appeared without notice on my doorstep, I would probably not want to talk just at that moment. In short, I was simply unprepared for her willingness to do the interview right then and there. So I tried another tack, explaining that I'd forgotten my tape recorder and that because I thought she had important and interesting things to say, I wanted to be sure to record our conversation. These explanations seemed to confuse Mrs. Ramaswami all the more, but her daughter assured us that she understood we wanted to record the interview and that her mother would be prepared the next day. With some awkwardness, I made our excuses, cursing again my bad American thought habits, but most of all my negligence in leaving behind the tape recorder.

The next evening Geetha and I returned, and to our surprise found the entire family waiting for us. All seven of Mrs. Ramaswami's children were assembled, and the oldest son, a loud, heavyset man with an imitation MGR[2] hairdo (greased and slicked up high) was clearly in charge.

"Yes?" he queried us in English, "you have come from the TV station to talk to amma about our father?" I could hardly contain my startled exclamation as I realized that my emphasis on the tape recorder had led them to expect a major technical production. The next half hour followed with slow explanations: that I'd come from a university in the States, and Geetha from a university in Delhi, to write our Ph.D.s on women in India's Freedom Movement, and that this was why we wanted to talk to Mrs. Ramaswami.

MGR had interrupted, "But I don't understand why you want to talk to *her*. She did not do anything; it was our father who was involved in the movement and went to jail: once in 1930, once in 1932, and once in 1943." At this point he pulled a recent request for his father's jail record from a file, and a petition to the government of India for a freedom fighter pension. We shuffled through the papers with feigned interest, and then stressed again, politely, that we understood his mother had also gone to jail, and that we wanted to talk to her.

MGR continued to insist upon his father's achievements. About the room I could hear the buzz of his sisters' Tamil. Finally one of them asked me in halting English, "You've come from the TV, isn't it?" "No, no, she's not from TV, she's from University," MGR said to his sister scornfully. "Yes," I said to her in Tamil, somewhat apologetically, "we've come from the University."

Geetha and I turned to the now anxious and intimidated Mrs. Ramaswami and began to ask her a series of basic questions. After another half hour, we learned that she had indeed gone to jail, but only, she said, with a nervous glance at her son, because her husband had wanted her to follow him. At this point her son began a long story about how difficult it was to secure the pension due his father as a freedom fighter. Geetha, fully impatient with the man, practically shouted, "We've come to talk to *her*!" One of the sisters, sensing our frustration, offered again hopefully, "You've come from the TV, isn't it?" Geetha and I, with a glance at each other, decided that the situation was hopeless, and extricated ourselves as quickly as possible. Leaving the house, we concluded that the whole thing had been a disaster, a complete failure.

*

One may read into this anecdote a number of lessons: the interference, however well meaning (or hostile), of male members of the family when attempting to constitute a woman as her own subject, the embarrassing misunderstandings about the relationship of technology to the interview genre, the misapprehension of rules and norms governing Indian hospitality. Or, more concretely, in emphasizing the tape recorder I had forfeited the trust and spontaneity of a moment of introduction. I had insisted upon my tape recorder, hoping to "capture" women's words, and in so doing was caught by the desire to capture. Yet even if I had been less fixated on my tape recorder, and more accepting of the immediate hospitality Indians often offer to complete strangers, a "successful" interview, I want to argue, would only have masked substantially a more fundamental level of failure. The account I have given is neither typical nor especially enlightening. It does, however, illustrate a particular moment when feminist intentions "fail."

Even so, accounts of "failure" frequently function to suggest better ones. In one collection of essays on fieldwork edited by Philip De Vita, an essay titled "Fieldwork That Failed" is found under a section called "Learning from Mistakes."[3] The second section of the book, however, recuperates those mistakes as "Lessons from Fieldwork." Similarly, a recent collection on feminist oral history, *Women's Words,* edited by Sherna Gluck and Daphne Patai, reveals a series of painful or difficult situations faced by the feminist researcher, replete with strategies and problem-solving advice. For example, "If the narrator is to have the chance to tell her own story, the interviewer's first question needs to be very open-ended. It needs to convey the message that in this situation, the narrator's interpretation of her experience guides the interview." Or, "Try not to cut the narrator off to steer her to what your concerns are."[4] Another author suggests that "prior to the initial meeting, interviewers can discard their own research-oriented time-frame in favor of narrators' temporal expectations." Still another author emphasizes that "feminist interviewers will not try to elicit a repertoire of attention-getting monologic narratives, especially narratives that originated in previous communication contexts and are well-polished from repeated rehearsals."[5]

The collection, then, begins to read like a manual on feminist malpractice. What happens repeatedly, however, is that a problem, initially described as a failure, is finally recuperated as a success, for of course, future feminist researchers benefiting from this experience will not go on to commit the same errors. They will arrive at an interview, tape recorder in readiness, or with a small notebook held discreetly in one hand. The assumption is that "better" methodology will mean better accounts.[6]

While these examples indeed reveal failures of method, there is a sense in which any discussion of methodology diverts attention from more fundamental issues of epistemology. Thus I am more interested in tracking failure at another level, at once ethnographic and epistemic. I will argue that we use our "fields" of failure as a means of pointing up the difficulties in our own epistemological assumptions and representational strategies. Rather than referring to the *Women's Words* collection as yet another advice manual, I argue that we read it as yet another sign that all is not well in the field of feminist research, and that this malaise is as historic as it is epistemic. It is here that I find Gayatri Spivak's notion of "cognitive failure" instructive.

Based on Ranajit Guha's premise that the history of India is inevitably the failure of a nation to come into its own, Spivak's notion of failure extends to those moments when a project is faced with its own impossibility. Normative historical description shields those moments of cognitive failure (when interpretation is unattainable), leading to its interpolation as "success" ("success-in-failure"), the belief that one has provided a satisfactory interpretation. Yet this shielding, she tells us, is an actively sanctioned ignorance and a form of colonial domination. She tells us, too, that the historians of

India "fail" to ascertain the consciousness of the subaltern for reasons as "historical as those they adduce for the ... subjects they study."[7]

I suggest that Spivak's analysis holds true as well for feminist ethnography. Normative ethnographic description, even of the feminist kind, also propagates a sanctioned ignorance, for to continue to even talk about women as "women" (or to assume that the subjects of feminist ethnography are "simply" women) represents a not unfamiliar success-in-failure. And like the subaltern studies historians, feminists too fail for historic reasons: the displacement of the very epistemological center of feminism (gender) means that we can no longer describe women as women, but as subjects differently and sometimes primarily constituted by race, class, and sexuality. Again, the problem is not that feminists don't recognize the importance of race, class, and sexuality—what Kobena Mercer has dubbed the mantra of liberal multiculturalism[8]—but rather that considerable confusion exists about *how* to consider these "multiple axes of oppression."[9]

What I am arguing, then, is that the breakdown, or, more properly, reconstitution, of feminist theory is a historic moment, and so, too, is feminist "failure." Let me be clear, however, that I do not advocate or call for a "politics of despair," as have some recent theorists.[10] What I urge is rather the acknowledgment of failure through an accountable positioning, one that I will argue takes us homeward rather than away. In this reconstituted feminist project, the practice of failure is pivotal.

Not surprisingly, this historical moment is also marked by the failure of an entire genre of description: ethnography. Clifford Geertz marks anthropology, "a task at which no one ever does more than not utterly fail,"[11] as subject to the same conditions of questioning and crisis that characterize feminist debates. For "at the same time as the moral foundations of ethnography have been shaken by decolonization on the Being There side, its epistemological foundations have been shaken by a general loss of faith in received stories about the nature of representation, ethnographic or any other, on the Being Here side."[12]

This notion of ethnographic and epistemic failure influences the practice of feminist fieldwork. For our failures are as much a part of the process of knowledge constitution as are our oft-heralded "successes." Failure is not just a sign of epistemological crisis (for it is indeed also that), but also, I would argue, an epistemological construct. Failure signals a project that may no longer be attempted, or at least not on the same terms.

Rereading one of my favorite books, I was struck again by Laura Bohannon's notion of ethnographer as trickster in *Return to Laughter:* "One who seems to be what (s)he is not and one who professes faith in what (s)he does not believe." I need not belabor the point that tricksters are admirable even as they are equal parts clever and treacherous, or that the art of the trickster is manifestly to *faire semblant,* to act "as if."[13]

The art of speaking "as if" (that is, from the "native's point of view") has been finely honed by practitioners of anthropology from Malinowski through Geertz. Yet perhaps because this locution was so firmly grounded in realist assumptions, the ethnographer has historically denied *his* role as trickster.[14] Thus in one of Geertz's later assessments, "Writing ethnography 'from the native's point of view' dramatized for Malinowski his hopes of self-transcendence; for many of his most faithful descendents, it dramatizes their fears of self-deception."[15]

What I propose is a transformation of Bohannon's phrase so that the feminist ethnographer as trickster becomes one who does not profess faith in what she believes. This notion of feminist trickster hinges on the supposition that we can "give voice" and the knowledge that we can never fully. Here I argue for a suspension of the feminist faith that we can ever wholly understand and identify with other women (displacing again the colonial model of "speaking for," and the dialogical hope of "speaking with").[16] This requires a trickster figure who "trips" on, but is not tripped up by, the seductions of a feminism that promises what it may never deliver: full representation on the one hand, and full comprehension on the other. In this scenario, the feminist as trickster mediates between cognitive failure and its success; it is trickster agency that makes the distinction between success and failure indeterminate, alerting us to the "possibilities of failure."[17] I believe that holding these two terms in tension—the desire to know and the desire to represent—gives us the means, as Spivak suggests, to "question the authority of the investigating subject without paralyzing her, persistently transforming conditions of impossibility into possibility."[18] Feminist ethnographers, then, seek out new possibilities engendered by the recognition of failure, as well as the limiting features of its acknowledgment.

A failed account, I argue, occasions new kinds of positionings. Yet a "failed" account resting on claims to totalizing explanation (in this case, the narrative primacy of gender) gives way to partial accounts, which in turn "fail" for new reasons (usually for providing inadequate information or "context"). If the response to a partial account is inevitably the demand for a fuller one, to refuse such a desire is immediately to jeopardize one's status as ethnographer. To counter the request for more information, I usually pose the question of returning to the library.

Homework, Not Fieldwork

If a movement to decolonize anthropology still exists, surely its arrival was heralded by two collections published almost simultaneously in the United States and Britian: Dell Hymes's *Reinventing Anthropology* (1969; paperback edition, 1974) and Talal Asad's *Anthropology and the Colonial Encounter* (1973). A number of recent collections memorialize this moment with undying persistence. Consider, for example, the introductory essays by Richard Fox for *Recapturing Anthropology* (1991), Michaela di Leonardo for *Gender at the Crossroads of Knowledge* (1991), and Faye Harrison for *Decolonizing Anthropology* (1991). Interestingly enough, the two collections that initiate the feminist anthropology of the seventies, Michelle Rosaldo and Louise Lamphere's *Woman, Culture, and Society* (1974) and Rayna Rapp's *Toward an Anthropology of Women* (1975), do not mark that decolonizing moment.[19] Even with the appearance of Eleanor Leacock and Mona Etienne's *Women and Colonialism* in 1980, as late as 1988 one author could still proclaim *Women: The Last Colony*.[20] Nevertheless, what I bring into focus with this juxtaposition of texts is the question of decolonizing feminist anthropology; to ask, as does Marnia Lazreg, "What is the nature of the feminist project? What is its relation to women in other places?"[21]

To my mind, *Reinventing Anthropology* remains the classic statement of a post-sixties anthropology, which sought simultaneously to denounce the continuing colonial role played by the discipline and to urge the project of "bringing it all back home." It is no accident, I think, that two positions appear in the same collection, for indeed, each in a sense presumes the other. Anthropology at home (otherwise known as Sociology) was not acceptable until the move to decolonize anthropology arose; a decolonized anthropology assumed that a critical eye would necessarily be cast on a whole range of practices at "home" that authorized American intervention in the "Third World." Indeed, a number of anthropologists who had begun their careers abroad now turned homeward. I think particularly of Rayna Rapp, Sherry Ortner, Renato Rosaldo, and Paul Rabinow,[22] among others. I think too of a number of ethnographers who have worked in homes they have not always recognized as familiar: Faye Ginsburg, Judith Stacey, Carol Stack, and Sylvia Yanagisako. It is perhaps only a coincidence that a number of these ethnographers are women, or that most of them are white.

While I find this trend encouraging (if it can indeed be called that), and I applaud and admire the efforts of these ethnographers, I would not argue that we stop with what is more properly a beginning. For it seems to me that an uncompleted project embodied in the title *Reinventing Anthropology* was actually not so much fieldwork at home, as "homework."

James Clifford, in a recent essay, attempts to explore the epistemological weight fieldwork carries for the practice of anthropology.[23] He sees fieldwork as a "specific kind of localized dwelling" where the field becomes a "home away from home, a place of dwelling." Clifford is concerned that anthropology has tended to "privilege relations of travel over relations of dwelling";[24] his project in opposing the two terms is, I think, to dislodge the prominence of travel as metaphor for anthropology. In emphasizing "dwelling," the act of staying in one place, over traveling, the act of moving from place to place, Clifford transforms Geertz's polarity (Being Here/Being There) by problematizing the relationship between "being there" and "getting there."

Clifford worries about the dangers of construing ethnography as fieldwork. I, too, share his concern. Recent proclamations that "the field is everywhere," even when coupled with critiques of fieldwork,[25] do little to unsettle the epistemological weight fieldwork signifies for the discipline. Yet in opposing dwelling to travel, Clifford inevitably stresses the meaning of "dwelling" as verb rather than noun. For "dwelling," as he himself suggests, is also a site of habitation, a potential "home." Were Clifford to stress the second sense of the term, "homework" might well emerge from his analysis as vital epistemological terrain for anthropology.

"Homework" is, I contend, the actualization of what some writers have termed "anthropology in reverse." David Scott has noted that the ethnographic project is characterized by the anthropological journey, which entails a recursive movement between departure and return.[26] It is this "going and returning that organizes the epistemological and geographical disposition of the anthropological gaze." Scott explains:

This movement ... has never been an innocent or unmarked one.
The very possibility of the anthropological journey has been linked to
the historical occasion of Western expansion. And this expansion has
not only enabled, facilitated and authorized the specific
anthropological problematic of difference ... but also established its
epistemological standpoint.[27]

Scott then reminds us that the idea of "return" that marks the generative concept of anthropology always insinuates the "presence of the social imaginary of the West."[28]

However, it is Mary John's recent essay "Postcolonial Feminists in the Western Intellectual Field" that begins to unsettle these distinctions by suggesting the practice of an "anthropology in reverse." She notes, "Unlike the western anthropologist who has to undergo specialized training to ready herself for fieldwork in a distant place, one that her culture does not prepare her for, isn't it clear that in sharp contrast everything can collude to bring (the postcolonial) westward, and hardly for anthropological reasons?" John reminds us that our subjectivities are forged in "sanctioned ignorances," and the positioning she describes for a postcolonial intellectual is, I think, equally descriptive of First World positionings, especially the anthropological:

Education is more obviously a process by which we learn to avow
and remember certain knowledges and devalue and forget others. We
grow up repudiating the local and personal in favor of what will get
us ahead and away—thus coming of age in an intellectual field that
by no means arbitrarily creates disinterest and oversight in some
areas while directing desire elsewhere.[29]

In this way, John identifies the "West" as a kind of field, and asks, "What kinds of fieldnotes would I like to see carried back to a third world nation like India?"[30] And still later, "What would it be like to read Harriet Jacobs or *This Bridge Called My Back* in India?"[31]

These are indeed important questions, but I think the more valuable implications of John's own argument are obscured by her framing of the West as field as a kind of direct reversal. It seems that John struggles with the nostalgia of "India as home," and for this reason identifies the West only as a kind of field, and not also as a kind of "home." This, despite her suggestion that we learn to recognize as both "home" and "historical choice" our sites of enunciation.[32] Indeed, John herself wonders whether an "anthropology in reverse" is intelligible at all.

I believe that her notion of anthropology in reverse is intelligible, given a different reading of some of its implications. John speaks of "learning to desist from offering ventriloquistic fantasies" of speaking from a place she is not. Speaking from a place where one is not, where location and locution are tightly bound by a distant imaginary, is, of course, the normative practice of anthropology. "Anthropology in reverse" then means speaking from the place one is located, to specify our sites of enunciation as "home." The neglected insight of John's essay is that she urges anthropology to enact a different politics of location, one that redirects its gaze homeward rather than away. That John has, in fact, undertaken a kind of "homework" and called it "fieldwork" (for reasons as complex as most strategies of resistance) should not prevent us, I think, from seeing the radical utility of her notion.

It is true that those of us called upon to be experts on everything from ethnic cooking to multicultural curricula often find the response "Do your own homework" sticking in our throats. Nevertheless, if I suggest a return to the library, I am not being frivolous, for I consider it one viable site for the conduct of "homework."

Fields of Failure

Grade school days notwithstanding, what I want to address with the notion of "homework" is precisely our own methods of schooling. Why is it that despite recent critiques of place and voice in anthropology,[33] we have yet to turn to our own neighborhoods and growing-up places?[34] This is precisely what much contemporary antiracist work and feminist writing does, in particular a well-known essay by Minnie Bruce Pratt in which a rigorous interrogation of what constitutes "home" takes "place." This questioning of heretofore unexamined points of privilege and blindness forms the basis of an accountable positioning that seeks to locate itself in and against the master discourses of race, class, and sexuality that inscribe it.

In Chandra Mohanty and Biddy Martin's discussion of Pratt's essay, " 'being home' refers to the place where one lives within the familiar, safe, protected boundaries; 'not being at home' is a matter of realizing that home was an illusion of coherence and safety based on the exclusion of specific histories of oppression and resistance."[35] Yet once that questioning of the "enclosing, encircling, constraining circle of home"[36] begins, and once one understands the ways in which identity is sandwiched between home and community, homogeneity and comfort, between skin, blood, heart, "then comes the fear of nowhere to go" that one can never have a safe place like "home."

Many years ago, in *Tristes Tropiques,* Claude Lévi-Strauss wrote of "dépaysement."[37] The root of the word is *pays,* French for "country," and describes two processes: the act of sending away from, or leaving home, and one's feeling of loss or unease in being away from home. At least one writer has seen Lévi-Strauss's notion as a "distancing that would allow one to return more profoundly home."[38] While this understanding evokes a nostalgic mode, I suggest that anthropologists return more profoundly home if we view dépaysement as one strategy for what Spivak has called "unlearning our privilege as loss," that is, as an interrogation of our reasons for travels afar.

One way in which "loss" mediates between home and field is suggested by Laura Nader in her essay on "studying up" for *Reinventing Anthropology.* She references "the traditional alienation from their own society that characterizes anthropologists," which relates to their lack of "intense commitment to social reform."[39] Anthropology, then, trades on the reversal of the terms *safety* and *danger.* Following her point it would be only too easy to say that "going away" is a way of masking that there is "nowhere to go." One has only to think of the opening lines of Paul Rabinow's *Reflections on Fieldwork in Morocco:*

> I left Chicago two days after the assassination of Robert Kennedy.... I had been mildly anxious about leaving, but the news of the murder had buried those feelings under a wave of revulsion and disgust. I left America with a giddy sense of release. I was sick of being a student, tired of the city, and felt politically impotent. I was going to Morocco to become an anthropologist.[40]

But psychologizing here is not quite appropriate, for like Mary John (and indeed Nader herself), I agree that this "going away" is the product of institutional mechanisms of power.

Citing Gloria Anzaldúa's "borderlands," Emily Hicks's "border writing," Deleuze and Guattari's "deterritorialization," and Edward Said's "traveling theory," critic Caren Kaplan advises us that "as we begin the last decade of this century we may have no better terms to describe our wordly activities than those which refer us to the atlas."[41] Yet there are times when an atlas is less useful than a road map. For if it is geography that symbolizes the field, and anthropology's problematic epistemological site, then (as Martin and Mohanty suggest) it is demography that radically symbolizes "home," and, I would argue, anthropology's reterritorialized epistemological site: who lives in what neighborhood and why; who went to what school and why. ("Also erased: the university home of the researcher.")[42]

In a recent article, Angie Chabram has called upon us to acknowledge "pre-institutional histories, histories that originate in the fields, the border, the family, the oral tradition, factories, public institutions, and research designs,"[43] urging scholars to study their communities, not only from the outside, but from inside, within the academy.[44]

As I think through my own "preinstitutional history," the ways in which I come to my current institutional site, and the ways in which some of my students arrive, I remember again the differences in neighborhood and demography that send some to school and turn others away; that my questions about college were not whether, but where, to go; not whether to stay, but what to study. One of my students, Lara Angel, has written quite movingly about the process of negotiating privilege as loss:

> The minute I came to the New School I realized what relating to privilege meant, and how I was privileged.
>
> I went to a mostly all black college in Oakland—it was a community college and the people there did not really have money—in fact very few of us had money at all. All of us (well, not all) were people who grew up in ghettos, el Barrio, "little Viet Nam" or "little Chinatown." We knew we were privileged, and some went as far as to say "lucky" because we were "given" a chance.
>
> I remember walking home at night (I worked full-time during the day), completely afraid that I would get my ass kicked by the people in my neighborhood because I was a *"college* stu-dent." They could tell by my backpack and my dream of upward mobility that came out of every stitch of my clothing. I was afraid I'd get my ass kicked because I was trying to escape "funk-town" (fighting town—place in Oakland—18th Street—the "other side" of Lake Merrit). I was privileged and I was scared. *But* not all the people in my neighborhood disapproved of what I was doing. In fact, I had a lot of support—as long as I "stayed in the community" and "not sell out." I was warned by the African Student Association that the minute I sold out, I could never come back. Yeah well . . .
>
> Not long after, I moved to New York and went to an elitist school (go to an elitist school). But what has this got to do with anything? My bitter sense of *never* being able to be fully accepted in my community after I achieved a certain sense of upward mobility tells me how I relate to my privilege. How embarrassed I am to talk to my grandparents and find myself using words that they never heard of, and yet knowing that I am not truly a product of privilege.

What crosscutting axes of race, class, and gender connect Lara's story of home with my own? Or is it only that a particular institutional site of power throws us together as teacher and student? What are my own sites of privilege and loss?

I am only "second generation" for one side of my family in this country. The other side has been on American soil so long that counting the generations has become difficult. I was born thousands of miles from my father's place of birth, and yet my own birthplace, Chicago, is not so far from where my mother and many of her family were born. A certain spatial proximity obtains, and yet if I could speak across the generations to my great-great-grandfather, would he recognize me as kin?

"Matthew Miller, the original member of the Miller family in the United States, was born in northern Ireland 1722–32, and came to this country during the great Scotch-Irish Emigration 1700–50."[45] He entered Philadelphia first, and later settled in Carlisle, Pennsylvania. His son John Miller was born near Carlisle in 1752. After serving in the revolutionary war, and earning the rank of major, John Miller immigrated to Kentucky in 1778 and founded the town of Millersburg some twenty years later. His son James Miller was born there in 1791. After serving in the War of 1812, James Miller decided to immigrate with his family to northeast Missouri in 1838. Harry Middleton Hyatt has recorded some of the stories of this journey he heard from his grandfather, one of James Miller's sons. These are slapstick tales that will not draw laughter:

> An amusing episode occurred during the overland trip to
> Williamstown. The negro slaves, the older of whom had witnessed
> Indian raids in Kentucky, were rather nervous about an unsettled
> country like northeast Missouri, though they had been assured that all
> Indians had been driven further West. The first night out from
> Louisiana (Mo), a band of wandering Indians chanced upon the
> Miller camp. Never having seen negroes before, the Indians
> immediately exploded into warhoops and wild gesticulations. Dogs
> barked and growled, and tethered horses reared and neighed; the
> white children were filled with awe; and the slaves were thrown into
> a panic, crawling under wagons and hiding behind trees. The crisis
> began when the Indians began to pinch and rub the faces of the
> negroes, demanding with suspicious grunts what kind of warpaint
> they used.[46]

Upon arriving in Lewis County, Missouri, James Miller purchased 600 acres of land, and later became the owner of 2,000 acres. In a "compromise" state, and a local area that had a station on the underground railroad by 1830, James Miller was also one of the largest slave-owners in northeast Missouri, though the exact number of slaves he possessed is not known.

James Miller was my great-great-great-grandfather.[47]

To celebrate that in some sense I am a "Daughter of the American Revolution" is to erase the fact that I am the product of a settler history, a history whose narratives are staged by the encounters with "slaves and Indians," a history shaped by the violent practices of slavery, deceit, and genocide. My mother's family is a large and loving one, and I have always felt "at home" with them, but claiming my American heritage has never been easy.

*

The loss or absence of a cultural heritage (sometimes called "acculturation") is deeply felt by second generations around the world. Yet demography was also surely part of the reason I went to, and studied, India. Growing up in a white middle-class neighborhood, and attending mostly white middle-class schools, yet racially marked as "other," I had no recourse to an identity that is now variously (and I might add unfortunately) called Indo-American or Indian-American; in a California city whose farming interests and racial politics marked "brown" as Mexicano or Chicano, farmworker: possibly undocumented, possibly trouble. How many times in my childhood was I left speechless by school-yard taunts — "Dirty Mexican!" — knowing that to reply I was Indian would affirm what they already believed: I must be ashamed of my heritage.

Later, in school at Berkeley, where some make a fetish of cultural difference, my long and winding South Indian name was eagerly remarked upon, and the insistent but well-meaning questions began: What were the secrets of Indian cooking? How many untouchables lived in India? What did I think about V. S. Naipaul?

In desperation I turned to anthropology. "Indianness" was now being constructed for me, and in turn I was forced to construct it for myself. I could no more argue with my well-meaning interlocutors by insisting that I was as "American" as they were (therefore equally ignorant and unable to answer their questions), than I could with grade school tormentors who called me names for being brown.

To this day, I am not sure that I "chose" to work on India. Surely the reasons I didn't do fieldwork in Nicaragua are inversely related to my reasons for going to India. For part of what led me to India was the necessity of being "Indian," of being already inscribed as "Indian." Is this why such a radical change in field (normally evoking at least the surprise, if not consternation, of one's adviser), occasioned no comment from any of my professors at Stanford?

I do not mean to elide the differences between Mary John's postcolonial positioning and my own as a second-generation person of Indian descent, but it seems to me that our trajectories, opposite as they are, were determined long before she or I occupied the subject positions that constitute them, and, as well, are linked by the shadowy figure of the NRI (nonresident Indian). John returns to India in part to avoid becoming the NRI, and I return as the daughter of one. If Mary John's generation is going west, so is mine going east, and not only, to turn on John's phrase, for "anthropological reasons."

As differently positioned subjects, both of us "return" to India in different ways. Nevertheless, I have not meant to claim India as home for one of us and field for the other, for I, too, want to claim India as a "home." As Ursula Le Guin reminds us, one can return home after realizing that home is a place never before seen.[48]

*

Reterritorialization, an emphasis on the demographics of home, is not obviously anthropology's new epistemological center. Some ethnographers, notably Arjun Appadurai, among others, have identified an urgent need to study the cultural dynamics of "deterritorialization," asking, "What is the nature of locality as lived experience in a globalized, deterritorialized world?"[49] I am in sympathy with the impulse driving this question, but less confident that its resolution hinges on a "fresh approach to the role of imagination in social life,"[50] as Appadurai argues. Appadurai recognizes that there are divergent interpretations of what locality implies, and yet in arguing that the *ethno* in ethnography takes on a slippery, nonlocalized quality, I believe he has called too quickly for an ethnography "not so resolutely localized," one that "focuses on the unyoking of imagination from place."[51]

In so doing, it appears to me that Appadurai valorizes deterritorialization as a mode of being, or as an imaginative act. Deterritorialization is studied not to understand the powerful forces of oppression unleashed by it, or that it is unleashed by, but because it "illustrates the workings of the imagination."[52] How, then, do we understand the pain of the deterritorialized, the ones constantly in transit, like Aurora Morales, a Puertorriqueña who writes of being?

> The immigrant child of returned immigrants who repeated the journey in the second generation. Born on the island with first-hand love and the stories of my parents' Old Country — New York; and behind those, the secondhand stories of my mother's father, of the

hill-town of his long-ago childhood, told through my mother's barrio childhood. Layer upon layer of travel and leaving behind, an overlay of landscapes, so that I dream of all the beloved and hated places, and endlessly of trains and paths and roads and ships docking and leaving port and a multitude of borders and officials waiting for my little piece of paper.[53]

Akhil Gupta and James Ferguson have recently observed of the ethnographic situation that the familar lines between "here" and "there" have become increasingly blurred.[54] However, if Morales's narrative depicts not a one-way migration, but a migration never completed, a continual two-way exchange, she does not describe so much a blurring as being caught between *places*. The "here" (New York) and the "there" (Puerto Rico) matter.

Even Gilles Deleuze and Félix Guattari's initial formulation attempted to strike a relationship between deterritorialization, "the connection of an individual to a *political immediacy,* and the collective assemblage of enunciation."[55] Yet Appadurai's "Global Ethnoscapes" evaporates into an undertaking in which very different works shaped by distinctive political traditions and histories — a short story by Julio Cortázar and a film by Mira Nair, "India Cabaret" — are made to stand as "ethnographic profiles of deterritorialization" or displacement, and, by extension, the predicament of particular postcolonial anthropologizing.[56] Caren Kaplan's warning "against a form of theoretical tourism on the part of the first world critic, where the margin becomes a linguistic or critical vacation, a new poetics of the exotic"[57] reflects tellingly on Appadurai's global ethnoscapes.

Appadurai's project partakes of a transnationalism devoid of any politics of location or constituency, for it is difficult to discern in his schema whether subjects choose deterritorialization, or deterritorialization has chosen particular subjects.[58] While transnationalism practiced as a critique of the nation-state may indeed prove a useful endeavor, it seems that we would do well to heed R. Radhakrishnan's distinction between a "theoretically avant-garde transnationalism and a historically fraught transnationalism, between transnationalism as easy deracination, and transnationalism as a sensitive mode of commitment and accountability to past histories and experiences."[59] Radhakrishnan argues that transnationalism "has to be actively and critically implicated in the very histories that it seeks to deconstruct and go beyond.... The transnational space should have room for fundamental disagreements and contestations." Thus, "it is essential that each of us ask the other, 'Where do you come from?' and listen rigorously to the answer."[60]

In my view, deterritorialization is too often coupled with a kind of transcendent transnationalism often found in various calls to cosmopolitanism. Indeed, Appadurai's objective is to advance a doubled vision of transnational cultural studies, and what he terms "genuinely cosmopolitan ethnographic practices,"[61] with the result that "natives" are reinscribed unproblematically as cosmopolitans in the process.[62] While there may be much to recommend Paul Rabinow's "critical cosmopolitanism,"[63] or Bruce Robbins's "comparative cosmopolitanism," it is disquieting to learn that such calls are coupled, as in Robbins's (or Appadurai's) case, with declamations of the "manifold abuses of thinking local" or the "pieties of the particular."[64] Thus even if we agree with Robbins that "distances are really localities," and that "not enough imagination has gone into different modalities of situatedness-in-displacement," it does seem to me that one of the worst abuses of thinking about the local was to assume that we gained more than we lost by leaving it behind. For as Robbins himself says, "There is no alternative to belonging."[65]

Richard Fox has recently noted that "the close-to-home constantly intermixes with the far-from-home, and often it is not worthwhile deciding which is which."[66] I would argue that not only is it worthwhile, but imperative, for it is the generative processes of constituting home that matter. A blurring of boundaries between "here" and "there" does not mean that we need jump immediately from the local to the translocal, but that we rethink the construction of the local "here," reimagining "home" as an "oppositional image of place"[67] instead of valorizing a certain placelessness.

Uncritically theorized notions of deterritorialization project too comprehensively a "global homelessness" and displacement, trivializing the political particularities of the phenomenon and erasing the "resolutely local" homesites necessary both for First World anthropologists to interrogate their own privilege and for less privileged subjects to claim home as a place of nurturance and protection.[68]

Is it coincidence, then, that while many feminist theorists identify home as the site of theory, male critics write to eradicate it? Is this because, as Marilyn Strathern wryly remarks, "our cosmopolitan at home seems unable to hold the center"?[69]

bell hooks tells us of a childhood where "houses belonged to women, were their special domain, not as property, but as places where all that truly mattered in life took place—the warmth and comfort of shelter, the feeling of our bodies, the nurturing of our souls."[70] hooks juxtaposes the homes of white folk and black folk in order to focus on the black women who worked in both. Yet she emphasizes that "this task of making homeplace was not simply a matter of black women providing service; it was about the construction of a safe place where black people could affirm one another and by so doing heal many of the wounds inflicted by racist domination."[71]

hooks goes on to make poignantly the connections between the "homeplaces" of black Americans, however historically fragile (the slave hut, the wooden shack), and the homelands of South African racial apartheid:

> It is no accident that the South African apartheid regime systematically attacks and destroys black efforts to construct homeplace, however tenuous, that small private reality where black women and men can renew their spirits and recover themselves. It is no accident that this homeplace, as fragile and as transitional as it may be, a makeshift shed, a small bit of earth where one rests, is always subject to violation and destruction. For when a people no longer have the space to construct homeplace, we cannot build a meaningful community of resistance. [72]

hooks concludes her essay by linking decolonization and homeplace (the site of resistance and liberation struggle), allowing us to pose Caren Kaplan's question "Reterritorialization without imperialism?"[73] as a concrete statement.

Conclusion

My own narrative has begun with the "field" and worked its way steadily homeward. If I have not told you anything of the women with whom I worked, I have at least told you something of why it was that I attempted to work with them. My opening account of "being there" has been displaced by an emerging narrative of "getting there." Such a movement enables me to think through more clearly the act of "being here." In enacting a trickster agency of the "as if," I also seek to avoid speaking "as," undercutting the polarities of identity politics that led me to India in the first place. This essay, then, has been a part of my own homework exercise, an attempt to understand how one anthropologist, enabled by a particular kind of "field," attempts to rewrite the terms of "home" and "world" through a regenerated feminist praxis.

I have argued for the convergence of two distinct epistemological shifts, one where gender ceases to hold the center of feminist theory, and one where the field fails to hold the center of anthropology. One shift signals the failure of feminist thinking, and the other, the failure of ethnography. Both shifts, I believe, mark decolonization as an active, ongoing process—incomplete, and certainly not one to be memorialized as past historical moment.

None of the problematics raised here will be resolved in this essay, but if I have strategically theorized home in order to unearth the hegemonic "field" of feminist anthropology, I also recognize that *field* and *home* are dependent, not mutually exclusive, terms, and that the lines between fieldwork and homework are not always distinct. I have suggested that a feminist ethnography based on "fieldwork" will not produce a substantially different (or "decolonized") ethnography, but a feminist ethnography characterized by "homework" might. Am I also saying that anthropologists, once they do their homework, will have "nowhere to go"? Yes, but not entirely. Home once interrogated is a place we have never before been. This sense of "being at home," I suggest, allows feminists and anthropologists alike to travel in radically new ways. For "indeed the countryside 'at home' has always held promise of dangerous journeys."[74]

7

Identifying Ethnography

"I too call myself I."
— Kamala Das

The offices of the Indian Consulate, Paris
June 1991

Trying to get a tourist visa to travel to India, I am called again to the counter, surveyed, finally asked, "Are you of Indian origin?" An immediate freezing, and then a slow stammer, "I don't know what you mean. I was born in the United States; my father is Indian, that is he used to be ... now he's an American citizen ..." my voice trails off. I begin again, unable to control the pitch of my voice, a register too high. "Why do you want to know? What difference does it make? ... "

I am cut off before I can make a proper offensive. "Just one moment, please be seated," says the consular official coolly as she turns from the window. A few minutes later I am informed that the Head Consul would like to speak with me. Would I wait until five P.M., when the Consul has finished with his meetings? It is only 3:30 P.M. I wait. At 5:30 P.M. I am told that the Consul has already gone home for the evening and am asked to return the following morning.

The next morning my appearance causes a stir. I hear variously in French, English, and Hindi the same question and confirmation: "That's her?" "That's the one." In the next few minutes, half a dozen people enter the booth on one pretext or another. I am made to repeat why I had not been able to obtain a visa for visiting India before leaving New York; how I'd left it until the last minute, how the Indian embassy in New York had been closed because of Rajiv

Gandhi's assassination, the last three days in May before I left for Paris.

The consular official frowns at me and studies my application. I look down and find penciled in large letters across the top: NO PROOF OF INDIAN ORIGIN. Farther down the page in red ink I can make out the scrawl, "Applicant became hostile when asked about her origin. Refused to answer question in straightforward manner."

I look up. The consular official fondles my passport, then stamps it aggressively before delivering a short lecture on applying for visas well in advance of departure. I never see the Consul, nor am I told why I was made to wait.

*

Certainly the question "Where are you from?" is never an innocent one. Yet not all subjects have equal difficulty in replying. To pose a question of origin to particular subjects is to subtly pose a question of return, to challenge not only temporally, but geographically, one's place in the present. For someone who is neither fully Indian nor wholly American, it is a question that provokes a sudden failure of confidence, the fear of never replying adequately.

The consular official's questioning highlighted in a brief moment a series of contradictions about how we understand and talk about identity. By "origin," was she referring to my parentage, place of birth, or both? If she meant to emphasize my parentage, was it because I "looked" Indian, thus invoking concepts of "race" and "blood" I am usually at pains to dispute? Did it matter that one parent was Indian by birth and the other not? Was it important to know that both were American citizens? Did it matter what I called myself, or with what culture(s) I claimed affinity? For me, race, nationhood, culture, and identity were as surely entangled in the consular official's question as she had seen it to be "straightforward."

I am aware of a potentially productive conflation of second-generation positionings with postcolonial subjectivities. Airports and consular offices are increasingly marked as the sites for the enunciation of postcolonial identities.[1] Airports, of course, mark the geographical space of liminality, while consulates and embassies signal (at least) the discourse of citizenship and rights in foreign territory. At such sites arrival and departure scenes are immanent, but suspended by what is now departmentalized as "international relations." Although there are obvious similarities between second-generation and postcolonial positionings, I think it makes sense to underscore further points of contact, to mark those differential, though contradictory, predicaments of the hyphen.

Hyphe-Nation

When I was growing up, no discrete identity existed that I could claim. Faced with a questionnaire, I never knew which box to check, "Asian," "White," "Other"? I was among the first-born to that second wave of Indian immigrants to the United States that began as a trickle in the early sixties when immigration restrictions were relaxed. As Gauri Bhat notes, the date of our parents' arrival in this country is important, because it limited our cultural options.[2] This slice of the second generation was raised without "Indian friends, Bharatanatayam dance classes, Karnatic music recitals, Hindu temple societies, or Hindi films," because the large Indian communities of the Los Angeles or San Francisco Bay areas, Dallas, or New York were not firmly established until the mid-seventies.[3] Bhat argues that "Indian-Americans have had no distinctive creative voices of their own, probably because that generation of (second)-wave immigrant offspring is still maturing, now swelling the college ranks."[4]

The increasing currency of terms such as "Indo-American" or "Indian-American," even given the maturing of a generation seeking its voice, does not reassure me. Rather, it signals for me the continual virulence of identity politics in the United States as newer groups rush for their hyphens, even as some groups begin to abandon them and others, such as U.S.-born or immigrant Puerto Ricans, have never adopted them.[5]

The Indian-American hyphen retains the imaginary of the nation-state, its mobile diaspora with increasing (if complicated) choices about whether to go or stay. It is a hyphen that signals the desire (and the ability) to be both "here" and "there." Yet the postcolonial nature of this particular hyphen should not obscure other processes of hyphen formation, or prevent us from seeing how, in the African-American context, the notion of a "diaspora" with a "land of return" is problematic. Such a notion must be located equally in post-Civil War "repatriation" schemes launched by whites to return American blacks to Africa, and in social movements like Marcus Garvey's, which viewed this return as a form of empowerment.[6] Then, too, there is the fact that too few Anglo-Americans recognize the political etymologies of the words "Native American" or "American Indian." Five hundred years after Columbus, too few "Indian-Americans" recognize how their hyphen participates in the erasure of those on this continent long before Columbus got lost.

I do not mean to suggest that claiming the hyphen has not also been difficult, or without worthy elements of struggle. For there are other, more derogatory ways of naming my generation. We of the alphabet soup[7]—the ABCDs (American-Born Confused Deshis), the ABCDEFGs (American-Born Confused Deshis Emigrated From Gujerat), the HIJ (House in Jersey)—are the ones who cannot properly pronounce our own South Asian names:

> "There was a t.v. reporter here some days back," said George
> Miranda. "She said her name was Kerleeda. I couldn't work it out."
> . . . Zeeny interrupted. "He doesn't know what freaks you guys
> turn into. That Miss Singh, outrageous. I told her, the name's Khalida
> dearie, rhymes with Dalda, that's a cooking medium. But she couldn't
> say it. Her own name. Take me to your Kerleader. You types got no
> culture. Just wogs now. Ain't it the truth?"[8]

If Rushdie's caricature of South Asians in Britain rings true, so does Bhat's account of attending a Hindi language class at the University of Texas—"wall to wall ABCDs" with slack-jawed West Texas drawls.[9]

There were, however, other reasons for not knowing who I was; it was not simply the lack of some ready-made identity when I was growing up in the sixties and seventies. There was also the fact that my father rarely spoke of India, except to punish one of his willful daughters: "If we were in India you would never speak to me like this!" Nor did he ever speak to us in Tamil, his mother tongue. It was only later that I learned an Indian birth would not have prevented English being my first language (given trajectories of a certain South Indian caste, the privileges of an aspiring class). Please note that I use the term "first language" advisedly. Although English was my mother's tongue, I cannot bring myself to call it my mother tongue.

Bharati Mukherjee speaks of being born into a class that did not live in its native language.[10] And I puzzle over the relationship between postcolonial South Asian friends who are illiterate in their mother tongues (what must it be like to be so supremely literate elsewhere, but to stumble through intimate geography in a Madras or Bangalore, unable to read street signs, buses, storefronts?) and someone like me, with a clumsy, accented tongue, who after years of language study can read and write—enough Hindi to tell whether the bus is going to Janakpuri or Chanakyapuri, enough

Tamil to skim the newspapers and write to my grandmother. Are we "midnight's children," postcolonial and second-generation, born that some might speak, and others read and write, that some be blind, and others deaf and dumb?

Meena Alexander speaks of a "treasured orality," a "cherished illiteracy" in her mother tongue, Malayalam.[11] She records memories: a Scottish tutor who over and over makes her say "duck, duck," "pluck, pluck," "milk, milk," "silk, silk," the "split sense of writing in English."[12] And finally, in spite of her attempts to rationalize the "privilege of illiteracy," a sense of rage:

> Come ferocious alphabets of flesh
> Splinter and raze my page
>
> That out of the dumb
> and bleeding part of me
>
> I may claim
> my heritage.[13]

*

For a postcolonial critic, writing about an "over-there" enacts a certain similarity with the anthropologists' "Being There"—the act of writing about one place from another. And yet, as Nasser Hussein argues, the act of "going home" subjects the postcolonial critic to a particular vulnerability, a loss of the immunity that exile affords.[14] Thus Salman Rushdie confesses, "However I choose to write about over-there, I am forced to reflect the world in fragments of broken mirrors.... I must reconcile myself to the inevitability of the missing bits."[15]

This fractured or hyphenated identity marked by the geographical site, "over-there," is also marked temporally by the term "post-colonial." Hussein continues:

> Hyphens are radically ambivalent signifiers, for they simultaneously connect and set apart; they simultaneously represent both belonging and not belonging. What is even more curious about a hyphenated pair of words is that meaning cannot reside in one word or the other, but can only be understood in movement. "Post-colonial" then, shifts a movement away from, yet (retains) a vital connection to colonialism.[16]

Hyphenated identities in the United States share with postcolonial identities "a movement between cultural identity and nation-states,"[17] revealing important limits about the specification of difference. For it is not possible to hyphenate all identities. If it seems strange to speak of Bengali-Indians (or Bengali-Americans), Punjabi-Indians (or Punjabi-Americans), Tamil-Indians (or Tamil-Americans), it is not absurd to note that a Gujarati Samaj, a Singh Sabha, Tamil Sangam, or American Federation of Muslims from India (AFMI) finds potent expression on American soil.

The hyphen enacts a violent shuttling between two or more worlds. Trinh Minh-ha, however, argues that "the challenge of the hyphenated reality lies in the hyphen itself: the *becoming* Asian-American; the realm in-between, where predetermined rules cannot apply."[18] Trinh continues:

> The becoming Asian-American affirms itself at once as a transient and constant state: one is born over and over again as hyphen rather than as fixed entity, thereby refusing to settle down in one (tubicolous) world or another. The hyphenated condition certainly does not limit itself to a duality between two cultural heritages.[19]

All identities are intrinsically coalitional, in that they seek to establish grounds of affinity. "Asian-American," however, is a deliberately constructed coalitional identity, an inclusive political term of solidarity for those of diverse Asian backgrounds that attempts to distance itself from the logic of nation-states. Other coalitional identities such as "South Asian" or "women of color" function similarly.[20] It is important to recognize, though, that coalitional identities are by nature unstable, and may also, as in the case of "becoming Asian-American," set into play a necessary set of exclusions when talking about Affirmative Action criteria and the specific histories of different immigrant groups in the United States.

The hyphenated ethnic identity in the United States, however, has more often than not signaled a move toward the center. The hyphen in "Indian-American," then, must be seen not simply as a conflict of identities, but as a political signifier, not, as Bharati Mukherjee put it, as a "form of ghettoization," a "temptation to be avoided."[21] For hyphenated identities have typically marked a politics of assimilation in this country, at least formally different from experiences in Canada or Britain, where South Asians may form part of a coalitional identity termed "black."

In fact, the place of South Asians in the United States has often been to work against coalitions with people of color. "Affirmative Action alibis,"[22] South Asians are often unwitting or willing mediators between the white power structure and other communities marginalized by it. We find it easier to condemn the racism that is sometimes directed against us than the hypocrisy and racism in South Asian communities directed against American people of color.

Indeed, I wonder if the unwarranted attention given Dinesh D'Souza's book *Illiberal Education* isn't related to the politics of the hyphenated Indian, many of whom are members of a large and increasingly powerful business community anxious to prove to the conservative interests who run this country that it, too, stands for the same liberal values—"competition," "free market"; ready to emphasize that the "race" recorded on some South Asian passports is still "Aryan."[23]

A recent article in *Indian-American* magazine, an emerging voice of such hyphenated interests, reports triumphantly that Indian small businesses in San Francisco qualify for the "Minorities and Women Business Enterprise Program," allowing them to compete with well-established firms for lucrative public contracts by taking 10 percent off a minority bid.[24] In order to be considered, the Indian community had to present evidence of historical discrimination in California. This, no doubt, was done by pointing to two groups settled in the state in the early 1900s, the "Mexican-Hindu" community of the Imperial Valley[25] and the Sikhs of Yuba County, many of them agricultural workers, small orchard owners (or, more recently, low-paid cannery workers in Stanislaus County).[26] The irony of the Indian victory in San Francisco should not be lost. The less well off Sikhs of Yuba County may never be in the position to benefit from such Affirmative Action policies,[27] yet Indian businessmen are not only given preferential treatment in the United States, as NRIs (Non-resident Indians) they are also awarded higher rates of interest to invest in India. Thus even as they proclaim historical victimization, they enact the power of privilege. The hyphen is indeed an ambivalent signifier, for it includes under its umbrella first-generation immigrants, both citizens and noncitizens, second and third generations born on American soil, born as well to different experiences of racism and discrimination.

I wonder at the ease with which Bharati Mukherjee can proclaim "I am an American,"[28] words that were forced back down my throat in grade school, words I was never permitted to say with any amount of certainty. How is it that Mukherjee's postcolonial transition from "graduate student to citizen"[29] acknowledges neither a process of immigration long problematic for India nor the conflicts of second-generation subjects who have often found the promises of unmarked citizenship elusive at best?

Kalpana Vrudhula's poem "Do Not Belong to This or That, but I Am Here" expresses some of the ways in which second-generation Indians handle the presumption that they are not American:

> "Are you from India?"
> "No my parents are."
> > "Oh, how exciting. You know I saw
> > the movie Gandhi, I thought it
> > was great ... Have you been?
> "Oh, Yes, of course!"
> *I've only gone once, I was already 23.*
> > "The guy I work with is from
> > India. You must know him? His
> > last name, uh ... let me think,
> > oh yes, Patel?"[30]

Vrudhula is effectively able to convey the ignorance with which most white Americans view India through her repetition and variation of these lines throughout her reflections. Her continual polite reply to the ignorant questioner, "Oh, Yes, of course!" is a means of underscoring both the nature of the question and her own (lack of) response, for she is not able to say, as the title of the poem suggests, "I'm from here."

Yet if second-generation Indian voices are coming to terms with citizenship, Americanness, and cultural belonging, they must also face questions of race, and in ways that immigrant parents have not often been forced to confront. If the failure of the first generation to address race is inflected by class positioning, second-generation subjects, because they have been interpolated from early childhood into the racialized structure of U.S. identity politics, are compelled to engage race in their narratives. Indeed, I would argue that race is perhaps the most crucial juncture distinguishing South Asian postcolonial from second-generation subjectivities. That is, second-generation writers confront by necessity rather than choice, directly, however deplorably, their relationship not only to white Americans, but to American people of color as well. The second stanza of Vrudhula's poem painfully manifests what Mira Nair's *Mississippi Masala* portrays so clearly about racism in Indian communities (whatever else might be said of the film):

> "Say baby is you mixed?"
> "Mixed?"
> > "You know, I knows you black,
> > but you're sometin' else too?

"No, I'm not **mixed**."
         "Yes you is. You're black 'en?"
Why the hell should I answer
this guy? I could, but he probably
would ask me what tribe anyway.
         "Come on baby, what else is ya?"
Ah . . . The Bus.[31]

It is instructive that Vrudhula objects not to being addressed as "baby" but to being called mixed. Here she repudiates an attempt to establish affinity on the basis of color. Instead of the polite replies profferred her other interlocutors, she provides no information at all to her black questioner, responding instead with a silently inscribed stereotype that is far more offensive than her questioner's attempts at conversation.

Gauri Bhat's essay, on the other hand, attempts sustained reflection on the complexities of color and identification both within and outside of the Indian community, showing both a willingness to recognize points of contact with other communities of color and an unwillingness to use color as a means to appropriate the experiences of those less privileged. She calls the Indian-American child's benign sense of difference "the form without the content of prejudice."[32] And although there is room for disagreement on the levels of racism immigrant and second-generation Indians face in the United States, the very unevenness of the community's exposure to racism points largely to the protections afforded by class privilege. Bhat writes:

> In the classrooms of radical discourse, the darkness of my skin is like
> a badge of honor. I am marked as an empath. Guilty and solicitous
> white male scholars tiptoe around my privileged understanding of
> texts. And I think: I was not raised in the barrios, in the ghettos,
> under the British colonial empire, so how is my color a window?[33]

*

My Illinois birth certificate registers my mother's race as "white," and my father's as "Indian." The very appearance of the category "race," and the responses it elicits, somehow surprise me. And yet in California, miscegenation laws remained on the books until 1951, mandating a predominantly Hispanic origin for the women with whom immigrant Punjabi men formed families.[34] "Men and women applying to the County Clerk for a license had to look alike, and most often it was Hispanic women who satisfied that requirement. Many a license application has 'brown' and 'brown' in the blanks for 'race.'"[35]

Yet I cannot forget that my childhood in Fresno (as daughter of an immigrant who arrived in the United States in 1960) was not that of Kartar Dhillon's, whose father arrived at the port of San Francisco in 1899, and whose family faced life-threatening racism. As Dhillon recounts, "My mother was sure she would die after surgery. A doctor told her she would have to go to the county hospital in Fresno to have a tumor removed. Her first sight of the doctor in the hospital confirmed her fears. 'That man does not like Indians,' she told us. 'He is the one who let Labh Singh die.'"[36] Dhillon's mother was right. She did die a few days after the surgery. The year was 1932.

Second Wave, Second Generation

The accounts of women from the second wave of Indian immigration to the United States are, of course, markedly different. They traffic hugely in the idioms of class privilege, and unless one is knowledgeable about conditions of the everyday in India, it is easy to mistake such markers for the generalized oppression of women in India. Thus when Bharati Mukherjee proclaims "I was born into a religion that placed me as a Brahmin, at the top of its hierarchy, while condemning me as a woman to a role of subservience" and later says, without a trace of embarrassment, "I'm a person who couldn't ride a bus when she first arrived," it is easy for an American audience to misunderstand that the sheltered life evoked here refers not so much to being shut away as to the privilege of being driven from one place to another.[37] Likewise, in Indira Ganesan's novel *The Journey,* the narrator reflects on how her mother weathers the transition from a small South Indian village to the United States, wondering how, "as a young girl who had family and servants to cater to all her needs, a woman who had never been to the market by herself, her mother had held her breath," leaving willy-nilly for America, "Land of the self-serve," to bravely face supermarkets, kitchen appliances, and car washes.[38] Ably conquering self-service America, Ganesan's character does not lament the loss of servants in India.

I do not mean to suggest that all narratives that mark later periods of Indian immigration to the United States are so steeped in the language of adjustments to material, rather than emotional, conditions; or that all such transitions are easier rather than difficult. A recent documentary by Indian feminist Indu Krishnan, *Knowing Her Place,* poignantly addresses some of the emotional crises of identity among second-generation and immigrant Indians in the United

States. The film opens with a middle-aged woman naming the pain of a "second-generation immigrant child": "It takes a long time to figure out where you belong."

Krishnan presents a dramatic subject, a woman who oscillates continually between the questions "Are you Indian?" "Are you American?", never able to answer either. Vasu, the wife of an NYU mathematics professor, is tortured by this question cycle, which enacts a vicious attack on her fragile hold on selfhood and identity. In order to escape the endless repetition of these questions, Vasu attempts suicide while the documentary is being made.

Vasu's family moves to New York when she is a baby, and her childhood is affectively American (she avidly describes her passion for "rock and roll"). So, too, is the racism she experiences at age seven or eight: children who spit on her to see if the "dirt" will rub off. Although her family returns to India when she is twelve, she spends only four years in India, returning to the United States at age sixteen with a husband. Yet those four years, the years of adolescence, must have been as formative as her American years, deepening what Vasu calls "the dualism within her." She movingly, if obliquely, describes her experience of puberty, shut away for several days in a dark room, as is the custom among orthodox groups, part of her knowing this was unacceptable in the country she had left behind, and part of her accepting the isolation; afraid, and at the same time understanding that it was impossible to ask questions.

Before returning to India at age twelve, Vasu entertained the hope, encouraged by her father, that she might attend the Sorbonne. Her hopes were cruelly dashed, however, upon her father's death when she was fifteen, the event that provokes her early marriage. Vasu tells her audience, "My feeling about marriage is very bitter. . . . I just didn't want to get married at sixteen."

As a historical subject, Vasu's particular experience of immigration to the United States falls between two major waves of Indian immigration to American shores—one at the turn of the century, and one later in the 1960s.[39] Yet perhaps it is Vasu's very particularity as a subject that instigates experiences of identification across very different audiences. Although she is in her mid-forties, since Vasu's childhood was American, she speaks to a second-generation, college-age audience. Her being trundled off to India at the age of twelve also signals the powerful gender differential that marks second-generation experiences in South Asian communities. Girls face more restrictions than boys, are not allowed to date, and, to this day, may be sent "home" during their teenage years to ensure a protected environment and proper marriage. The response of Vasu's mother to the question "What would happen if boys and girls dated?" ("They would slowly start kissing . . .") marks a moment of heartfelt laughter among audiences, yet it also dramatically underscores the different way in which female as opposed to male second-generation subjects return "home."

Vasu is, however, also an adult immigrant to the United States, and this aspect of her identity, named by Krishnan, but not Vasu herself, provokes another range of identifications, including the complicity of the filmmaker in erasing certain questions about postcolonial identity by subsuming it too easily into its second-generation counterpart. However, the particular dualism of Vasu's historical positioning says something about the nature of second-generation identities in general, pointing to an oscillation between postcolonial and racialized American subjectivities.

The film generates strong responses from three other (not always distinguishable) groups of people: South Asian women, South Asian mothers, and Anglo-American mothers. It is not uncommon to hear from a cousin's mother-in-law or an Indian friend's aunt that Vasu's sense of an unfulfilled life, her plight in raising (male) children, and the lack of sympathy from her husband resonate powerfully with their own experiences. It is also not uncommon to hear older Anglo-American women in the audience (particularly those who have parented teenagers) say that the film engages their experiences as well. And it is true that Vasu's interactions with her teenage sons (lack of respect, being taken for granted) are not atypical of mothers' experiences in a variety of cultural and historical contexts. The film, then, addresses that generation of women who were first emboldened by Betty Friedan's *Feminine Mystique,* revealing that the middle-class woman's "housewife dilemma" is far from resolved.

Although it is Vasu's middle-class status that enables different groups of women to identify with her across cultural space (and the film does not signal this as an issue or problem), it would certainly be wrong to reduce Vasu's conflicts to an American "housewife's dilemma." Although Krishnan's own focus unwittingly plays to this interpretation (ordering Vasu's life into a therapeutic narrative: identity crisis, attempted suicide, counseling, increased self-confidence, new job, functional subject, functional family), Vasu's own diagnosis of "cultural schizophrenia" is a compelling one.

Vasu plays the dutiful Indian daughter when she visits her mother at home in Madras, and the dutiful Indian wife at home with her husband in New York, but with her two sons, she struggles to be an

American mother. For holidays she prepares elaborate American meals, rather than the sambar or rasam she prefers to cook. (At a Thanksgiving meal her younger son says a mock grace: "Thank you, Vishnu, for this food ...," then complains that the roast is too mushy.) Her older son dates, plays in a rock band (and has his own apartment at age seventeen). He, too, says that his mother's cooking doesn't suit his "utility function."

This is perhaps the axis that should have been more thoroughly explored by the filmmaker. Vasu's children appear as cardboard examples of assimilation to the materialist values of the Reagan era. The older son, explaining that he couldn't live in India because he wants to be comfortable and happy, says, apparently without an ounce of self-consciousness, "Money can't make you happy, but if someone gave me a million dollars right now, I'd be the happiest guy in the world." Later when he is asked "Do you feel Indian or American?" he says "both" too quickly, then challenges, "What's the conflict? I am how I am. Just like Popeye says, 'I am what I am what I am.'" Vasu's younger son tells her, too, that even if she went from Queens to India, then back to Queens, "She has no conflict."

Why is it that Vasu's children so strenuously resist acknowledging her conflict? (Her husband resists, too, but at least acknowledges that "the conflict may be real for the person experiencing it.") Is it only a matter of patriarchy in the household, or is this a juncture the filmmaker might have explored more deeply? What is it that Vasu's children and by extension, Krishnan herself, repress?

What is advanced by the film is the fantasy of assimilation (and, indeed, as "new ethnics," Indians seem to be among the recent "model minorities"). What is repressed is the question of the children's Americanness, precisely because it is assumed. The children assume it, possibly because the fear of not being fully American is very powerful (Vasu's comment that she knows what her older son feels when people call him Go-pal instead of Gopal is telling). Krishnan herself assumes the children's Americanness because she continually presents "Indian" and "American" as essentialized identities, never broken down into further specificity. (During the scenes filmed in India, for example, the voice-over never identifies that the language spoken is Tamil, or the community, Brahmin.) Thus in Krishnan's eyes, the children must be American because they lack Indian markers: language, religion, appreciation of food, and so on. I suspect that if Krishnan had probed further, she might have unearthed second- (in this case third-) generation sensibilities that are not articulated in the film.

To Krishnan's credit, the hyphenated identity "Indian-American" is neither offered nor proposed as a solution to Vasu's dilemma. Vasu herself never articulates it as a possibility. Instead the film closes with an affirmation of Vasu's duality: she has not chosen, nor can she ever choose, one culture over the other. "Growing up in two different cultures, or coming from one to another, is like moving in two different directions at once; or being in two places at once." The final words of *Knowing Her Place* remind us that one definition of biculturality is not being at "home" in either place.[40]

Hyphenated Ethnography

Normative ethnographic practice, founded in the ethic of the participant-observer, produces an intrinsically "hyphenated ethnography,"[41] but there is another kind of hyphenation that, I would argue, stands to encourage a very different form of ethnography. I offer the term "hyphenated ethnography" not to elevate the phenomenon of hyphenated identities, but because a Japanese-American doing work in Japan, or a Palestinian-American doing work in the Middle East, suggests more than accidental academic trajectories. Dorinne Kondo, for example, writes that "culture and meaning ... lay in an awareness of assumptions, deeply felt, that shaped everyday life in the Japanese-American community where I grew up."[42] Renato Rosaldo similarly affirms, "For me as a Chicano, questions of culture emerge not only from my discipline, but also from a more personal politics of identity and community."[43] This is the juncture at which I want to reflect further upon how my particular identity formation influenced not only where but also how I chose to study; to understand, if only partially, how the anthropological resources available to an American of South Asian descent might shape a return "home."

*

I had anticipated that the recent literary works about India would fail me. I knew that the streets filled with poverty and despair so effectively described by a V. S. Naipaul (or a Bharati Mukherjee, for that matter) would give way to warm if always complicated relationships, namely, those of my family. I could see, roaming through West Delhi neighborhoods of Mayapuri, Hari Nagar, or Janakpuri, that the endless blocks of LIG (Low Income Group) and MIG (Middle Income Group) housing painted shades of wan distemper yellow would only have reminded Naipaul (if comparisons were to be made) of tenements in urban American cities.

Yet each day as I returned from pushing onto overcrowded DTC buses to and from the archives and libraries of central Delhi, I would thread my way through apparently indistinguishable blocks of LIG flats broken only by dusty lots and struggling trees to find flat D2A-27C, where my aunt and four of my cousins lived. Once inside I would be met with a cup of hot coffee, rapid questions about my day, incessant chatter in three languages, and fast insults between siblings. But first my arrival would be announced by a doorbell playing "London Bridge Is Falling Down" at top volume, and the frenzied barking of two absurdly fluffy white dogs, who, like everyone else in the house, were driven mad by the doorbell, which began ringing with the 6 A.M. arrival of the dudhwallah and did not stop until well past 10 P.M. The doorbell had been the bright idea of an excessively generous cousin, so that in any family house we visited in Delhi or Madras we could not escape the sound of London Bridge falling down. It was impossible, even had I wished it otherwise, to see India through Naipaul's eyes.

Yet when I arrived in India, I had the distinct feeling that the ethnography had also failed me. I had dutifully studied the ethnographies of India before boarding the plane in September 1987 and thought that by reading descriptions of codes for behavior I, too, would understand how to proceed in India. Why, then, did nothing in the books prepare me for what I saw and felt there? Take, for example, my first Hindu wedding.

South Asianists, and anthropologists in particular, are fond of studying ritual. They write books and books about the structural, the latent, the manifest rules of ritual; its symbolic, hidden, or overt meanings; the distinctions between its form and its content. Above all, anthropologists tell us, ritual is formality. It is precisely the formal nature of the rite that reassures us, even as it reinscribes us within culture.

This wedding as a Brahmin affair, should have conformed most closely to what I had read in the literature. (I should note that anthropologists who work in India are overly fond of studying Brahmins.) Yet what I saw was intense sensuality and beauty: a proliferation of sounds, colors, and wondrous intoxicating smells, and also mass confusion.

Rituals, the anthropologists say, are orderly. But here at a most serious and sacred occasion, small children chased one another everywhere, and toddlers safely out of their mothers' gaze routinely wandered through the rite to poke at a priest or pluck a flower from the altar. Old, crafty grandmothers patrolled the rooms relentlessly searching for comely unmarried young women, hoping to make a match for grandsons or nephews before the day was done. Businessmen cut deals in a corner, and, of course, there was the never-ending gossip of the women, their gales of laughter periodically inundating the chants of the priests. At some point, one of the shastris winked at a cousin of mine, and amidst a chorus of giggles was immediately dubbed "the naughty pundit." Even the bride and groom seemed more interested in getting away from the small, smoky fire than in the ritual itself.

There I sat, stiff-backed in a new silk sari, wondering why no one else was paying attention. I decided then and there that I would not study ritual.

*

As I think back now to the subject of my dissertation, an ethnographic and historical study of women's positioning and participation in the Indian nationalist movement, it strikes me as significant that my own analysis of early Indian feminist thought situated it between Indian nationalism and Western feminism, yielding a hybrid subject position not so far removed from my own. Written as partial refutation of the claim that the Indian women's movement was "Westernized," my argument was that such a formulation obscured the important ways in which "first-wave" Indian feminists positioned themselves according to issue and context during the latter period of the nationalist movement.

I am reminded, also, that what I send to be published in India seeks direct interventions in a series of debates about feminist practice and history. What I intend for American audiences often entails a more deconstructive approach, in part to resist the tremendous demand for knowledge about "Third World women" that American middle-class feminism places on scholars like me.

Lata Mani's essay "Multiple Mediations: Feminist Scholarship in the Age of Multinational Reception" remains one of the first attempts to address the problematics of identity and reception across diverse audiences.[44] Here, however, I focus on Kirin Narayan's anthropological study *Storytellers, Saints, and Scoundrels,* which also explores some of the complexities of addressing different audiences. In the 1992 Indian edition of this work, she asks, "Is there really any such thing as one 'Indian audience' even if one has narrowed this to those fluent in English?" and acknowledges that "for someone brought up, like me, in urban India, attending English medium schools ... the existence of a sadhu telling folk stories through a mouthful of tobacco may seem exotic, even embarrassingly 'traditional.' "[45] She challenges her Indian audiences to navigate their own uneven exposure to Indian folklore, religion, and Hindu aesthetic traditions when coming to terms with her text.

Narayan tells her readers that were she to have written the book only to be read in India, she would have changed two things. Her first concern — that she may have too strongly emphasized Western devotees' lack of cultural context to understand the "wisdom or wiles" of Hindu gurus — seems strangely oversolicitous:

> Just as Swamiji affectionately mocked his foreign devotees by holding up a mirror highlighting gullibility and earnestness in his stories, so I attempted to reflect back certain facets of popular, predominantly American, interest in Hinduism for readers outside India. Yet I fear I may have engaged in a kind of reverse Orientalism, parodying "Westerners" and not sufficiently sorting out the differences in insight, dedication, and sophistication. I want to make it clear that I respect people whose quests for self-understanding take them across the ever more permeable borders between cultural traditions.[46]

Narayan's second concern is perhaps easier to understand. Given that hers is a study of one form of popular Hinduism, she would have reminded her Indian audience of the "precedents for empathy across differences at a time when some of the loudest Hindu voices deem it 'religious' to infringe on the persons and property of neighbors who practice different religions, or even those who share the same religion yet are set apart by caste, gender, regional identity."[47] Narayan's gesture toward locating the reading of her text within the current climate of Indian communalism is an important (though not wholly adequate) one. (It is, I think, doubtful that a more sincere reading of Hindu religious practices or texts can combat the highly interested pronouncements of Hindutva ideologues.)

It is, of course, striking that while Narayan has attempted to negotiate the vagaries of her Indian audience, her American audiences are assumed and no attempt is made to delineate them. Is this in part responsible for her sense that parody or critique of American interest in Hinduism can only be addressed to American audiences? That some kind of compact is broken if such parody is conveyed explicitly to Indian audiences? How many of Narayan's own "shifting identifications," as child of a Gujarati father and German-American mother, raised in India then settled in the United States since the age of sixteen, are entangled in the quandary of audience?

> Although I was partially assimilated as a local woman, I did not altogether "pass." While in Nasik I dressed in a sari, with earrings, bangles and anklets, my hair in a braid, and kumkum on my

forehead. But I was a little too fair; a little too tall; my Hindi accent betrayed that English was my first language; and my taperecorder gave away my affiliations with a project that would not concern most local women. Everyone who visited Swamiji sooner or later figured out my ties to another continent. Among his visitors was a handful of Westerners from England, France, the United States, and Australia who stayed for short periods of time. I shared many references with the Westerners present, especially those who lived in America. But even as I identified with them I was acutely aware of the cultural faux pas they good-naturedly made and was anxious not to be lumped together with them, the "foreigners."[48]

Reflections like these are increasingly common, as hyphenated ethnographers negotiate the terms between shifting alliances. A recent essay by Lila Abu-Lughod attempts to highlight some of the problematics of positioning by drawing on Narayan's term "halfie-ethnography." According to Abu-Lughod, the halfie, one "whose national or cultural identity is mixed by virtue of migration, overseas education, or parentage," suffers (along with the feminist ethnographer) a "blocked ability to comfortably assume the self of anthropology."[49] She argues that the split subjectivities of feminist and halfie anthropologists entail an uneasy traveling between "speaking for" and "speaking from,"[50] creating new problems and strategies of audience:

> Halfies' dilemmas are ... extreme. As anthropologists, they write for
> other anthropologists, mostly Western. Identified also with
> communities outside the West, or subcultures within it, they are
> called to account by educated members of these communities. More
> importantly, not just because they position themselves with respect to
> two communities, but because when they present the Other they are
> presenting themselves, they speak with a complex awareness of and
> investment in reception.[51]

While Abu-Lughod's analysis points in several promising directions, it is possible that the "halfie" as she defines her stands for too many subject positions. Abu-Lughod collapses too easily a second-generation positioning with the "indigenous" (or one might more productively say postcolonial) anthropologist, and doesn't explore how conflicting citizenships and loyalties are imbedded in different processes of movement. Amitav Ghosh's work stages an ethnographic encounter between "delegates from two superseded civilizations," revealing that an Indian working in Egypt (as opposed to an Arab-American like Abu-Lughod) is defined by a different set of historical experiences and expectations, his identity determined by

different national axes of alignment or "nonalignment."[52] Narayan
herself notes that while she might be identified with the postcolonial phenomenon of the indigenous or native ethnographer, her situation is actually "more complex."[53]

In fact, Abu-Lughod's essay remains wedged between rather
heavy binarisms. Narayan's most recent intervention, however, has
been to question, "How Native Is a Native Anthropologist?"[54] arguing that anthropologists must be situated in fields of interpenetrat-
ing communities and power relations. Narayan draws on what Rosaldo has termed "multiplex identities,"[55] contending that because
anthropologists negotiate the world of scholarship and that of
everyday life, they should be seen as minimally bicultural, enacting
a form of hybrid subjectivity. While I am in full agreement with
Narayan's move to problematize notions of "authentic" identity, I
am wary of valorizing a generalized hybrid condition. Such a generalized hybridity, coupled with theories of multiple positioning, runs
the risk of inaugurating, once again, the freely choosing modal subject that is at once everywhere and nowhere. While all identities
may ultimately be multiple and shifting, surely there are also hier-
archies of hybridity. Not all identities are equally hybrid, for some
have little choice about the political processes determining their
hybridization. It is my claim that identifying ethnography asks us to
see how identities are determined by the political exigencies of history, compelling us to take sides. Identifying ethnography asks that
we exhibit and examine our alliances in the same moment.

The process of how language creates or fractures affinity is a crucial one to understand. Abu-Lughod's analysis suffers from some
inattention to the relationship between language and these split (or
multiple) subjectivities, although many have written with insight on
the subject. Valentine Daniel, for example, describes how his early
experience with multiple languages precipitated his move to anthropology:

> I am a native Tamil speaker, born in the Sinhalese-speaking south of
> Sri Lanka to a South Indian Tamil father who changed his name from
> something divine to something daring in order to marry my mother, a
> Sri Lankan Anglican whose mother tongue was English. My father's
> English was poor, his Sinhalese reserved for servants. (They have
> been married for over almost half a century.) For me at least,
> anthropologizing began early.[56]

Anthropology is, of course, the act of translating one language or
culture into another. Yet colonialism has shaped a diaspora and lin-

guistic power differential anthropology has often inadequately apprehended. Gilles Deleuze and Félix Guattari begin their discussion of "deterritorialization" with the question, "How many people live today in a language that is not their own?"[57] Native American critic and writer Paula Gunn Allen has written movingly of the strategies of the resisting self thrust into an alien language:

> She knew that everything moved and everything balanced, always, in her language, her alien crippled tongue, the English that was ever unbalanced, ever in pieces, she groped with her words and her thought to make whole what she could not say. She was obsessed with language, by words. She used the words she had lavishly, oblivious to their given meanings. She did not give them what was theirs, but took from them what was hers. Ever she moved her tongue, searching for a way to mean in words what she meant in thought. For her thought was the Grandmother's, was the people's, even though her language was a stranger's tongue.[58]

Chicana writer Gloria Anzaldúa writes of English as the "rip-off of my native tongue,"[59] and Sephardic writer Anton Shammas speaks of writing in his "step-mother tongue." While all ethnographies are properly "bi-lingual," to speak of a bilingual or multilingual ethnography is to challenge the translation of a subordinated language into the dominant tongue. Anzaldúa's *Borderlands* is one text that utilizes several languages, not all of them translated, or translatable, producing an ethnography that speaks in tongues. She addresses directly the imbrication of identity and language, forcing her readers to confront the politics of reception:

> Ethnic identity is twin skin to linguistic identity. Until I can take pride in my language, I cannot take pride in myself. Until I can accept as legitimate Chicano Texas Spanish, Tex-Mex and all the other languages I speak, I cannot accept the legitimacy of myself. Until I am free to write bilingually and to switch codes without always having to translate, while I still have to speak English or Spanish when I would rather speak Spanglish, and as long as I have to accommodate the English speakers rather than having them accommodate me, my tongue will be illegitimate.[60]

*

If Abu-Lughod's essay leaves more questions about language and identity asked than answered, she does address questions of representation. For it is also true that some of the issues confronting second-generation as well as postcolonial anthropologists involve the exigencies of writing about communities under political attack. It is in this context that Abu-Lughod raises the possibilities of a "tactical humanism" for representing Middle Eastern cultures in a time of intense hostility toward Islam.

In his discussion of Edward Said's *Orientalism,* James Clifford observes certain methodological difficulties in Said's use of Foucault, noting Said's equivocation between a critique of unacceptable representation and a Nietzschean critique of representation itself, and, in general, Said's attempt to utilize antihumanist theory while remaining deeply enmeshed in the habits of Western humanism.[61] Clifford contends that such methodological ambivalences typify an increasingly global experience,[62] and suggests that they are characteristic of "hybrid perspectives."[63]

Thus it is not surprising that Dorinne Kondo, in a moving conclusion to her study *Crafting Selves,* invokes her paradoxical use of antihumanist discourse for humanist ends by arguing that her emphasis on "power, contradiction, discursive production, and ambiguity is invoked in part to demonstrate complexity and irony in the lives of people (she) knew, in order to complicate and dismantle ready stereotypes that erase complexity in favor of simple, unitary images":[64]

> The current disturbing tendency to use martial metaphors—invasion, trade wars, beach heads—in descriptions of U.S.-Japan relations underlines the embeddedness of such representations in specific historical, political, and economic situations. As a Japanese American, and as an Asian American, whom some will see as inevitably foreign and whose fate is intimately tied to the state of American relations with Asia, I see the political weight of these representations take on vivid and searing immediacy.... What and how I write is no mere exercise; for me it matters and matters deeply.[65]

And yet, the dilemma over use of humanist or antihumanist representational strategies is resolved differently depending on the problematic to be addressed. Some critics of "Betrayal," for example, have wondered at my jettisoning a symbolically textured understanding of Tamil personhood in favor of deconstructive analysis. My response has been that erring in favor of agency (however staged or overdetermined) is not unwarranted given a dominant textualist tradition in South Asian studies that still holds that the concept of the individual does not exist in India (Louis Dumont is only one of the more sophisticated proponents of this position). As Kondo reminds us, anthropological accounts that rely on concepts of the self, or notions of personhood "with no reference to the contradictions and multiplicities within 'a' self, the practices creating selves in concrete situations, or the larger historical, political, and institutional processes shaping those selves, decontextualize and reify an abstract notion of essential selfhood, based upon a metaphysics of substance."[66] Kondo's words underscore Gayatri Spivak's observation that "the person who knows has all the problems of selfhood. The person who is known seems not to have a problematic self."[67]

Renato Rosaldo understands that the "process of knowing involves the whole self" and articulates "identification as a source of knowledge."[68] These are not new insights for feminists or oral historians, but I would argue that the increasing elaboration of "identifying ethnography" signals that the process of claiming the identity of the group studied has important consequences for the representational practices of the discipline.

While "identity politics" subsumed much of academic discourse during the decade of the 1980s, anthropologists by and large forgot that the production of their own identities mattered, could no longer be taken for granted. Stating one's commitments and how one came to them was formerly seen as a luxury (at best "confessional"; at its worst a symptom of "diary disease"). Now the question seems to be, How can such commitments be ignored? As "hybrid" or "hyphenated," "halfie" or postcolonial anthropologists begin to renegotiate the terms of distance and intimacy informing social analysis, theory itself begins to change, leading often to a strategic redeployment of the category of experience. As Dorinne Kondo puts it,

> Meaningful axes of identity, such as race and gender, loom large in American society as they do in Japan, and my shifting positionings as a Japanese American woman crafting a self within a particular historical and cultural matrix have informed (my) work subtly but unmistakably. Certain modes of explanation and exposition seem especially comfortable or strategically important in light of these shifting positions. More specifically, "experience" leads me to a theoretical concern with the place of meaning and power in social life.[69]

Kondo concludes that "theory" also lies in enacting particular writing practices and strategies.[70]

Indeed, members of groups on the margins of power have begun to redefine the fields of anthropology and cultural studies in the American academy, reappropriating the genre of ethnography in the process.[71] Angie Chabram notes that "mainstream ethnographies undermine the impact of differences of race, class, gender, and educational access on ethnographic discourse, especially as these differences have privileged the cultural formation and interpretation of the ethnographer. Mainstream ethnographies have also honored methods and assumptions which presuppose a geographical, geopolitical, and intellectual distance between the world of the researcher and the subject of his or her analysis."[72]

Chabram's provocatively posed "revised oppositional ethnography" has much to offer anthropology, though she is at pains to distinguish her project, "the critical re-examination of the writing of cultures through oral histories and ethnographies ... (as) a basis for grasping a condition which does not appear in textbooks ...," from "trendy perspectives within specific anthropological discourses."[73]

Chabram argues:

> Few are the ethnographic revisionists who have contemplated the possibilities that the objectified subject "object" write his or her own culture ... without the central mediating presence of the Anglo ethnographer....
>
> And few are the revisionists who contemplate what happens to the ethnographic genre itself when this formerly nonlegitimated subject-object of color "talks back," i.e. what types of novelties, problems, and adjustments emerge within this genre of human speech as a result of this reformulated, self-generated, newly positioned (inter)ethnographic dialogue across disciplines, cultures, races, and ethnicities.[74]

Chabram suggests, and I agree, that "even the idea of such revised oppositional institutional ethnographies ... taking place within national university settings suggests a break with the traditional ethnographic situation under scrutiny."[75]

Yet some, like the historian Joan Scott or the philosopher Linda Alcoff, worry that appeals to experience stymie interpretation. Scott asks, "What could be truer than a subject's own account of what he or she has lived through?" maintaining that "it is ... this kind of appeal to experience as uncontestable evidence and as an originary point of explanation—as a foundation on which analysis is based—that weakens the critical thrust of theories of difference."[76] Scott cautions against experience being used to establish the fact of difference, rather than seeking to explain how difference is established.[77] She urges us to attend to the historical processes that mold subjectivity and experience:

> Making visible the experience of a different group exposes the existence of repressive mechanisms, but not their workings or logics;

we know that difference exists, but we don't understand it as relationally constituted. For that we need to attend to the historical processes that through discourse, position subjects and produce their experiences. It is not individuals who have experience, but subjects who are constructed through experience.[78]

Scott's concern seems not unwarranted, yet it is also true that experience directs us to ask certain questions of theory that theory alone may not enable us to ask.[79]

Borrowing a phrase from Roland Barthes, Clifford Geertz has dubbed the autobiographical trend in anthropology "diary disease."[80] Such a cursory dismissal, however, ignores the insights of a writer like Toni Morrison, who recognizes that a large part of her own literary tradition is the autobiography, which actively constitutes a "site of memory."[81] Or, as Stuart Hall puts it, identities are stories we tell about history, a retelling of the past.[82] Thus, the autobiographical is not a mere reflection of self, but another entry point into history, of community refracted through self. As Janet Varner Gunn says,

> If self-realization must be gained from the ways the self is known by others, authorship of autobiography is always multiple. The story told through the convention of the first person narrative is always a story which both discovers and creates the relation of self with the world in which it can appear to others, knowing itself only in that appearance or display.[83]

Some of the most powerful social analysis now being written deliberately instigates autobiography. Patricia Williams's essays in *The Alchemy of Race and Rights* are good examples of how autobiography may frame larger social questions.[84] Another example of first-person narratives that evoke the larger community can be found in the work of the cultural studies task force at Hunter College's Centro de Estudios Puertorriqueños in New York City.

In the team's first working paper, "Stories to Live By: Continuity and Change in Three Generations of Puerto Rican Women," women's stories of arrival, resettlement, hardship, discrimination, and struggles to get ahead in New York City are elicited as "threads to the past, . . . personal history, and to a collective identity."[85] These testimonies explore the historical legacy of the first wave of Puerto Rican women migrants, in many cases, the mothers, grandmothers, or fictive kin of the researchers, who began work in New York's garment industry. History is continually elaborated in order to reveal the formation of an identity in resistance. Life stories of older

Puerto Rican women highlight the colonial nature of U.S.-Puerto Rican relations, "enabling young Puerto Ricans to begin reconstructing and reinterpreting their own history," and reminding the community that "For Every Story There Is Another Story Which Stands before It" (the title of Rina Benmayor's essay in this monograph).[86]

The next two studies, "Affirming Cultural Citizenship in the Puerto Rican Community: Critical Literacy and the El Barrio Popular Education Program" (1991) and "Responses to Poverty among Puerto Rican Women: Identity, Community and Cultural Citizenship" (1992), elaborate on the notion of "cultural citizenship" developed by the Cultural Studies Working Group of the Inter-University Program for Latino Research. As the authors note,

> Bringing together culture and citizenship into a single analytical framework underscores the dynamic process whereby cultural identity comes to bear on claims for social rights in oppressed communities; and at the same time, identity is produced and modified in the process of affirming rights. The cultural citizenship concept also frames responses to subordination in terms of collective rather than individual action. It directs attention to how people affirm their existence, perceive their common interests, structure their connections to each other, and build their group identities and binding solidarities.[87]

They conclude by arguing that "citizenship is culturally constructed and not simply legally defined.... The affirmation of cultural difference and cultural rights does not imply abrogation of the duties, responsibilities, and contributions attached to membership in the polity."[88]

Much of the analysis in the last two studies focuses on the use of memory and testimony in classroom literacy work. Spanish adult literacy classes created by the Centro as both a research site and a service to the Puerto Rican community of East Harlem gave participants (most of whom were women) a break from family responsibilities, but at the same time allowed them to re-create a "second family" in the program. Shared stories of childhood reminded participants that they engage a common history. The ethnographic notes of the research team report that one day,

> the teacher asks Ana whether she wants to read the first part of her autobiography. Ana says, "No, lo que escribí no tiene importancia" (No, what I've written isn't important). With the encouragement of her classmates, she reads a descriptive account of her life in the countryside. When she finishes, everybody applauds. Felix (the teacher) tells her, "Has escrito muy bien. Todo lo que has escrito son

cosas a las que hay darle valor" (You've written very well. All that you have written about are things we have to learn to value).[89]

The process of narrating a personal experience that can be understood as part of a shared history or community memory is also empowering, not only for the speakers, but also for listeners. Such work represents a radical departure from the way in which most anthropology is practiced, and it is in that sense not at all surprising to learn that none of the researchers themselves are professional anthropologists.

The work of the Cultural Studies task force at the Centro de Estudios Puertorriqueños presents rich opportunities for rethinking the parameters of history, identity, and community, in short, for identifying ethnography. The act of working through the relationship of identity to ethnography allows oppositional ethnographers new ways of remaking the genre, one that may not inappropriately be slipping from the hands of its most disciplinary practitioners.

Conclusion

In calling for an identifying ethnography, I have not wanted its foundations to seem supported by essential notions of identity. The understanding of identity advanced here is conjunctural, one continually in process, as much a matter of becoming as being.[90] Thus, the first half of this essay has attempted to describe some of the consequences of theorizing the local in demographic, rather than purely geographic, terms; how my own identity is constrained by the limits of American identity politics, which pushes subjects like myself toward the hyphen. My "second-generation" hyphenated identity is, however, formed in the process of negotiating political affinity and alliances, of coming to terms with whom I owe allegiance, and where my accountabilities lie, activating, at times, membership in Asian-American and South Asian coalitional identities; at other times identification as a woman of color, or "Third World Woman."[91] The second half of this essay attempted to explore how particular "hybrid" identity formations may be linked to particular theoretical dilemmas or representational strategies engaged by post-colonial and second-generation subjects alike. In so doing, I have sought to foreground the conjuncture between hyphenated identity and hyphenated ethnography.

In identifying an ethnography of particular conjunctures, my argument has not been that in order to practice anthropology, one must be a member of the group studied. Nor would I claim that relations of power disappear when one is a member of the group researched. As Nita Kumar reminds us, "A cultural encounter can and does take place between classes, and the difference marking conflict, domination, and objectification that go on within 'a' culture are as resounding as those between 'a' culture and 'an' other."[92] The relationship between research and accountability is perhaps more acute, but hardly less complicated.

Rather, I have wanted to detail how those of us engaged in identifying ethnography may be moved by different sets of questions concerning power, domination, and representation; how we may ourselves be positioned (and not always by choice) in opposition to dominant discourses and structures of power. The oppositional sense of such ethnography shows that these questions are not only important, but indeed vital for reshaping the practice of anthropology, and point again to the double sense of "identifying ethnography."

> While I was waiting to board a flight, a young woman who was also a student began a conversation. As every student does, she asked the inevitable question, "What's your major?" When I apologetically responded that my "major" was Anthropology, her eyes lit up. She proceeded to tell me that her brother studied Anthropology at Yale.
>
> "Oh," I commented, trying not to sound like an underachiever because I went to a lesser known school.
>
> "Where do you study?" She flipped her blond hair over her shoulders.
>
> "I study at The New School, in New York."
>
> "No, I mean, which country?" she asked.
>
> "Country?" I was confused and I was sure I looked foolish.
>
> "Yeah, like my brother studies Thailand, he's been there three times already. So, where do you want to study?"
>
> I pointed to myself and said, "I want to study here."[93]

Family wedding, 1961.

Subbalakshmi with her son Raja, about 1915.

8

Introductions to a Diary

First Introduction: August 1988

In a crowded English classroom at Indraprastha College, Delhi University, a group of students and their teachers are waiting for a lecture titled "Interpreting Women's Writing: A Feminist Perspective." I begin hesitantly, offering a few tentative definitions, hoping to turn a lecture into a discussion. I suggest a few questions for discussion: What is it that counts as "women's writing"? What is literature? The students are slow to respond, shy, unused to being asked direct questions by a guest speaker. I try another tack: what do they think about the Ameeta Modi case?

Their interest is piqued. Everyone has heard of Ameeta Modi, a young woman married to a sports hero murdered by (some say) her lover (a local politician), or (some say) by her lover's political enemies in the Congress-I. In any case, Ameeta Modi's relationship with her lover (and thus her potential involvement in the murder) is under intense scrutiny. Her diary is confiscated as evidence in the case.

An intense young woman seated in the front row who has taken issue with my American accent decides to bait me. She begins a monologue about the political machinations of the Congress-I. I deflect her commentary by saying that of course I don't support the confiscation of Ameeta Modi's diary and ask whether a diary can be considered evidence — legal, historical, or other. A few hands go up; there are dissenting opinions. I ask the students (all of them women) if any of them keep diaries. More hands go up. More questions: What is a diary, who keeps them, in what language(s) are they written? A genuine discussion has arisen. I ask the students if they would help me analyze a diary written in English by a Tamil woman who lived in Madras. I introduce them to Subbalakshmi's diary by telling them a little of her background, about my conversations with her daughter Pankajam, and by reading aloud passages of the diary. Of course, I have not at that point used Pankajam and Subbalakshmi's real names, but we all wonder whether a private document is ever intended for a public audience. And yet we discover that Subbalakshmi has written little of domestic affairs. The world of which she has so deliberately and painstakingly written about in English is a public world, marked by journeys to other towns, letters sent and received from other parts of India, trips to city schools, libraries, art shows, khadi exhibitions, and political gatherings, displacing some of our assumptions about diaries and their female keepers. The students apply themselves eagerly to the task of analyzing Subbalakshmi's diary, and at that moment are the ones directing questions to me.

I cannot yet claim to have answered all the questions that arose in that discussion, but I would like to thank the students, and their teachers, for posing them. I cannot help but think that Pankajam, and Subbalakshmi herself, would be pleased to know of the enthusiasm and pleasure one group of young women, college women, showed in learning about the life and struggles of one woman during the second decade of this century.

*

I came to know of Subbalakshmi through her daughter Pankajam, the mother of an acquaintance of mine in the CPI-M (Communist Party of India-Marxist). There is a photo of Subbalakshmi and her son Raja taken when Subbalakshmi was about eighteen or nineteen. She was only fourteen when she gave birth to Pankajam, her oldest child. Despite her youth, Subbalakshmi's eyes are serious and grave. Still, there is a kind of defiance in the set of her jaw that draws one away from the sadness of her gaze. It is a beautiful, unmistakably intelligent face, but frustration and resentment are already etched into the contours of her drawn mouth.

Subbalakshmi's family remembers her as being unconventional. She was a woman who rarely offered kumkum to departing guests, and who wore khadi to the end of her days, even to weddings where silk saris were again the post-Independence norm among former nationalists. Later in life, when her asthma did not respond to allopathic treatment, she decided to try naturopathy. Her family recounts that she followed devoutly an entire switch of dietary regimen, curing herself of the affliction. Subbalakshmi was a woman who refused to refer to or address her husband by anything but his initials, P. R. G. Still later again, she narrated over and over to her young grandchildren the dream of an Indian woman in South Africa being beaten while on satyagraha. One of her granddaughters felt that the recurring images of women fighting for their freedom must have been extremely potent ones for Subbalakshmi.

Subbalakshmi's husband was a serious and scholarly man who wrote poetry ranging from the spiritual sublime to a lighter vein. He was remembered as affectionate and loving. He laughed, told Shakespearean stories, and occasionally wrote humorous poems, like "The First Kiss," which one granddaughter recalled fondly.

Yet Subbalakshmi, by anyone's reckoning, was a genius. Educated in Tamil only to the third standard, she also learned English and Sanskrit, then taught herself Bengali because she wanted to read Tagore's poems in the original.

One day as I was sorting through the various scraps of yellowing and cracked paper in Subbalakshmi's remaining files, I noticed a newspaper article from the *Hindu* newspaper dated May 25, 1929, titled "American Letter: Praise for Indian Ideals, Dr. and Mrs. Cousins' Lectures." It is a long article reporting on the Cousinses' trip to Iowa and their lectures on Indian art and women's issues. Margaret Cousins, in explicating the Indian nationalist response to Katherine Mayo's notorious book, *Mother India,* argued,

> In the 13 years I have lived in India ... I have known of only one case where a girl was a mother under 14 years of age. The preponderance of evidence is that the average girl does not become a mother before 17.
>
> Child motherhood is common among the Brahmins who comprise 15,000,000 or only 5% of India's total population.... By overemphasizing these Brahmin marriages the entire population of India has been misrepresented and a wrong picture given to the world about a nation of 320,000,000 people.

The irony of these passages could not escape me given the context of Subbalakshmi's life. Subbalakshmi was exceptional in two ways. She was an unwilling mother at the age of fourteen, a member of the minority community projected as the majority. And, as the statistics in the remainder of the article indicated, she was one of only 345,000 literate women in the entire Madras Presidency.

In what follows, I try to understand what the diary as a historical document might tell us about the parameters of a woman's agency. If, however, we hoped to learn something of Subbalakshmi's family life through her diary, we would be disappointed, for her family is mostly absent from the pages of her diary. (What, indeed, we might ask, has led us to expect it to be there?) Yet in considering other sources about Subbalakshmi's life — papers, letters, and her daughter's testimony — partial outlines of her life emerge. Subbalakshmi was an upper-middle-class Brahmin woman who came of age during the nationalist movement, only to have the seeds of her political awakening crushed by the patriarchal authority of the household.

*

Perhaps the very meagerness of Subbalakshmi's diary is the clearest reply we can make to the historians of India who assume that the participation of women in the nationalist movement was at best only a story about middle-class women. For such an assumption obscures the important questions about women's agency, as if marking them as middle class allows us to "know" the story more easily.

Judged by the standards of a national archive, Subbalakshmi was marginal indeed. She was not one of the many women who picketed foreign cloth shops, made speeches, leafleted, marched on salt satyagrahas, or went to jail. And yet Subbalakshmi's muted voice betrays the emergence of a nationalist subjectivity that can be gleaned from her entries on spinning khadi or discreet contributions made to nationalist causes. Perhaps more important, her writings on, and interest in, the subcontinent's major religions reveal an unusual secular consciousness, one sorely missing in the current communal climate.[1]

I want to begin by speculating about what we can learn from the diary and private papers of a woman who lived on the borders of the nationalist movement. It is true that those who live in the margins often evoke a critical voice at odds with that produced at the center. Yet were we to read Subbalakshmi's diary as it is written, we would not immediately discern its critical voice. Subbalakshmi's marginality was forced on her, and the diary hints of her efforts to circulate in elite nationalist society: of her trips to local art exhibitions, or to Marina beach to hear Gandhi speak, of her attempts to have her daughter enrolled in Santiniketan, the school founded by Rabindranath Tagore.

What is most striking about the diary is, as already noted, the absence of any description of familial relations. Yet a reading of these absences coupled with that of her other writings makes it possible to construct her critical voice. It can be found in a sole surviving letter from her friend Grace, in the letters and poems her daughter wrote for her, in the precise chartings of her desire for knowledge(s): lists of books she planned to read; elaborate, almost scientific descriptions of temples and archaeological sites she visited; detailed passages on Buddhist philosophy and Islamic poetry. There are, too, the stories her daughter and youngest granddaughter tell of her frustrated life and longings.

Subbalakshmi's diary, begun when she was twenty-seven years old, is difficult to read apart from other sources about her life. It is not typical of some diaries kept in India, that is, as a record of public affairs or as a form of financial or chronological accounting (indeed, "diary" more often designates a calendar or datebook). Nor is it typical of many Western diaries, that is, as a medium for expressing one's innermost thoughts, feelings, and fantasies. Rather, Subbalakshmi's diary is itself a mixed medium. It contains an account of her expenditures during the year, her thoughts on contemporary Indian art, her descriptions of the setting sun, wind-whipped trees, and flocks of roosting cranes. Perhaps we can better understand what Subbalakshmi might have told us if we first contrast it with Pierre Bourdieu's notion of "habitus" or the realm of the "unsaid"[2] in which the diary is constructed.

Subbalakshmi lived for many years as part of a joint family when she joined her husband after marriage. Her diary does not describe any of the mundane activities that comprise the bulk of housekeeping—cooking, cleaning, or shopping for food—though it is likely that servants or other female relatives carried out these tasks. We also know from her daughter's testimony that Subbalakshmi's brother-in-law (her husband's brother) disapproved of Subbalakshmi's English education and knowledge. If she left the house for an activity that did not concern shopping or visiting the temple, she was also sharply criticized by the other women in the house. Lack of privacy, or the chance that one of the men literate in English might stumble across the diary and read it, perhaps accounts for the cryptic and somewhat coded nature of most entries, for the diary studiously avoids any mention of these interpersonal relations.

Subbalakshmi's diary etches the lives of herself and her daughter Pankajam at "Ramananda Vilas" on Sunkuvar Street in Madras over a period of twenty-seven months. It records faithfully a mother's worries over a daughter's childhood illnesses (measles, eye infections, influenza); the day Pankajam wins a prize at school; and two of Pankajam's birthdays—a new pavadai or wardrobe bought, and evening visits to the temple. There are also frequent references to visits or gifts from members of her natal family she was closest to: her mother, sister Kanakam, and "Brother" (Ananthakrishnan). Even so, her relations with people are not described in any detail. For the two-year period of the diary, there is not a single reference to her husband, even by his initials.

The diary was written in the years 1924–26, after Subbalakshmi had gone through three major traumas—the birth and death of her two sons in infancy and a two-month period in the hospital, where she was treated for a "descended uterus." Her husband did not visit her once during that period, which saddened her, although her daughter Pankajam says "she was by then used to his indifference."

The diary also contains no record of any of Subbalakshmi's friendships. Her closest friend, Grace, an Indian Christian woman she met during her stay in the hospital, is mentioned only once, after Subbalakshmi receives a letter and a lace collar from her on January 24, 1924. And there is no mention of the friendships she was beginning to form with prominent nationalist leaders Kamaladevi Chattopadhyay and Mrinalini Devi, although there is an entry on March 24, 1924, for twelve rupees paid for a subscription to *Shaa'ma*, the publication run by Mrinalini Devi, and a notation for March 22, 1926, "Went to H. Chattopadhyaya's 'Sleeper Awakened.' The closing song was good." (Harindranath Chattopadhyay, a playwright and actor, was married to Kamaladevi.) Still another entry (April 20, 1925) notes that she "received Tagore's 'Red Oleanders' from Calcutta," suggesting a gift or that one of her friends had taken the trouble to procure a copy for her from Calcutta. Thus the diary reveals only the barest outlines of Subbalakshmi's family life and friendships.

I have described what is not in Subbalakshmi's diary so that what is actually in the diary stands out more clearly. Of a total of 188 entries made from January 1924 through March 1926, 80 entries are about nature, in particular Subbalakshmi's observations of birds, sea, sky, trees, and flowers in her garden. The next major portion of the diary (50 entries) concerns financial transactions: money loaned out and returned, money given to her by her mother or sister, money spent for dentists or doctors; money spent on gifts or small pleasures such as sweets or candy. Beginning in January 1925, however, this type of financial notation ceases completely save for the lone entry in March 1926 near the end of the diary: "Received rs. 5 from Pankajam and 13 from Kanakam." Thus at first, Subbalakshmi's diary was probably her primary means of keeping track of expenditures. While it is possible that men at this time were beginning to ask their wives to keep track of family expenditures as part of a modern domestic regime articulated by nationalism,[3] all of the sums of money Subbalakshmi records receiving are from her sister Kanakam, her mother, or her daughter. This implies that she was more concerned with accounting for the sources of her independent funds.

A number of entries concern Pankajam's periodic school fees—money spent on her stationery, books, and school supplies—as well as the small indulgences for a cherished child: rs. 1-8-0 for a paint box, or a trip to the circus. Despite Subbalakshmi's own love of books, it seems she rarely bought herself any. The diary records two trips to the library and the occasional purchase of books, never for large sums of money, and usually with money given to her by Kanakam: "Bought Aravinda Ghosh's 'Essays on the Gita' from the 4 rupees given by Kanakam" (March 12, 1924); "Bought Tolstoy's Plays out of Kanakam's present money" (April 19, 1924). One entry records that she spent "rs. 3-6-0 for 'Tagore's Letters From Abroad,' Ghosh's 'Yogic Sadhan,' and Mahatma's 'Guide to Health.'" Another entry of December 24, 1925, records a trip to Adyar to buy a number of books for her brother, "very good ones, on art, travel, etc." Reading through Subbalakshmi's several financial notations, one does not have the impression that she ever spent much money on herself.

Subbalakshmi's funds seem to have been limited. There is only one deposit recorded, a sum of twenty rupees (out of twenty-five rupees given to her by her sister Kanagam) on February 1, 1924. On April 1 and 20, 1924, and again on June 3, 1924, she records changing "rs. 1-0-0" for miscellaneous expenses, suggesting that even small sums represented a significant expenditure for Subbalakshmi. The nine recorded withdrawals of money from the bank for the year 1924 were also usually for small sums of money, five or ten rupees. It is possible that Subbalakshmi had her own bank account. If not, the very fact of going to a bank and withdrawing money on her own must have been highly unusual. While it underscores her comfortable class position, it also points to Subbalakshmi's independence of thought and action.

It is difficult to adduce much more about Subbalakshmi's domestic economy from her diary, but I am struck by the fact that it was written on a child's exercise book (perhaps one bought originally for Pankajam), and that the often cryptic, yet precise, form of Subbalakshmi's observations was in part due to the fact that the number of entries for any one month never exceeded more than a page. For this reason, Subbalakshmi's already meticulous handwriting, in small cursive letters, neatly and clearly defined, often has a cramped quality. It seems that Subbalakshmi intended that this book be a record of her life for many years. The exercise book was only a third of the way filled when she stopped writing in it. That Subbalakshmi thought a great deal about what she was going to write before she wrote it is also evident from the fact that there is not a single crossed out word or letter in the entire diary. A remarkable exercise in days without erasers or ballpoint pens.

Interspersed throughout the financial entries for the year 1924 are several cryptically elegant descriptions of nature: "Strangely lovely night, after ten o' clock the clouds from the North threw long streamers southwards over the eastern half of the sky through which the newly risen moon shone" (January 26, 1924). And again, on November 7, 1924:

> Saw a gorgeous sunset, masses of mauve clouds like a mountain-range low in the horizon. Then a strip of green sky in which a golden wisp of a cloud was floating, orange-colored clouds then interposing, after which came a bit of blue sky and then purple and grey clouds.

Yet the diary after 1924 is dominated by descriptions of nature, in particular of birds and their nests, the planting of evening jasmine flowers in her garden, her sadness when a cherished mango tree is cut down by vandals. There were no entries made for May 1925, but the sole entry for the following month (June 28, 1925) describes the wilderness of the rocks and falls at the Cauvery near Chanaikal before summer vacation in Dharmapuri in May.

It is possible that Subbalakshmi was a poor sleeper, or perhaps her impressions of the night made a deeper imprint on her than did her daytime activities. In any case, many of her entries are about the positions of the planets in the sky, the presence of the star Rohini, the moon rising or setting "in the midst of white clouds, the sea glittering" (March 23, 1924). "A glorious full moon, like a golden shield some time after rising. Later it turned the fresh young mango leaves into dreams of silver" (April 8, 1925). This vignette of July 23, 1925, is not atypical of her writing during this period:

> Magnificent sight at evening, in the West, against a background of dark heavens, there formed a bow-like whitish mass of clouds stretching from North to South, which rapidly moved eastward with

great thunder and dissolved in furious rain. Verily, "In the rainy
gloom of July nights on the thundering chariots of clouds, he comes,
ever comes."

Subbalakshmi's habit of combining natural description with the
poetry of others, I would argue, both evokes and masks her own
emotional states. For example, the entry for August 30, 1924, is an
unattributed quote (perhaps from Tagore): "I forget, I ever forget
that I have not the winged horse, that the gates are everywhere shut
at the house where I dwell." Significantly, on January 20, 1925, Subbalakshmi records, "Made a resolve. God help me to keep it." Later
entries, however, testify to an ongoing internal conflict or anguish.
Through another unattributed quote she asks, "When shall my heart
find its haven of rest, where shall my heart find repose?" (April 8,
1925).

Leila Ahmed in a recent analysis suggests that women autobiog-
raphers turn toward their gardens as a means of foregrounding
unexpressed pain.[4] The contrast evoked is that between the beauty
of inherent possibilities in nature and the wantonness of human
arrangements that cripple or destroy life. Perhaps it is this contrast
that infuses, in part, Subbalakshmi's moving words about the
wilderness around her.

It is also true, however, that Subbalakshmi's descriptions of nature
often convey her own particular religious sensibility. Were we to
attempt to gauge this sensibility through the obvious references in
the diary (as I initially did), we would miss much of what makes
her unique. For there is little description of the numerous pujas that
make up the life of a pious Hindu woman. Even major events of the
Hindu Tamil calendar such as Nava Ratiri, Deepavali, or Pongal
(times of gift-giving, worship, and arduous food preparation) are
omitted. Entries about Subbalakshmi's journeys to temples outside
of Madras are prominent, however, even if a journey to the famous
temple in Tirupati (one of the major sites of pilgrimage in southern
India) on December 26, 1924, and her return to Madras four days
later are unremarked.

Subbalakshmi makes passing references to Andal or Maham pro-
cessions (on August 3, 1924, and February 27, 1926), to images she
has seen at the temple: "Went to the temple and saw the beautiful
vision of Sri Rama with Sita and Bharata" (January 2, 1925); "the
vision of the divine flute-player enchanted the eye and the mind"
(January 3, 1925); "saw the beautiful get-up of the Divine Charioteer,

a feast to the eyes" (January 31, 1925); or notes gratefully, "Went to the temple and had the luck to get tulsi and mangal" (October 24, 1924). But the most impassioned comment is about Saraswati (goddess of wisdom and learning), which reads simply, "Saraswati puja; may her grace never fail." It is poignant, if fleeting, testimony to Subbalakshmi's own reverence for knowledge.

Aside from these scant references, Subbalakshmi's spirituality often appears accentuated by her aesthetic appreciation of natural settings. For example, her entry for December 8, 1924, juxtaposes the temple as a site of worship offered God and nature as the manifestation of God: "Went to Thiruvanmiyoor [a village then on the southern outskirts of Madras] with all. Was lucky enough to be in time for the festival evening worship and procession. Back in Madras, beautiful moonlight night with frog chorus instead of the cries of the night-herons of Thiruvanmiyoor." Still later (December 21, 1924) she records,

> Went to Thiruvuthiyur with all. Saw Pattinathar's tomb in a grove full of the cries of birds and the roar of the sea. Returning through flower-bordered lanes to the temple, wandered among the numerous tiny shrines which lie in the grass-grown prakasam where tumbai and yellow alamander flourish. Then went inside and saw mother's archanas to God, Goddess, and Kali.

Subbalakshmi's spiritual and aesthetic sense is also expressed through her interest in temple architecture, a subject she researched heavily at the Madras University library. In February of 1925, she records a trip made with her mother, sister Kanakam, and Pankajam to Rameswaram:

> A memorable trip, Devipatnam, Rameswaram and Dhanuskodi visited. Found the famous corridor at Rameswaram temple as impressive as expected. Saw the delightful garden temple of Sri Rama on the outskirts. The approach to Dhanuskodi, for some distance composed of sandy plains and dunes covered by luxurious flowering creepers and then of shallow lagoons in which millions of gull(s) and a graceful white bird with pink legs, shall never be forgotten. Halted at Madura and saw the exquisite figures on the pillars of the 1000 pillared hall, also the statues of Thrumala Raya and his queens, all in the great temple.

A lesser, but still substantial, portion of Subbalakshmi's diary contains brief comments on the nationalist movement that only hint at her steadfast support. One entry of April 12, 1924, says simply,

"Went to the Tilak Ghat meeting on National Education. Mr. Sarma's speech in chaste Tamil good." Another entry of March 7, 1925, says, "Went to the beach in the evening to see Mahatma Gandhi. Could not hear a word and got only a brief sight of him." Remembering Pankajam's words that her mother had deferred to family pressure not to actively participate in the movement so that her father's position under the British would not be jeopardized, I can easily picture Subbalakshmi at the edge of a crowd or meeting, but never quite in the middle of one.

And yet in spite of Subbalakshmi's marginality, it is likely that she was a regular reader of newspapers and was well informed of nationalist activity and issues. The entries for April and May of 1924 show that Subbalakshmi was experiencing trouble with her eyes, "pupil dilation" and a "dragon-fly apparition," which prevented her from her usual reading. She made several trips to the Ophthalmic Hospital. On May 2, 1924, she wrote, "Tried to read, after two weeks' enforced rest. Read 2 newspapers but was obliged to hold at arm's length. Eyestrain after reading."

It is clear from the diary that Subbalakshmi contributed money to various causes, some of them nationalist. The clearest entry is that of June 2, 1924—"Sent 1-0-0 to the Moplah Relief Fund," again revealing an unusual sympathy for the victims of the ill-fated "Moplah Uprising" of 1921. While this Khilafat-oriented movement is now seen by historians as a "massive, armed anti-imperialist revolt," Hindu opinion then "generally condemned the Moplahs as being no more than communal fanatics."[5] A February 24, 1924, entry shows she donated one rupee to the "V.R. Fund"; an entry of April 13, 1924, shows another one-rupee donation to the "Barathas-raman"; and still another one-rupee donation to the "PRF" is noted on August 6, 1924.

Other entries record Subbalakshmi's efforts at spinning and weaving khadi, a key element of Gandhi's "Constructive Program," and a task he argued was especially well suited to women since they could contribute to the nationalist movement while sitting at home. Subbalakshmi's first entry on this subject is April 8, 1924, when she notes that she "bought Gita Govindam for 1-4-0 and cotton for 0-7-6." On April 11, 1924, she notes, "Began spinning after many months. So the yarn is not as fine as before." This entry tells us that this was not Subbalakshmi's first time spinning, and that she was an experienced enough spinner previously to have spun a finer thread, something not accomplished without many hours of practice. Judging from her entries it seems Subbalakshmi often spun when the weather was too bad to go outside: "Rain fell for the first time this season. The whole day was cloudy and the evening full of quiet beauty, the sky and the sea blending together. Began spinning once more" (June 8, 1924). Another entry of July 14, 1924, noted,

> Cut out the Khaddar cloth (mine) into a shirt for Pankajam. Heavy rain in the evening accompanied by wind mirroring Tagore's song, "Last night clouds were threatening and amlak (here, mango) branches struggled in the grips of a gusty wind. . . . Last night when the darkness was drunken with storm, and the rain like the night's veil was torn by the winds into shreds."

On July 21, Subbalakshmi notes that she "finished the Khaddar shirt." The following day, Subbalakshmi records that she "cut out the printed Khaddar into a shirt for Pankajam," and on July 29, "finished it." On October 19, 1924, Subbalakshmi reports that she saw a "Khaddar exhibition," and later that year, that she "cut out a bodice from the Khaddar spun by me" (December 6, 1924). She records finishing the bodice on December 15, 1924, and beginning to embroider it on January 1 of the new year, 1925. The last reference in the diary to spinning occurs on January 28, 1925, where she says, "Began spinning out of the second cotton bundle."

Yet the diary also charts Subbalakshmi's intellectual interests. While her recorded purchases of books only hint at the breadth of her intellectual curiosity, Subbalakshmi also records her attendance at several art exhibitions, unusual for a woman of that time. Her reflections on art are some of the most extended in the diary. An entry on June 6, 1924, reports that she "went to the Picture Exhibition organised by Mrs. Adair." Another entry on April 3, 1925, reads,

> Went to the "Parent's Day" show at the training college. Saw also the exhibition of pictures by famous artists. The gem of the collection, "Flight" entrancing in its beauty. To own this masterpiece of Nandalal Bose is preferable to possessing a gallery of lesser paintings. Amongst other pictures, those of D. Battacharya and A. P. Bannerji (new names) were good, especially the latter's "Krishna" and "Rasalila." But Chatterji's "Sarada" is not so beautiful in treatment. His "Durga" is better.

A last entry on this subject for December 28, 1925, observes,

> Went to the International Arts exhibition at Adyar, a very fine collection of pictures, textiles, ivoryware, etc. Among the pictures, G. Tagore's Himalayan studies were superb. P. K. Chatterji and A. P.

Banerji also contribute a number of fine paintings, "Vanadeva and Devi," "Lotus Blossoms" being typical. Among the newer artists Vasudevan and Raju are the most promising, the "Comrades" and "Reapers" of the former being very good, both in expression and technique. In the European section, Delftware from Holland was particularly attractive. The Japanese section was also interesting, such tiny painted incense-burners.

It is difficult to emphasize how much these blocks of text, like her temple descriptions, stand out in a diary that is only twenty-seven pages, the majority of entries being just one or two lines long. Yet each of these entries is almost a full page.

Reading Subbalakshmi's diary, then, gives us the contours of her life and thought. It is helpful, however, to read the diary against other documents. Subbalakshmi kept dozens of files and notebooks filled with press cuttings, intricate descriptions of temple architecture, birds, and landscapes; lists of books she wanted to read in psychology, Buddhism, geography, and neurobiology; as well as translations of Kabir's poetry into English and of the devotional Devaram songs in Tamil. These songs, and various philosophical or religious teachings, were the only notebooks of Subbalakshmi written in Tamil, much of it classical Tamil. Everything else is in English. The fact that Subbalakshmi chose to write her diary in English suggests that she never intended it as a record of her innermost feelings, but perhaps as testimony of her superb literacy. Of all her papers and notebooks, we are left with only her diary from 1924-26 and one of Pankajam's old copybooks (the pages on the right bearing Pankajam's third- or fourth-standard compositions on beetles and frogs, and the left-sided pages filled with Subbalakshmi's notes on religious texts in classical Tamil). There are also scattered notes, and a few letters saved by Pankajam, her only surviving child. They are sadly inadequate fragments, many of them lists of books she wanted to read. For example, one list is simply titled "Books from the Library":

Hindu Realism by J. Chatterji
The Child's Unconscious Mind by W. Lay
Psychoanalysis by Tridon
Creative Evolution by H. Bergson
Textbook of Psychoanalysis by W. Games
Education for Self-Realization by Watts
History of Creation by Haeckel
Discourses, Biological and Geological by Huxley
Aesthetics (B. Croce) D. Ainslie

Positive background of Hindu Sociology by Sarkar
Rg Veda-Bramana, Aetreyi Kausitaki
Buddhist Legends, no. 28
Buddhism in Translation, no. 31
Dawn of Civilization by Maspero
A General Survey of European Literature by Magnus
Persian Literature under Tartar Domination by Prof. Browne
Prose and Poetry of Modern Persian by   "   "
History of Russian Literature by Kropotkin
Book of the Epic by Gerberer
Picturesque Nepal by Percy Brown
Antiquarian Remains at Sopara by B. Indraji
Ancient Geography of India by A. Cunningham
Maha-Bodhi Temple by   "   "
Ancient Khotan by Aurel Stein
Java, Sumatra and D. E. Indies, Cabaton
The Altar of the Dead by H. James
An Ideal Husband by O. Wilde
A Woman of No Importance O. Wilde
Plato and Platonism by Walter Pater
A Child's Garden of Verse by R. L. Stevenson

Two notations on the page indicate dates and the number of books read. The first says, "4.2.25 47/130, 12 extra," and the second, "28 books read 18.7.26." Subbalakshmi's files show that she received a reply from the Madras University librarian regarding the list of Buddhist Gathas available in English translation on September 30, 1939. The short reply Subbalakshmi received from the university librarian a year later in response to another request says quite a bit about her voracious literary appetite:

12/7/40

Dear Madam,
    There are more than 1,000 books in Psychology. If you can send somebody here, I should be glad to give him facilities to copy the list.

In order to get a full accounting of the breadth and depth of Subbalakshmi's interests, one would have to reproduce all of the lists she has left us with, which is not possible here: lists of books in English, lists of books in Tamil, lists of books wanted from the Madras University library, receipts for books bought (including one for *Red Star over China* in April of 1948 from Higginbotham's bookstore in Madras). Suffice it to say that her interests were inexhaustible. Many of Subbalakshmi's writings are actually notes taken from other texts, or her own comments on what she was reading. For example, she began her study at age twenty-four, of Sankaracharya's text *Vivekachudamani* by commenting,

Ellore 10/6/21

Note: Viveka means discrimination, Chuda is crest, and Mani, jewel.
Hence the title means "Crest jewel of Discrimination." Just as the
jewel on the crest of a diadem is the most conspicuous ornament on
a person's body, so the present treatise is a masterpiece among works
treating of discrimination between the real and the unreal.

One of her notebooks is filled with descriptions of birds, their mating habits, nest sizes, number of eggs laid, and distinguishing colors. Another consists of elaborate descriptions of the human body in different stages of maturation. Still another is filled with precise notations about recent archaeological sites.

These fragments only hint at Subbalakshmi's aesthetic and intellectual interests. Yet the pain in her life, both physical and emotional, is to be found in other forgotten bits of paper. The only remaining letter from her closest friend, Grace, tells us much about Subbalakshmi's married life. It begins:

November 5, 1926

My Dear Lakshmi,

I have been feeling it a crime to have kept silent for so long, but
many changes have taken place since you wrote to me last, and we
both have not forgotten to remember you day and night that God
may grant you His own comfort and fill your heart with the peace
that passeth all understanding. How we both feel for you dear
Lakshmi! We who know what ideal married life is and enjoy its
blessings every moment of our lives! You have indeed a heavy cross
to bear, but God in his great Mercy, has given you your little
Pankajam to be a comfort in your sorrow. May he bless her little life
in this world, so that, through her you might have some joy even in
your disappointments.

How I long to be near you just now! The whole world seems to
be full of joy for me even though I am childless and considered a
very unfortunate, perhaps accursed one in this world; simply
because of the hope I have in St. Jesus, who is all to me. If only
you knew and loved him. You would never more be unhappy in
spite of all.

While Subbalakshmi's stay in the hospital afforded her the opportunity to meet the woman who was to become her best friend, she never fully recovered her strength after that operation. The diary itself records her poor health and numerous bouts with illness, and later letters to her daughter reveal the same:

Dear Pankajam,

  I have been receiving your letters all along but as you may have
guessed, I could not reply to them owing to the bad state of my
health. And because that reply is not a thing to be bottled up in a
few lines. I was waiting and hoping for a day of improvement all
these times. But no, instead of that I have worsened in some
respects. My nerves have become very weak all over the body for
some time and lately pain too has set upon them in great
measure.... But after seeing your letter today, I feel that somehow I
must try to get the suffering fingers together so as to be able to pen
a few lines at least each day and manage to send a sort of reply to
you in a week or so.

As earlier suggested, much of the poetry Subbalakshmi so carefully transcribed potentially reveals something of her varying emotional states. One in particular, a poem by Kabir, perhaps reveals
some of her strategies for coping with the troubles she experienced.
By turning the literal into metaphor, she also turned her intellectual
and aesthetic pursuits into a spiritual quest:

How hard it is to meet the Lord!
The rainbird wails in thirst for the rain: almost she dies of her
longing, yet she would have none other water than the rain. Drawn
by the love of music, the deer moves forward: she dies as she listens
to the music, yet she shrinks not in fear.

Subbalakshmi's intense but unusually progressive spirituality (as a
practicing Hindu with a Christian friend, a woman well read in
Bakhti poetry and Buddhist and Persian texts) was founded on several sources, but was consolidated, according to Pankajam, during
the time Subbalakshmi lost her small sons.

Second Introduction: July 1991

This is why I have found fault with what you have written the first
time. You have not represented my mother correctly. I want only for
people to know her as she really was. She was a far greater person
than either you or I. But it will be difficult for you to understand, no?
You have come from a different culture, western. You may not
understand our culture and customs.... Suppose I were to go and
start writing about your culture, just like that? Without properly
understanding. What would people think? You see, it is like that.

My notes tell me that Pankajam made this comment on July 13,
1991, as we sat drinking coffee in the front room of the house
where she stayed with her youngest daughter's family. I had come

to discuss a series of corrections Pankajam wanted made to my analysis of her mother's story. Pankajam had written me earlier, on September 10, 1990, and in spite of her eighty-odd years, had either typed or seen this letter typed to me. I had sent back a revised version of her mother's story with corrections, but Pankajam had not received it. So we picked up where Pankajam's earlier letter left off, she emphasizing again the importance of getting her mother's story right, of understanding Subbalakshmi's spiritual nature and religious devotion.

I asked Pankajam why her mother didn't record her frustrations with family in the diary, and, as on other occasions, she responded that if someone in the family happened to read the diary years later (as was indeed the case), her mother would not have wanted to hurt the people close to her. Pankajam's interpretation of her mother's reticence to reveal herself in the diary raises important questions of audience, piety, and self-expression. Even in English, Subbalakshmi's writings were not immune from scrutiny. However, Pankajam offers another explanation of her mother's reticence to reveal much of her inner conflicts:

> Some women from Delhi had come—they said (on reading the diary) that it must have been written by a westerner, because of the sensibilities she had. But people in the West will be more extroverted than people in the East, isn't it? This is why she does not write about her feelings, because people in the East are naturally more introverted. They don't discuss such things. It is not our habit.

Pankajam's analysis is reminiscent of what some historians have also claimed, namely, that Indian "autobiographies in the confessional mode are notable for their absence."[6] And yet it is not quite true, as Dipesh Chakrabarty argues, that "Indian autobiographies are remarkably 'public' when written by men ... and they tell the story of the extended family when written by women."[7] Chakrabarty limits this generalization to autobiographies produced between 1850 and 1910, and he is right to suspect that "once women join the public sphere in the 20th century, their self-fashioning takes on different dimensions."[8] For Subbalakshmi assiduously avoids any description of familial relations, and this fact is significant, whether we impute it to respect for the living, to cultural norms, or even, perhaps, to a form of belated resistance. Yet I would argue that neither is Subbalakshmi's diary a strictly public account. Even if Subbalakshmi does not use the language of emotions to describe her inner states, it seems possible to gauge a sense of interiority emerging out of the aesthetic in her writings: her choices in poetry, architecture, and art, her luminous descriptions of nature that set her apart from most women of her caste or class. This is to say that Subbalakshmi's diary does reveal a distinct, though muted, sense of self, one caught up in, but not fully vocative of, changing times.

Much more could be said here, but I think it is important to conclude this essay with Pankajam Sivaraman's own biographical narrative of her mother's life. Although it is a work in progress that Pankajam plans to publish as a separate article, she has kindly agreed to let what she has written so far be reproduced here.

Birth and Childhood of Smt. Subbalakshmi Ammal
By Pankajam Sivaraman

Smt. Subbalakshmi Ammal was born in Trivandrum (Kerala) in 1897. Her father happened to be serving in Travancore state as a surveyor. But Mr. Sundaram Iyer (Subbalakshmi's father) belonged to Kumbakonam (Tanjore District). Their native village was Kurukkai, a small seaport. Subbalakshmi Ammal's mother and her ancestors lived in Thiruvayaru. Before I go further, I must say a few words about Subbalakshmi's mother and her ancestors.

One Mr. Nilakanta Iyer, Subbalakshmi's forefather of seven generations past, lived in Thiruvayaru on Sannidhi Street. This Nilakanta Iyer was very poor and he had a large family to support. But he was very spiritual and unworldly and was in the habit of standing on one leg in the temple Pragara doing tapsya, or meditation. People passed him by, talking in hushed voices, watching him standing on one leg without the slightest movement, like a statue. Slowly his fame spread and people referred to him as the "Rishi" of Thiruvayaru temple. The Raja of Tanjore presented lands to him.

Kamakshiammal, Subbalakshmi's mother, was herself an extraordinary woman. She had an uncommon memory. She could read and write three languages: Tamil, Telegu, and Malayalam. Her mother, Kalyani, educated by her father as well in Tamil and Sanskrit, used to read and recite the *Puranas, Ramayana,* and *Mahabharata* to the crowd that gathered before the pial (front porch) of their house to listen to her. She came to be called "Storytelling Kalyaniammal."

Kamakshi was very much interested in politics and history. She used to read the Tamil newspapers avidly and discuss politics first with her husband, Sundaram Iyer, and later (after he died) with her own aged father and then with her own children when they grew up.

Sundaram Iyer, her husband, was a scholarly man and very modern in outlook. He had two daughters and two sons. He had strange notions for that age, for he wanted to educate his children in Western ways. He employed the very teachers who taught the Royal family at Travancore. He sent to London for books and toys like the "Magic Lantern" to educate his children in modern ways.

One day, it seems, when Subbalakshmi was an infant, he picked her up high and told his wife, "Do you know that a college for women has opened in Madras called the 'Queen Mary's College'? It is built only for my daughter Subbalakshmi. She will one day study there." But alas! For all his pride and planning for his family, he died young; soon after he became the father of three little children, and one not even born then. The family faced a tragedy then, or rather Kamakshi Amma faced it as her kids were too young to understand the consequences of the death of their father.

The old gentleman Mr. Nilakanta Iyer (named after the family's forebear), who was the father of Kamakshi, brought his daughter and her infants to his house in Thiruvayaru from Trivandrum. From then on he began to take upon himself the responsibility of looking after his daughter's family. It fell to his lot.

While Kamakshi's children were all very bright and very healthy, one child, our Subbalakshmi, was not very strong like the others. She was delicate and caught cold and fever frequently. Hence she was not sent to school but was taught the three R's at home by her grandfather.

When Subbalakshmi was as young as five, her grandfather began to develop eye trouble and eventually lost his sight. When he was losing his sight, he got his young granddaughter Subbalakshmi to read him the newspaper. By then she was able to read English and Tamil well, for being at home and lonely she got into the habit of looking into books for amusement. And when her grandfather made her read out the newspaper to him, at first she refused and shirked like all children. Although she liked to read stories, she did not at first like the newspaper reading to her grandfather. However, while resisting and protesting, the little girl Subbalakshmi read on and on and eventually she began to develop an interest in what she was reading. . . . Soon the little girl began to thirst for more reading. English literature and poetry attracted her.

She pestered her older brother Ananthakrishnan to bring books from the college. She became a voracious reader. From English classics, she soon became a very good translator, for her mother, Kamakshi, did not know English but was interested in the classics of that language and books on history. Therefore she depended on the daughter for translating them into Tamil.

When Subbalakshmi was eight the family moved close to Tiruchirapalli town, for her elder brother Ananthakrishnan had to join college. Her brother was only twelve then (four years her senior), but in those days there was no age limit for getting into college. So they settled in Tiruchirapalli and he joined St. Joseph's College there. This coming to Tiruchirapalli was much disliked by Subbalakshmi because she yearned for the silver sands of the Cauvery, where she used to play with her brother and friends, and also the temple. [But] soon she found that she had reason to be happy in Tiruchirapalli too. For her brother brought her great books to read, though she missed the freedom of movement in the bigger town.

Once when Ananthakrishnan was returning his library books, he found one book missing. He obtained permission to run home and get the book, as home was close to college. When he explained to his teacher about how he forgot to bring it because his sister had taken it, the Jesuit priest was astonished that his sister could read such serious books. Indeed, he did not believe that so young a girl could understand those books. He evinced an interest in meeting the girl himself and came to their house. He plied the girl with questions and, finding her quite able to comprehend him and replying back in good English with eloquence about what she had read, he was astounded and understood here was a genius before him — a prodigy.

Well, when Subbalakshmi was about ten, her mother began to worry about her marriage. Those were days when girls were married off very young. The grandfather began to search for a bridegroom. Mr. Rajam Iyer happened to hear of Mr. Nilakanta Iyer's family and his granddaughter. So he contacted the grandfather and asked for the hand of the girl for his second son, Gopalakrishnan, as his eldest son was already married. My father, Gopalakrishnan, was twenty-three when he was married to my mother, who was only eleven!!! In those days, disparity of age was ignored for other conveniences.

Two years after her marriage, Subbalakshmi went to live with her husband and his people when she was thirteen. She lived in that joint family for two years. I was born to my mother when she was barely fourteen!! Unluckily, just before I was born, my great-grandfather died. Subbalakshmi gave birth to two other male children in the course of time, but the boys died in their infancy. That was a cruel blow to Subbalakshmi. The misery and agony of the loss of her two boys made her turn to philosophy, which was inherent in her heart since childhood.

While these events were happening to Subbalakshmi, equally great tragedies were taking place in the country. The country was in a ferment. Those who rallied to the Mahatma's call had to sacrifice jobs and home. Indeed, they did so happily with full faith in their leader. At this juncture, Subbalakshmi's life underwent a complete change. Here also fate intervened. She had to come to Madras to enter her daughter in a school. The Swadeshi movement attracted her, so also the noncooperation movement of Mahatma Gandhi. She immediately joined these two movements and threw her heart and soul into their programs. She received once a lathi charge and frequently the police sprayed sewage water into the faces of those who resisted the police. She became bold and wrote articles for a well-known magazine called *Shaa'ma,* edited by Mrinalini Devi, sister of Sarojini Naidu, the famous poetess of India. By picketing and acting thus for the country, she helped both political workers as well as the poor. The receipts from those who had received her money are still in her box. She had sent money to those in the Congress, and others who had no money to campaign for the freedom struggle.

I ought to have mentioned before one fact. My mother had an Indian Christian lady as her friend who introduced her to many interesting things. It happened thus.

Subbalakshmi developed some serious trouble in the uterus after her son was born, and she had to be hospitalized in Conjeevaram for nearly two months. It was there that she met this highly interesting lady, Mrs. Grace Samuel, who happened to be in the same hospital along with my mother, occupying the next bed. This lady belonged to Thirunelveli District. Her husband was a reverend—a priest in Nazareth who lived afterward in Surandai. Both were nearly the same age and a great friendship was forged between them that was to last until Mrs. Samuel died years later.

Grace seems to have been an extraordinary woman, highly endowed with many talents. She was interested in everything around her, birds, insects, flowers, and trees. It was she who taught Subbalakshmi about how to watch birds and identify them; and how to watch and identify the constellations in the sky. Subbalakshmi's interest in nature now widened and they both corresponded regularly. They met only once after their first momentous meeting.

It was in Madras at my house when they had both become quite old. This friendship enriched my mother's life.

*

To go back to 1922–24, when Subbalakshmi was picketing and contributing articles and thus joining the Freedom Movement, she also began to visit the art exhibitions that were displayed in Madras. Subbalakshmi was an art lover, too, and had exquisite taste. While Subbalakshmi stood admiring silently the beautiful paintings of the great masters, she was not conscious of herself being noticed and discussed by others. Here I must explain certain things about our society in those times. Those were the years when our women had not started to go to school to educate themselves as they do now. There were colleges and schools for men, but very few schools for girls had started. So mostly our women were not educated in English, which was necessary then for being in society and coming out of their homes.... So it was such a surprise to see a lady wearing the sari in the old caste system fashion at the exhibition—a single woman with a small child. After a number of ventures like this, the conveners of the exhibition contacted her and spoke to her. One of those who noticed her was Mrinalini. Smt. Mrinalini and Subbalakshmi became great friends, and the former one day brought Sarojini Naidu with her and introduced her to Subbalakshmi. Sarojini Naidu and Mrinalini then learned how much my mother admired Tagore. They saw she had bought a Bengali and English dictionary to learn Bengali because she wanted to enjoy Tagore's poems in the original. On learning this they took her to hear Tagore recite his poems. I remember one such meeting where Tagore was seated in the center and some of the elite of Madras were sitting in a circle around him. I remember the names of a few only—they are Sir C. P. Ramaswami, Harindranath Chattopadhyay, and his wife, Kamala. Somehow Kamaladevi Chattopadhyay was attracted to my mother and invited her to her house. Kamaladevi was then living near the beach in a house called "The Blue Wave" where my mother and I were frequent visitors. I never understood what the friends were talking about, but used to immensely like and was moved by the grandeur of the organ that Harindranath was playing, as well as the ice cream that he bought me ...

A Last Introduction

Pankajam's emerging biography of her mother seems to me both an immense labor of love and a poignant exercise in humility. Pankajam has not wanted me to write anything of her own life, though she also struggled, as did her mother, for education and knowledge; she, too, had thoughts and feelings about the nationalist movement; she, too, appreciates and writes poetry. Years before I met Panka-jam, she had undertaken a similar biographical exercise for a festschrift honoring her father. She begins her essay "My Father Sri Swamiji" by saying,

> Before I begin to write down my father's life as I know it, I must at the outset say, that in general I am unfit to do it, as I have not had the privilege of higher studies at all, which was a subject of argument between my parents very often in those days. So it was that I never saw the portals of a college. Why, I was not even allowed to finish school before I was married off. So I beg to be pardoned for the many grammatical and other mistakes that might be there.

With only a fourteen-year difference in age, Pankajam and her mother must have been very close, sisterly even. Sometimes when Pankajam talked to me I had difficulty in distinguishing which life was being narrated to me, hers or her mother's. Perhaps Pankajam, too, recognizes that she has indeed, with great skill and compassion, narrated some of her own history through the telling of her mother's life.

9

Sari Stories

Somehow, during the course of that first year in India, I accumulated a lot of saris. I'm not really sure how. Various concerned mamis, surprised and delighted with how "Indian" I looked, determinedly gave me saris at all possible moments: old ones, new ones, cotton ones, and silk; torn, but still lovely ones; others in colors so gaudy I dared not wear them. The logic was, if I looked Indian, surely in a sari, I must be Indian.

I myself went through a batik phase and a craze for Bengal cottons. Then I entered my Kanchi cotton period, even traveling to Kanchipuram to buy saris. Once in a while, I spent a lot on a sari, but like any good female shopper, I delighted more in the bargains.

My grandmother and I had a ritual. Whenever she spotted me sneaking in the door with various paper or plastic parcels tucked under my arm, she would demand from her couch, "Enna velai?" My bargains met with her approval ("adu nala velai" — a good price), and my excesses with one word — "jasti" (too much). On the days when I did well I might be rewarded with a pre-Independence story about all the terrific saris she had once bought for ten rupees.

Once, however, I scandalized a group of aunties who were visiting with patti when I returned home. I'd come back with a superb Coimbatore cotton that cost only forty rupees, outdoing even their own standards for a bargain. They clucked excitedly over the find and demanded to know at exactly which Cooptex I'd found it. "Kalahala pen," they told me. "Good girl."

I soon discovered, however, that the wearing of saris was coded by factors such as age and class. A woman of any age might wear a Bengal or Kanchipuram cotton, but a woman my grandmother's age would never wear a batik or any of the northern cottons so popular among younger women. Nor would a younger woman wear any of the bright, durable cotton-silks in which Rangachari's on Luz Church Road specialized. The two-tone simplicity of such saris appealed to me, but when I took home a rust sari with a navy blue border, my cousins laughed at me for buying a "mami sari." And it was true that I never saw women of my age in these cotton-silk blends, but often witnessed stout middle-aged women going about their chores in worn versions of such saris.

Similarly, my grandmother didn't approve of the newfangled blends my cousins and I sometimes went in for at the numerous sari expositions held in Madras. There was the time a cousin talked me into buying what was called "artificial silk," a shiny combination of synthetic fibers that looked like, and even felt a bit like, heavy silk. "Ugh, adu artsilk," patti said, using the English word when she saw the sari. "I can even tell by the smell," she noted with disgust.

One week I brought home only green saris. Green was not a color I usually wore, but somehow the monsoon rains and air pregnant with promise made me feel as if a vital change in season had occurred. I bought saris with flowers and butterflies sprinkled over them because they reminded me of spring in the States. Patti took to calling me "pachai papa." I teased her too about quirky food preferences, in particular her evening cup of hot, milky liquid: "Horlick's baby," I called her.

*

Even distant members of the family commented on how much I looked like my grandmother. Depending on what side of the family they were from, they'd say: she has attai's smile, or she's tall like periyamma. The resemblance was undeniable, but I'd noticed some things. First, when my grandmother smiled, there was a gleam of white that lit up her entire face, perhaps because she was so often sad. Not obviously, but more philosophically so, as with a person who has seen many things, and who knows that she will see many more that will not surprise her.

Then there was granny's height. It was not really that she was tall. It was true, she was now stooped with age, but I thought that if she were to stand straight she'd still be not quite my height of five feet six inches. But patti gave the impression of being tall. Broad-shouldered and rangy, she was an intimidating figure. Sometimes I'd see her in the kitchen from the other end of the house, her arthritic knees causing her to rise slowly from the floor where she cooked, but with a dignity and grace I was not sure inhered in my own carriage. It was then that her size would impress me. I'd feel her at least a head taller than me, and I'd marvel at the strength of her bearing. Well-toned muscles from the daily labor of more than eighty years had not quite given way to sagging flesh, and her golden skin glowed from weekly oil baths. Patti's legs were bowed and her feet splayed in the manner of women who have squatted to work from a young age.

Yet I thought, and still think, she is one of the most beautiful women I have ever known.

*

Cousins and distant relatives always told stories about how beautiful patti was. But once she told me a story. About when she was first married and my grandfather had taken her from the village to Madras to live. Sometimes on Sundays he'd surprise her and take her on a stroll to Marina beach, about a twenty-minute walk from the house. Granny said people used to laugh at the couple she and my grandfather made: she tall and graceful, he, short, squat, and grizzled. "But he didn't care," my grandmother told me proudly. "He wasn't like other men that didn't take their wives anywhere and kept them locked up in the house." I smiled, and then realized that the stoop in her back and her grand slouching posture had not only come from cooking.

*

When the time came to hire a cook, what a pirachanai! It was becoming difficult for patti to bend and stoop in the kitchen, though she insisted she was fine. "What did we all want a cook for?" patti demanded to know. She was proud of her reputation as the best cook in the family—across three generations at that. Wasn't her cooking good enough? Besides, no one else could cook food to her taste. And how could she trust a strange woman in her kitchen? She'd had cooks before, and they were either lazy or they tried to steal food.

After months of arguing and cajoling, flurries of letters from my father in California, my aunt in Delhi, and from cousins all over India, a cook (or rather the first one) was found.

The first cook was a gaunt, surly woman. She spoke little and wasn't the type to take orders. She suffered patti's continual commands and inquiries in stony silence the first day, her every action conveying a kind of mute resistance. The second day while the cook was preparing the sambar, patti told her to add more salt. Cook ignored her and just kept cooking. Patti was furious at being so rebuffed and fired her promptly, the sambar still bubbling. "Does she think she gives the orders around here? Does she pay me a salary? No! It is I who pay the salary, therefore she should do as I say!"

Cook number two was a rather innocuous, pleasant-faced woman who cooked diligently for a few days before she dared an innovation to make her job easier. Patti had rebuked her sharply for cutting up all of the day's vegetables that morning, saying, "Can't you see that's too much for one curry? It will all go to waste!" The cook rallied to the occasion and declared boldly that she was going to cook the vegetables all at once; in my grandmother's refrigerator, the leftover curry would certainly keep until dinner. Patti was horrified. Anyone who was not willing to cook fresh food would simply not cook for her at all.

Two cooks in one week.

Then a third cook, plump, jovial, and overtalkative, followed. She bore patti's bossing with endearing good humor, to the point that patti was unsettled at not finding fault with her. Patti began to grouse that someone must be filching her Horlick's because there was less in the jar than there should be. Then she noticed that the cook seemed to spend an inordinate amount of time in the kitchen, sometimes remaining two or three hours after everyone assumed she'd already gone home. Patti was soon convinced that the cook was making more food than necessary and hanging around to have her fill of the leftovers. The idea of the already substantial woman getting rounder and fatter off her meager coffers was more than patti could stand. Then one day patti claimed she'd come upon the cook helping herself to some idlis that had been set aside for the afternoon tiffin, and that was that. Cook number three was gone.

More months lapsed, until an impoverished Brahmin woman down the street was found to cook. Somehow she fit right into patti's household, which in spite of a lone male cousin consisted namely of contentious women. Gnanam was an indifferent cook at best, but she always cooked what patti asked, with sometimes spectacular, and more often abysmal, results. She and patti would trade recriminations and tales of woe, and if granny went too far, cook would bunk for a few days to show her displeasure. Her excuses were ingenious only in their brazen execution: mysterious fevers or menses that had passed just ten days before would suddenly reappear. Gone were the days when patti could fire a cook every few days, for now there was no one else available.

Gnanam was a thin, spry woman with thick-lensed glasses, buck teeth, and a pinched nose that made her look like a less terrifying version of the bandicoot when she peered at you. In a good mood, Gnanam infected the house with her boisterous wisecracks and rowdy observations. But when she and my grandmother ganged up, they could badger me to the point of tears. Yet Gnanam could also be surprisingly tender in a gruff sort of way. Her manner of consulting me on what I might want to eat for the day (a formality, since I always said "edavadu") was to shout into my face, "ENNA VEN-DUM?" ("What do you want!")

I rather liked her.

In fact, I liked her so much that I felt I should buy her a new sari for Deepavali. It was thus that I presented her with a maroon cotton sari in a stylish print. Gnanam looked embarrassed but pleased at the gift. I was therefore surprised, when, after waiting patiently for her to wear my gift, some four or five days later she asked me brightly whether I liked the color of the new sari she was sporting, a yellow sari I had not given her. I wondered whether this was a way of telling me she preferred yellow to maroon, and thought perhaps she'd traded in the sari I gave her for a new one. "Oh no," said a visiting cousin. "Probably her husband gave it to her for Deepavali. Women like this begin guarding extra saris for their daughter's marriage years in advance. Each year they'll put away one or two saris as they can afford it. You know her oldest daughter is already sixteen. I'm sure Gnanam is saving the sari you gave for her daughter."

*

Patti was another one who hoarded saris. The senior women in the family had a kind of competition going to see whether patti ever liked one of the saris they had given her well enough to wear. Patti, with a crafty humility, would complain that she had more saris than she needed, and would quietly tuck her gifts away for future redistribution. In the whole time I stayed with her, my grandmother only let me give her three saris. To my great dismay, she always wore the ugliest one. Of course, I would never have intentionally given anyone an ugly sari. It happened like this:

I had decided to buy granny a sari, but there was another mami staying in our house whose son rarely spared her a considerate word, and who, with my cousin's two small children to care for, was treated mostly as a workhorse. I thought it would be unkind to offer only patti a sari, and besides, didn't mami deserve some small token of appreciation for her work in the house? So I walked into a shop on Mount Road and immediately spotted a sari in baby pink cotton for my grandmother, but I had difficulty finding one of comparable worth for mami. (I imagined that old ladies, like jealous sisters, might bicker over a gift, and I wanted to avoid a scene.) Then, with a sigh of relief, I spotted one at the bottom of the pile similar in design with a little jeri I knew patti wouldn't care for, but in a light blue cotton that I thought would complement mami's duskier complexion.

At home, I duly offered the pink one to patti, and the blue one to mami. Patti was delighted, but mami cast a baleful eye on hers. "It's a bit faded, isn't it?" she muttered. And to my dismay (since I had paid the same price for both saris), I realized it was, but hadn't noticed in the gloom of the shop. I quickly offered to exchange it, but mami just as quickly put on a good face and thanked me profusely for the gift. Two days later, however, I noticed patti had on the faded blue sari. I asked patti why, and she said it was because mami complained so much about the blue sari, she had offered to switch. "Enekku paravaillai," patti said with a shrug. "I don't care."

But I did.

Patti constantly offered everything she owned, including the house, to anyone who needed help, and this included the family who stayed with us. My blood boiled to see her walking around the house in the faded sari. And she wore it two or three times a week, as a work sari, because it wasn't fit for much else. Perhaps it was patti's way of acknowledging the gift, but often when I saw her in it, I felt it as a kind of reproach—that had I really the desire to offer a sari to mami, I would certainly have paid more attention to what I had bought. In wearing the faded sari, patti only underscored my missed motives: that the sari was not, in fact, a "gift." To this day, however, I am not sure who had the worse case of guilty conscience. I never once saw mami wear the pink sari. Some months later, in Delhi, I saw it on her sister-in-law at a family function.

*

There was no running water proper in our house. That is to say that unlike some Indian cities, the water situation in Madras has always been precarious, punctuated only by severe droughts and shortages, so that the water, when it came, ran quite improperly at odd hours of the night, on odd days, and was stored in large plastic buckets and a stone vat built into the wall at the back of the house. Needless to say, all of the house's activities centered on the circulation of buckets: for bathing, the cooking, and washing.

One night, after my cousins had gone off to Delhi, leaving patti and me alone in the house, the water began to run. Through the veil of sleep I could hear my grandmother rising awkwardly from her bed. I sat up and saw patti moving around, her hair hanging in loose white strings and her sari twisted around her in sleep. Women often wore the same sari to bed as they had in the day; the practicality of being fully dressed for early dawn chores meant that they'd already put in several hours' work before they bathed around 8 or 9 A.M. and put on a fresh sari.

"Patti, please go back to bed," I begged her. I was afraid she'd slip on the wet concrete, and where would I find a doctor at 2 o'clock in the morning? Patti ignored me, and grabbing a sloshing bucket trudged to the back of the house, as I followed.

When she stopped, her face was tensed, a combination of fatigue and irritation gnawing at her. "Sleep," she told me softly, but with an effort at control. I tried again, "Patti, *you* should sleep now, let me do this." Patti pushed past me and went to pick up another bucket.

Panic gripped me; I remembered that she had indeed slipped once before on the wet floor in the bathroom and injured her hip. I cursed her stubbornness and fretted that I hadn't even the vocabulary to give her a piece of my mind. The only Tamil expression I knew for "stubbornness" could be misunderstood as an insult, especially since it was generally used only with small children. I was anxious now, and struggling for words, loss of sleep inducing an equivalent loss of patience. So I blurted out in ragged Tamil, "Patti, how old are you? What age am I? Please go to bed. I'll do this."

Patti straightened herself slowly and with great difficulty. She was at her most imposing, and dwarfed me with the fire flashing from her eyes. "Amaam," said patti, sending exactly the same words back at me. "How old are you? What age am I?" She paused significantly, then quietly ordered: "Lie down."

I was beaten and I knew it. I was twenty-five or twenty-six, but I didn't dare reply. I retreated to my bed and miserably watched her empty and refill buckets for the next half hour. No matter how just my concern, I'd spoken out of turn to my grandmother. I was to remember that, even if I didn't hear about it in the morning ...

*

Sunday morning, 9 A.M. Time for the Ramayana. Time to go out and visit friends. A good time; the streets were always deserted and the buses empty. Entire neighborhoods glued to the nearest available television (on our street, my grandmother's old black-and-white set). I decided to wear a hand-painted sari I'd avoided because it was too stiff and starched. It was white and strewn with flowers but the effect was not too bad. Patti and company parked in front of the TV ignored me; they knew that whatever anyone else was doing normally, I would do differently. Granny threw me a glance as I said "poituvaren" and a big grin lit up her face. "Look at my grand-daughter," she said, "Oru devi illaiya?"

*

Sundays were also washing days for me, but washing saris is not so easy. There are tricks to learn once you decide to do it yourself to avoid the politics between one's grandmother and the maidservants that have lived, worked, and scrapped with her for more than thirty years.

The first time I stuck a sari in the bucket, all wadded up, I should have predicted trouble. For when I took it out and attempted to hang it on the line, it was impossible to do neatly: a hopeless num-ber of wet ends flapped absurdly in the hot wind.

The next time I watched my cousin. Her sari was already folded when she stuck it in the bucket. After soaping and rinsing, she took it out, wrung it, and let it sit twisted and dripping on the line for some time before skillfully shaking it out to hang.

This helped, but washing saris is hard work. I was usually exhausted after a Sunday wash, by the work women routinely did as one among many daily tasks. I started to put off this chore until a great pile had gathered, a failing that irked mami, and who, in a bad mood, might then complain that I'd used too much water for my washing.

*

Once the sari is washed it has to be pressed. There was a boy who came from the house down the street to pick up the clothes for ironing. Each time he brought the laundry back, mami would argue that the total should be rs. 10.25 instead of rs. 11.75. The boy was insolent (I could see why), and though I didn't like him much, mami was worse. She'd count the number of pants, shirts, hankies, nappies, and saris, then shake the addition at the boy and shout that he was an illiterate fool. And he'd usually mutter something nasty in reply.

The scenes depressed and embarrassed me, and for a time I took to wearing unironed clothes to avoid being implicated in the con-frontations. Yet mami, in spite of her failings, was a good-hearted soul. When she was rested from her chores, she smiled with gen-uine warmth and concern. The problem was that she was so infre-quently rested. Still, on the occasional days when I fell out of bed late, and struggled in bad temper to put sleep-tangled hair into some semblance of a plait, mami might braid it for me as she did often for her own daughter-in-law, who was known in the neighborhood for the thick, luxurious plait that swung like a silk cord well past her hips.

*

On days when it rained, women had the habit of wearing nylon saris. Usually an old one, one they didn't care if it were soaked and muddied in one of Madras's sudden downpours. Nylon saris, of course, also have the advantage of drying quickly. For some reason, although nylon saris (to my mind) were uglier than cotton ones, they were more costly. One could buy them fairly inexpensively in the States, and though I sometimes came with a suitcasefull for my aunts and cousins, I never bought one for myself.

On a summer day when the sun shone through magnificent purple-bellied clouds, I liked to think that it wouldn't rain on my fresh cotton sari. But that day it did.

As I stepped off the bus in Thiruvanmiyur, it began to pour. It was only a five-minute walk to the Institute, but by the time I reached it I was soaked. My red sari clung to me in all the wrong places. I stumbled into a strange office, hoping to find someone with a towel. One of the professors I had not seen before stared at me with obvious interest and motioned me into a chair. He asked me if my accent meant that I'd come from the States. Replying in the affirmative, he asked again, "And both of your parents are Indian?" "No," I said, "my mother was American."

"Ahh ..." he said, his tone implying certain stereotypes held about "Western" women, "but still you *look* Indian. What large eyes you have, such strong eyebrows, and very white teeth." I felt ridiculously like Little Red Riding Hood, or worse yet, a damsel in a bad Hindi movie. Professorji's eyes were now fixed on a point well below my chin. Shivering now, and with what shred of dignity a clinging sari might allow, I asked for a towel. Professorji handed me what might have been a handkerchief, and watched with amusement as I attempted to dry myself. Just then an office boy entered to ask a question, and I used the distraction to excuse myself and escape quickly upstairs.

*

Often waiting at the Mylapore bus stop, which bordered one side of the Kapaleeswara tank, I'd see the widows dependent on the temple for sustenance. Their vacant perambulations around the tank perimeter in search of alms only dramatized blouseless arms and mud-brown saris draped carelessly over withered skin and shaved heads. It was as if their slackened bodies had been ripped from the pages of a nineteenth-century treatise on social reform, arousing my anger and despair. It was as if nothing had changed, or ever would, for a penniless widow bereft or cast away from family.

Invariably at the bus stop I'd also see crowds of well-fed women in flashy, expensive silk saris, bejeweled by thick talis of braided gold, diamond nose-studs and earrings, plentiful bangles cutting into corpulent flesh. Many of these women were older, anywhere from fifty to seventy years of age, the morning's jasmine fresh on gray hair. Unlike other parts of India, women in the South did not, as a rule, cover their heads with their saris, and women of all classes garnished their plaits with flowers. Even the women I recognized as Muslim (by the long black garment they might wear over a sari) often left heads uncovered, and were never veiled.

Watching the groups of overdressed women preening and parading for each other, I reflected that whoever insisted women's clothes were determined by men's taste neglected the significant fact that women often dress to impress each other. I appreciated more and more my grandmother's simplicity—her lack of jewels and silks, her refusal to wear anything but cotton. Patti never called herself a Gandhian, but she lived like many Gandhians I knew.

Unlike the graceful flocks of reedy school girls in their uniform-colored pavadais, the gaggles of gaudily attired women at the bus stop both repelled and fascinated me. These were women who would pull their silks tightly around them when an unkempt child soaked in sweat and dust might sit next to them on the bus; who refused equally to abandon their seats to pregnant women trailing toddlers behind them. I soon learned never to ask such women for directions or bus information. Their knowledge was limited to the single bus they would take to the puja they were attending, the mami they were visiting, or the sari store offering holiday discounts.

My own schedules were as erratic as they were hectic, and days were often spent riding buses from one end of Madras to another. Sometimes as I recounted to patti the litany of places I'd been to during the day—Adyar, Nandanam, T-Nagar, Triplicane; Teynampet, Nungambakkam, Egmore; Kilpauk, Georgetown, Ayanavaram—she'd stop me to ask where a particular neighborhood was located. My grandmother had been all the way to the United States and back, but like many sheltered women of her community did not know the geography of the city in which she had spent the better part of her life.

Patti herself felt this irony all too keenly. She would say that tata told her not to worry about where things were. "You need to know the way to the temple, and the way back home," he told her. Sometimes when she recalled tata's words it was with resignation and a sigh; sometimes with brittle tears in her eyes; and sometimes as a way to underscore her pride in my self-sufficiency. On one occasion when well-meaning family members tried ineffectually to give unsolicited directions to far-off Anna Nagar, she waved them all away, announcing, "She knows where she's going. She knows Madras very well."

*

On the day I was to leave Madras, nothing was packed. That is to say, I'd futilely thrown piles of books and papers in my suitcases, and there was no hope of closing them anytime soon. A colleague dropped in to say good-bye but, frightened by the disarray, and the prospect that I might actually accept her offer to help me pack, beat a hasty retreat. Finally I decided to buy a trunk to store my saris. I knew I wouldn't wear them in the States and I planned to be back in India the next year anyway.

I searched the neighborhood surrounding the temple tank where we lived, but it was hopeless. I couldn't find a store selling trunks anywhere. I returned home to ask my grandmother if she knew of a place. "Ennadu? Why do you want to buy a trunk?" she demanded. She did not understand the logic of leaving behind several nice saris. "They'll all be ruined by the rains," she scolded me. Remembering how mold appeared on clothes in the almirah after only a few days of rain, I knew she had a point. But patti took me to the only place in the neighborhood that sold trunks, and I bought one, paying too much money and irritating her a bit more.

We went home, and I packed the cotton saris with naphthalene balls and shut the lid of the trunk. Somehow I got the suitcases closed. For the first time since I'd come, I put on a pair of jeans and went for a last walk around the siccant tank.

That was a drought-ridden year, so that when the rains came, if at all, it was suddenly, without warning. On that September day, the skies darkened with the capriciousness of a god's frown, and the rains broke with a loud belch of thunder, drenching everything in scant seconds. I sought cover under the narrow ledge of a storefront, elbowing myself a place between two potbellied nanny goats.

One of them began to butt at me systematically, but I held my ground, stamping my foot in return, hoping to show her that I, too, meant business. Instead she leapt at me head down, taking me by surprise and throwing me off balance into the furious rain. The nanny goat now stared wickedly at me from my place, yellow devil eyes flickering. It was hard enough to leave, but then to be aggressed by an evil-smelling goat—it was too much to bear. I turned my back on her and trudged home, tears and rain striking my face indiscriminately.

*

It was Pongal—January of the Tamil New Year—when I returned to Madras. I noticed immediately a change of attire, marked in a city described by all who leave it as one of the most provincial and least cosmopolitan examples of the Indian metropolis. Young women wearing the northern-style chudidar pajama or salwar-kameez used to be a rare sight, in part because they attracted the suspicion (usually borne out) that they were from elsewhere. I myself used to wear such clothes from time to time, which bothered patti no end. Although they had not yet learned the arts of flirting and wicked whispering behind dupattas or chunnis, it now seemed that the college-going women of Madras wore the ready-made suits so popular in cities of the North; it was more difficult to find women students in saris.

Such a change was not without contestation, however. In the late afternoons, when the buses were flooded with college students returning home, older, sari-clad women would prick at the girls' convent-school English and incessant boy-talk. The college girls stuck to each other clannishly, a gangling, giggling mass that banged heedlessly into people, no apologies ever offered. It was thus that I witnessed a tired office worker in crumpled sari give a literal dressing-down to the student who had stepped on her foot: "Look at you," she declared angrily. "You are living in the South and haven't even the decency to wear a sari."

*

When I opened my trunk to inspect the saris I'd put away the year before, they smelled noxiously of naphthalene, though the little balls tucked away into the folds had dissolved, leaving behind only traces of white powder. I had them aired on the roof of the house and wore several before the end of my short month's stay. Then I again had the saris washed, pressed, and packed in the trunk. My grandmother now understood, even if we both wept piteously every time I left, that as long as the trunk of saris remained in her house, I would return to see her.

"Your saris are still here," she would write to me. "When are you coming to wear them?"

Glossary

Attai: Father's sister; aunt.
Amaam: Yes.
Chitti: Mother's younger sister; aunt.
Chunni (H)*: Scarf covering the upper body.
Dudhwallah (H)*: Milkman.
Dupatta (H)*: Cloth, or scarf covering the upper body.
"Edavadu": "Anything."
"Ennadu" ("enna adu"): "What's that?"
Fall: A thin border of cloth sewn along the base of a sari to prevent it from tearing or ripping.
Idli: Steamed rice cake often eaten as a snack.
Jeri: Gold thread
Khadi: Homespun cotton. Part of Gandhi's program to boycott the importing of foreign cloth and promote Indian self-reliance.
Mami: Mother's brother's wife; otherwise a general term for aunt.
"Ore pirachanai": "What a problem!"
"Oru devi illaiya": "Isn't she a goddess?"
Pachai: Green.
Papa: Baby.
Patti: Grandmother.
Pavadai: Half-sari.
Periyamma: Mother's older sister; aunt.
Poituvaren: Good-bye; literally, "I'll go and come."
Ramayana: An Indian folk ethic popularly serialized in Hindi for Doordarshan television.
Shastri (S)*: Brahmin priest.
Tali: Marriage necklace.
Tata: Grandfather.

Glossary

Note: All words, unless marked by H (for Hindi) or S (for Sanskrit), are Tamil in origin or usage. I have not used standard forms of transliteration for the Tamil or Hindi words employed in this text, and have omitted all diacritical marks. Thus, I have not transcribed "pachai" as *paccai,* "patti" as *pāḍḍi,* "tata" as *tātā,* and so on, hoping that Tamil speakers will intuitively grasp my lay transliteration with more ease than they might the cumbersome academic forms. In keeping with my belief that English (as any language) is the product of particular historical, linguistic, or cultural collisions, and is continually being transformed by other vocabularies, I have also chosen not to emphasize the "foreignness" of Tamil or Hindi words in the text through use of italics or underlining conventions.

Notes

1. Introduction: Fictions of Feminist Ethnography

1. Barbara Babcock, "Mud, Mirrors, and Making Up: Liminality and Reflexivity in *Between the Acts,*" in *Victor Turner and the Construction of Cultural Criticism,* ed. Kathleen Ashley (Bloomington: Indiana University Press, 1990), 88.
2. My discussion here relies heavily on Phyllis Gorfain's essay "Play and the Problem of Knowing in Hamlet: An Excursion into Interpretive Anthropology," in *The Anthropology of Experience,* ed. Victor Turner and E. Bruner (Urbana: University of Illinois Press, 1986), 213.
3. See, for example, Jacques Maquet, "Castaneda: Warrior or Scholar?" *American Anthropologist* 80 (1978): 362–63; Stan Wilk, "On the Experiential Approach to Anthropology: A Reply to Maquet," *American Anthropologist* 80 (1978): 363–64.
4. See, for example, P. C. Joshi, "The Remembered Village: A Bridge between Old and New Anthropology," *Contributions to Indian Sociology* 12, no. 1 (1978): 49–56. Adrian C. Mayer, "The Remembered Village: From Memory Alone?" *Contributions to Indian Sociology* 12, no. 1 (1978): 39–48. David F. Pocock, "The Remembered Village: A Failure," *Contributions to Indian Sociology* 12, no. 1 (1978): 57–66.
5. See Oscar Lewis, *Five Families* (New York: Basic Books, 1959), *The Children of Sanchez,* and *La Vida* (New York: Random House, 1961 and 1965), among other works.
6. James Clifford, "Introduction: Partial Truths," in *Writing Culture,* ed. Marcus and Clifford (Berkeley: University of California Press, 1986), 6.
7. Clifford Geertz, *Works and Lives* (Stanford, Calif.: Stanford University Press, 1988), 140.
8. Clifford, "Introduction: Partial Truths," 4–6.
9. See Michael Fischer, "Ethnicity and the Postmodern Arts of Memory," in *Writing Culture.*
10. Arjun Appadurai, "Global Ethnoscapes: Notes and Queries for a Transnational Anthropology," in *Recapturing Anthropology,* ed. R. Fox (Sante Fe, N. Mex.: SAR Press, 1991).
11. Marilyn Strathern, "Out of Context: The Persuasive Fictions of Anthropology," *Current Anthropology* 28, no. 3 (June 1987): 269.
12. Elsie Clews Parsons, ed., *American Indian Life* (New York: Viking, 1922), 1.
13. Ibid., 3.

14. A number of the stories in the collection adopt the voices of children or adolescents, and could tell us (space permitting) much about the roughrider projection of American boyhood onto its Native American counterpart, and the all too predictable fantasies male anthropologists of this generation lavished upon the images of young Native American women. But that is another project.

15. Judith Friedlander, "Elsie Clews Parsons," in *Women Anthropologists: Selected Biographies,* ed. U. Gacs, A. Khan, J. McIntyre, and R. Weinberg (Urbana: University of Illinois Press, 1989), 286.

16. See Joyce Griffen, "Ruth Murray Underhill," in *Women Anthropologists: Selected Biographies.*

17. Helen Carr, "In Other Worlds: Native American Women's Autobiography," in *Life/Lines,* ed. B. Brodzki and C. Schenck (Ithaca, N.Y.: Cornell University Press, 1988), 145.

18. Ibid.

19. See Françoise Lionnet, "Autoethnography: The Anarchic Style of *Dust Tracks on a Road,*" in *Autobiographical Voices: Race, Gender, Self-Portraiture* (Ithaca, N.Y.: Cornell University Press, 1989), and Nellie McKay, "Race, Gender and Cultural Context in Zora Neale Hurston's *Dust Tracks on a Road,*" in *Life/Lines.*

20. Agnes Picotte, "Biographical Sketch of Ella Deloria," in *Waterlily* (Lincoln: University of Nebraska Press, 1988), 242.

21. See also Janet Finn's important paper "Ella Cara Deloria and Mourning Dove: Writing for Cultures, Writing against the Grain" for an analysis of Ella Deloria's work (forthcoming in *Women Writing Culture,* ed. R. Behar and D. Gordon).

22. See, for example, Nita Kumar's introduction in Nita Kumar, *Friends, Brothers, and Informants* (Berkeley: University of California Press, 1992).

23. See James Clifford, introduction, and Mary Pratt, "Fieldwork in Common Places," in *Writing Culture.*

24. Bronislaw Malinowski, *A Diary in the Strict Sense of the Term* (Stanford, Calif.: Stanford University Press, 1967), 190.

25. Ibid., 191.

26. Ibid., 248 and 272.

27. Ibid., 281.

28. James Clifford, "On Ethnographic Authority," *Representations* 2 (Spring 1983): 120.

29. Malinowski, *A Diary,* 161.

30. Ibid., 277.

31. Ibid., 291.

32. Ibid., 199, 237, 285.

33. Ibid., 249, original emphasis.

34. Ibid., 211.

35. Ibid., 245.

36. Ibid., 28.

37. See, for example, George W. Stocking, "The Ethnographic Sensibility of the 1920's," in *Romantic Motives,* ed. G. W. Stocking (Madison: University of Wisconsin Press, 1989), and Deborah Gordon, "The Politics of Ethnographic Authority: Race and Writing in the Ethnography of Margaret Mead and Zora Neale Hurston," in *Modernist Anthropology,* ed. Marc Manganao (Princeton, N.J.: Princeton University Press, 1991).

38. See Arnold Krupat, *For Those Who Come After: A Study of Native American Autobiography* (Berkeley: University of California Press, 1985), 11, and McKay, "Race, Gender and Cultural Context in Zora Neale Hurston's *Dust Tracks on a Road.*"

39. See Philippe Lejeune, *On Autobiography* (Minneapolis: University of Minnesota

Press, 1989), and Paul Smith, *Discerning the Subject* (Minneapolis: University of Minnesota Press, 1988). See also Caren Kaplan, "Resisting Autobiography: Out-Law Genres and Transnational Feminist Subjects," in *De/Colonizing the Subject: Politics and Gender in Women's Autobiographical Practice,* ed. J. Watson and S. Smith (Minneapolis: University of Minnesota Press, 1992), and Doris Sommer, "'Not Just a Personal Story': Women's *Testimonios* and the Plural Self," in *Life/Lines.*

40. Krupat, *For Those Who Come After,* and Krupat and Brian Swann, eds., *I Tell You Now: Autobiographical Essays by Native American Writers* (Lincoln: University of Nebraska Press, 1987).

41. See Sally Cole's paper "Biography as Historical Anthropology: Ruth Landes and the Early Ethnography of Race and Gender" for a discussion of ethnographies of race (forthcoming in *Women Writing Culture,* ed. R. Behar and D. Gordon).

42. There is now a body of work emerging on this subject, including Cole's paper "Biography as Historical Anthropology."

43. Gordon, "The Politics of Ethnographic Authority," 156.

44. See Cole, "Biography as Historical Anthropology."

45. Kumar, *Friends, Brothers, and Informants,* and Margaret Trawick, *Notes on Love in a Tamil Family* (Berkeley: University of California Press, 1990).

46. Richard and Sally Price, *Equatoria* (New York: Routledge, 1992), and Amitav Ghosh, *In an Antique Land* (Delhi: Ravi Dayal Press, 1992).

47. See Kaplan, "Resisting Autobiography."

48. See Michael Fischer, "Ethnicity and the Postmodern Arts of Memory," 195.

49. Ibid., 196.

50. Ibid., 201.

51. Talal Asad, "Ethnography, Literature, and Politics: Some Readings and Uses of Salman Rushdie's *The Satanic Verses,*" *Cultural Anthropology* (1990): 240.

52. Albert Wendt, "Three Faces of Samoa: Mead's, Freeman's and Wendt's," *Pacific Islands Monthly* 54, no. 10 (1983): 12.

53. See Finn's paper "Ella Cara Deloria and Mourning Dove"; Paula Gunn Allen's introduction to *Spider Woman's Granddaughters* (New York: Fawcett Columbine, 1989); and Jay Miller, ed., *Mourning Dove: A Salishan Autobiography* (Lincoln: University of Nebraska Press, 1990).

54. See Lila Abu-Lughod, *Writing Women's Worlds: Bedouin Stories* (Berkeley: University of California Press, 1993), 11, and Arjun Appadurai, "Putting Hierarchy in Its Place," *Cultural Anthropology* 3, no. 1 (1988): 36–49.

55. See, for example, Strathern, "Out of Context," 269.

56. Cited in Gorfain, "Play and the Problem of Knowing in Hamlet," 217.

57. I borrow this injunction from Ngugi Wa'Thiongo's book *Decolonizing the Mind* (London: Heinemann, 1986).

58. Leslie Marmon Silko, *Ceremony* (New York: Penguin, 1977), 132.

59. See, for example, Barbara Pym's novels *Some Tame Gazelle* (1950; reprint, New York: Dutton, 1983), *Less than Angels* (1955; reprint, New York: Harper, 1982), and *A Few Green Leaves* (New York: Harper, 1980).

60. George E. Marcus, "Contemporary Problems of Ethnography in the Modern World System," in *Writing Culture,* Marcus and Clifford, 191.

61. Ibid., 193.

62. James Clifford, *The Predicament of Culture* (Cambridge, Mass.: Harvard University Press, 1988), 9.

63. Ibid.

64. Ibid., 11.

65. Ruth Frankenberg and Lata Mani, "Crosscurrents, Crosstalk: Race, 'Postcoloniality,' and the Politics of Location," *Cultural Studies* (May 1993), 307. See also Judith Butler, "Contingent Foundations: Feminism and the Question of Postmodernism," in *Feminists Theorize the Political,* ed. J. Butler and Joan Scott (New York: Routledge, 1992), and Norma Alarcón, "Cognitive Desires: An Allegory of/for Chicano Feminists," in *New Essays in Feminist Criticism,* ed. S. F. Fishkin and Elaine Hedges (London: Oxford University Press, 1993).
66. Kamala Visweswaran, "Defining Feminist Ethnography," *Inscriptions* 3, no. 4 (1988): 27–47.
67. Judith Stacey, "Can There Be a Feminist Ethnography?" *Women's Studies International Forum* 11, no. 1 (1988): 21–27.
68. Lila Abu-Lughod, "Can There Be a Feminist Ethnography?" *Women and Performance* 5, no. 1 (1990): 7–27.
69. James Clifford, "Notes on (Field) Notes," in *Fieldnotes: The Makings of Anthropology,* ed. Roger Sanjek (Ithaca, N.Y.: Cornell University Press, 1990), 53. See also the introduction to James Clifford, *The Predicament of Culture* (Cambridge, Mass.: Harvard University Press, 1988).
70. See Strathern, "Out of Context," 261.
71. Zora Neale Hurston, *Mules and Men* (1935; reprint, New York: Harper and Collins, 1990), 63.
72. Margaret Mead, *Blackberry Winter* (1972; reprint, Glouchester, Mass.: Peter Smith, 1989), 149.
73. Arjun Appadurai's phrase in "Global Ethnoscapes: Notes and Queries for a Transnational Anthropology," in *Recapturing Anthropology,* ed. R. Fox, 197.
74. See Paul Smith's discussion in *Discerning the Subject* (Minneapolis: University of Minnesota Press, 1988), 103.

2. Defining Feminist Ethnography

I wish here to acknowledge some of the influences that have shaped this essay, but were not mentioned in the version that appeared in *Inscriptions.* Before *Writing Culture* appeared, I was fortunate to have attended one (very crowded) session of a seminar on experimental ethnography given by Paul Rabinow and James Clifford in the fall of 1984. Certainly some of my thinking here, in ways that I cannot fully detail, stems from that event and Deborah Gordon's very insightful presentation there.

1. Renato Rosaldo, "Where Objectivity Lies: The Rhetoric of Anthropology," in *The Rhetoric of Human Sciences,* ed. John Nelson and Donald McCloskey (Madison: University of Wisconsin Press, 1987).
2. In Marcus and Cushman's (1982) review of "experimental ethnography," for example, texts authored by women ethnographers account for only 9 of 117 references. Of those 9 texts, only Jean Briggs's *Never in Anger* is considered in this essay.
3. Audre Lorde, *Sister/Outsider* (Trumansburg, N.Y.: Crossing, 1984).
4. Susan Griffin, "The Way of All Ideology," in *Feminist Theory,* ed. N. Keohane et al. (Chicago: University of Chicago Press, 1982).
5. James Clifford, "On Ethnographic Authority," *Representations* 2 (Spring 1983): 121. See also Marilyn Strathern, "Out of Context: The Persuasive Fictions of Anthropology," *Current Anthropology* 28, no. 3 (June 1987).
6. Jane Atkinson, "Review Essay: Anthropology," *Signs* 8, no. 2 (1982): 236–58; Susan Geiger, "Women's Life History: Method and Content," *Signs* 11, no. 2 (1986): 334–51.

7. For example, Carol MacCormack and Marilyn Strathern, *Nature, Culture, and Gender* (Cambridge: Cambridge University Press, 1980).

8. See Jane Collier and Michelle Rosaldo, "Politics and Gender in Simple Societies," and Sherry Ortner, "Gender and Sexuality in Hierarchical Societies," in *Sexual Meanings,* ed. Sherry Ortner and HarrietWhitehead (Cambridge: Cambridge University Press, 1981).

9. See, for example, Sherry Ortner's 1983 paper "The Founding of a Sherpa Nunnery and the Problem of Women as an Analytic Category," in which women recede from the analysis as the primary analytic category. In *Feminist Revisions,* ed. Louise Tilly and Vivien Patraka (Ann Arbor: University of Michigan Press, 1983).

10. See Susan Kreiger's ethnography of a midwestern lesbian community, *The Mirror Dance: Identity in a Women's Community* (Philadelphia: Temple University Press, 1983), and more recently, Lila Abu-Lughod's *Writing Women's Worlds: Bedouin Stories* (Berkeley: University of California Press, 1993).

11. Marilyn Strathern, "An Awkward Relationship: The Case of Feminism and Anthropology," *Signs* 12 (Winter 1987): 276–92.

12. Ibid.

13. See, for example, Margaret Mead, *Coming of Age in Samoa* (New York: Morrow, 1928); Ruth Landes, *The Ojibwa Woman* (1937; reprint, New York: Norton, 1969); Phyllis Kaberry, *Aboriginal Woman* (New York: Humanities, 1939); Audrey Richards, *Chisungu* (London: Tavistock, 1956); and Marilyn Strathern, *Women in Between* (London: Seminar Press, 1972).

14. See, for example, Renato Rosaldo's analysis of Evans-Pritchard's *Nuer,* in "From the Door of His Tent," in *Writing Culture,* ed. James Clifford and George Marcus (Berkeley: University of California Press, 1986), and Barbara Tedlock, "From Participant Observation to the Observation of Participation: The Emergence of Narrative Ethnography," *Journal of Anthropological Research* 47 (Spring 1991).

15. See George E. Marcus and Dick Cushman, "Ethnographies as Texts," *Annual Review of Anthropology* 11 (1982): 25–69.

16. See Clifford, "On Ethnographic Authority."

17. Marcus and Cushman, "Ethnographies as Texts," 26.

18. Paul Rabinow, *Reflections of Fieldwork in Morocco* (Berkeley: University of California Press, 1977); Jean-Paul Dumont, *The Headman and I* (Austin: University of Texas Press, 1978); and Vincent Crapanzano, *Tuhami* (Chicago: University of Chicago Press, 1980).

19. Other examples are Morris Freilick, ed., *Marginal Natives: Anthropologists at Work* (New York: Harper and Row, 1970); George Spindler, ed. *Being an Anthropologist: Fieldwork in Eleven Cultures* (New York: Holt, Rinehart and Winston, 1970); Solon T. Kimball, ed., *Crossing Cultural Boundaries: The Anthropological Experience* (San Francisco: Chandler, 1972); T. N. Madan, ed., *Encounter and Experience* (1975); and M. N. Srinivas et al., eds., *The Fieldworker and the Field* (Delhi: Oxford University Press, 1979). However, not all the papers in Peggy Golde's edited collection, *Women in the Field* (Berkeley: University of California Press, 1970), represent the notion of anthropology as positivist science, especially those by Lederman and Briggs.

20. Kevin Dwyer, "On the Dialogic of Fieldwork," *Dialectical Anthropology* 2, no. 2 (1979): 121.

21. Clearly there are several exceptions, one of which is Robert and Yolanda Murphy's collaboration on *Women of the Forest* (New York: Columbia University Press, 1974).

22. Marion and Burton Benedict, *Men, Women, and Money in the Seychelles* (Berkeley: University of California Press, 1982), vii.
23. Zora Neale Hurston, *Tell My Horse* (1938; reprint, New York: Harper and Row, 1978); Ella Deloria, *Speaking of Indians* (New York: Friendship, 1944); Jean Briggs, *Never in Anger* (Cambridge, Mass.: Harvard University Press, 1970); Elizabeth Fernea, *Guests of the Sheik* (New York: Doubleday, 1969); Hortense Powdermaker, *Stranger and Friend* (New York: Norton, 1966); Elenore Smith Bowen (a.k.a. Laura Bohannon), *Return to Laughter* (New York: Doubleday, 1964); Manda Cesara, *Reflections of a Woman Anthropologist: No Hiding Place* (New York: Academic, 1982); and Marjorie Shostak, *Nisa: The Life and Words of a !Kung Woman* (Cambridge, Mass.: Harvard University Press, 1981).
24. Briggs, *Never in Anger,* 107.
25. Suzanne Kirschner's analysis of Briggs and Powdermaker emphasizes the place of women's empathy in cross-cultural understanding, derived from being placed more frequently in vulnerable roles (such as daughter), and suggests a different understanding of positionality than the one I employ. See her "Then What Have I to Do with Thee? On Identity, Fieldwork, and Ethnographic Knowledge," *Cultural Anthropology* 2, no. 2 (1987).
26. Powdermaker, *Stranger and Friend,* 112.
27. Ibid., 113.
28. Ibid., 116.
29. Bohannon (a.k.a. Elenore Smith Bowen), *Return to Laughter,* 123.
30. Ibid., 291–92.
31. Shostak, *Nisa,* 354. Emphasis mine.
32. Ibid., 356.
33. Ibid., 356.
34. Ibid., 50, 52, 62.
35. Ibid., 371; see also Mary Pratt, "Fieldwork in Common Places," in *Writing Culture,* ed. James Clifford and George Marcus (Berkeley: University of California Press, 1986).
36. Cesara, *Reflections of a Woman Anthropologist,* 112.
37. Ibid., 73.
38. Ibid., 86.
39. See G. Marcus and D. Cushman, "Ethnographies as Texts."
40. Edwin Ardener, "Belief and the Problem of Women," reprinted in *Perceiving Women,* ed. Shirley Ardener (New York: Wiley, 1972); Roger Keesing, "Kwaio Women Speak: The Micropolitics of Autobiography in a Solomon Island Society," *American Anthropologist* 87, no. 1 (1984): 27–39.
41. See Nicole-Claude Mathieu, "Man-Culture and Woman-Nature," *Feminist Studies International Quarterly* 1 (1978): 55–56.
42. Keesing, "Kwaio Women Speak," 27.
43. Adrienne Rich, cited in Joanne Feit Dehil, "Cartographies of Silence: Rich's Common Language and the Woman Poet," *Feminist Studies I* 6, no. 3 (1980): 539.
44. Clifford, "On Ethnographic Authority," 119.
45. Susan Griffin, *Women and Nature* (New York: Harper and Row, 1978), xv.
46. See Paul Rabinow, "Discourse and Power: On the Limits of Ethnographic Texts," *Dialectical Anthropology* 110 (1985): 1–22.
47. Marcus and Cushman, "Ethnographies as Texts," 44.
48. Paula Gunn Allen, introduction to *Spider Woman's Granddaughters: Traditional Tales and Contemporary Writing by Native American Women* (New York: Fawcett Columbine, 1989), 17.
49. Kevin Dwyer, "On the Dialogic of Fieldwork," *Dialectical Anthropology* 2 (1977): 143–51.

50. See John Gwaltney, *Drylongso* (New York: Vintage, 1982); Renato Rosaldo, "When Natives Talk Back: Chicano Anthropology since the Late 60s," Renato Rosaldo Lecture Series Monograph, vol. 2, series 1984–85 (Mexican American Studies and Research Center, University of Arizona, Tucson, Spring 1986); and Maxine Hong Kingston, *The Woman Warrior: Memoirs of a Girlhood among Ghosts* (New York: Knopf, 1976) and *Chinamen* (New York: Knopf, 1980).

In the 1988 version of this essay, I advocated reading the novels of women of color, including those of Paula Gunn Allen and Cherríe Moraga, as ethnography. While I feel this proposal has productive consequences for anthropology, I do recognize that for many such writers, the struggle is to have their novels read as "literature," and not automatically as sociology and anthropology. For example, Maxine Hong Kingston's novels *The Woman Warrior* and *Chinamen* were marketed as nonfiction when they first appeared. Zora Neale Hurston, responding to the criticisms of Richard Wright and others who accused her of ignoring the problems of racial oppression in her work, said "she had wanted at long last to write a black novel, and not a treatise on Sociology" (see Henry Louis Gates, "Zora Neale Hurston: A Negro Way of Saying," afterword to *Tell My Horse* [New York: Harper and Row, 1990], 294). Therefore in this version of the essay, I have decided to restrict my claim that the novel be considered as ethnography to a review of the writings of women like Ella Deloria and Zora Neale Hurston, who also worked as anthropologists.

51. However, see Michael Fischer, "Ethnicity and the Postmodern Arts of Memory," in *Writing Culture*, ed. James Clifford and George Marcus.

52. Zora Neale Hurston, *Dust Tracks on a Road* (1942; reprint, New York: Harper and Row, 1990) and *Their Eyes Were Watching God* (Chicago: University of Illinois Press, 1978).

53. Ibid., 117.

54. Mary Helen Washington, "I Love the Way Janie Crawford Left Her Husbands: Zora Neale Hurston's Emergent Feminist Hero," in *Invented Lives: Narratives of Black Women* (New York: Anchor, 1987).

55. Hurston, *Tell My Horse*. See also Deborah Gordon, "The Politics of Ethnographic Authority: Race and Writing in the Ethnography of Margaret Mead and Zora Neale Hurston," in *Modernist Anthropology*, ed. Marc Manganao (Princeton, N.J.: Princeton University Press, 1991).

56. Gwendolyn Mikell, "Zora Neale Hurston 1903–1960," in *Women Anthropologists: Selected Biographies*, ed. Ute Gacs, Aisha Khan, Jerrie McIntyre, and Ruth Weinberg (Urbana and Chicago: University of Illinois Press, 1989), 162.

57. Hurston, *Tell My Horse*, 16.

58. Ibid.

59. Ibid., 20.

60. Ibid., 57.

61. Ibid., 8.

62. Ibid., 59.

63. Ibid.

64. I refer readers interested in learning more about Ella Deloria to an excellent article by Janet Finn (Dept. of Anthropology, University of Michigan) titled "Ella Cara Deloria and Mourning Dove: Writing for Cultures, Writing against the Grain," in *Women Writing Culture*, ed. Deborah Gordon and Ruth Behar, forthcoming.

65. Ella Deloria, *Waterlily* (Lincoln: University of Nebraska Press, 1988) and *Speaking of Indians*.

66. Agnes Picotte, "Biographical Sketch of Ella Deloria," in *Waterlily*.

67. Ibid., 237.

68. Deloria, *Speaking of Indians*, 121.
69. Picotte, "Sketch of Ella Deloria," 241.
70. Ibid., 220.
71. Deloria, *Speaking of Indians*, 59.
72. Barbara Herrnstein Smith, "Contingencies of Value," *Critical Inquiry* (September 1983): 326.
73. Cornel West, "Minority Discourse and the Pitfalls of Canon Formation," *Yale Journal of Criticism* 1, no. 1 (1987): 194.

3. Betrayal: An Analysis in Three Acts

My debts to "Janaki," "Tangam," and "Uma" and her family, who spent time with me and shared their thoughts, are obvious. This essay is offered not as payment for a gift that cannot be returned, but as testimony to their generosity and as a token of my esteem for them.

I thank audiences at the University of Chicago and Centre for Women's Studies and Feminist Research at the University of Western Ontario for their critical responses to this paper. I thank also Jane Collier, Dipesh Chakrabarty, Nasser Hussein, Dorinne Kondo, Renato Rosaldo, David Scott, and Sylvia Yanagisako for their comments on early versions of this essay. I am especially indebted to Caren Kaplan, Ruth Frankenberg, Debbie Gordon, Inderpal Grewal, Mary John, and Lata Mani for their insightful and supportive close readings.

1. E. P. Thompson, *The Poverty of Theory*, cited in Denise Riley, *Am I That Name?* (Minneapolis: University of Minnesota Press, 1988).
2. Judith Stacey, "Can There Be a Feminist Ethnography?" *Women's Studies International Forum* 11, no. 1 (1988): 21–27.
3. Donna Haraway, "Situated Knowledges: The Science Question in Feminism and the Privilege of Partial Perspective," *Feminist Studies* 14, no. 3 (Fall 1988).
4. See Norma Alarcón, "The Theoretical Subjects of *This Bridge Called My Back* and Anglo-American Criticism," in *Making Face, Making Soul/Haciendo Caras*, ed. Gloria Anzaldúa (San Francisco: Aunt Lute, 1989); Teresa de Lauretis, "Eccentric Subjects: Feminist Theory and Historical Consciousness," *Feminist Studies* 16, no. 1 (Spring 1990): 115–50; Donna Haraway, "A Manifesto for Cyborgs: Science, Technology, and Socialist Feminism in the 1980's," in *Coming to Terms*, ed. E. Weed (New York: Routledge, 1989); Audrey Lorde, *Sister/Outsider* (Freedom, Calif.: Crossing, 1984); Chela Sandoval, "U.S. Third World Feminism: Oppositional Consciousness in the Postmodern World," *Genders* 10 (Spring 1991); Elizabeth Spelman, *The Inessential Woman* (Boston: Beacon, 1988); and Trinh Minh-ha, "Not You/Like You: Postcolonial Women and the Interlocking Questions of Identity and Difference," *Inscriptions* 3, no. 4 (1988): 71–78 and *Woman/Native/Other* (Bloomington: Indiana University Press, 1989).
5. James Clifford, "Introduction: Partial Truths" and "Ethnographic Allegory," in *Writing Culture*, ed. James Clifford and George Marcus (Berkeley: University of California Press, 1986).
6. I would like to thank Elena Feder for her comments on this subject.
7. See Edward Bruner, ed., *Text, Play, and Story: The Construction and Reconstruction of Self and Society* (Washington, D.C.: AES, 1984), and Clifford Geertz, "Blurred Genres," *Local Knowledge* (New York: Basic, 1983), 27.
8. Marilyn Strathern, "An Awkward Relationship: The Case of Feminism and Anthropology," *Signs* 12, no. 2 (1987): 276–92.
9. See also Emmanuel Le Roy Ladurie, *Montaillou* (New York: Vintage, 1979); Renato Rosaldo, "From the Door of His Tent: The Fieldworker and the Inquisi-

tor," in *Writing Culture,* ed. James Clifford and George Marcus; and Carlo Ginzburg, "The Inquisitor as Anthropologist," in *Clues, Myths, and the Historical Method* (Baltimore, Md.: Johns Hopkins University Press, 1989).

10. I am skeptical of the "feminist as hero" tone that runs through some analyses; see, for example, Frances Mascia-Lees, Patricia Sharpe, and Colleen Cohen, "The Postmodernist Turn in Anthropology: Cautions from a Feminist Perspective," *Signs* 15, no. 1 (Autumn 1989).

11. For a different discussion of these terms, see Mary E. Hawksworth, "Knowers, Knowing, Known: Feminist Theory and Claims of Truth," *Signs* 14, no. 3 (Spring 1989).

12. See also Mary John, "Postcolonial Feminists in the Western Intellectual Field: Anthropologists *and* Native Informants?" *Inscriptions* 5, no. 6 (1989): 49–74.

13. Gayatri Spivak, *The Post-Colonial Critic* (New York: Routledge, 1990), 59.

14. Ibid., 77

15. See Hawksworth, "Knowers, Knowing, Known."

16. See Elizabeth Weed, "Introduction: Terms of Reference," in *Coming to Terms: Feminism, Theory, Politics* (New York: Routledge, 1989).

17. Riley, *Am I That Name?,* 6.

18. See also Kamala Visweswaran, "Defining Feminist Ethnography," *Inscriptions* 3, no. 4 (1988): 27–47.

19. See Trinh Minh-ha, *Woman/Native/Other,* and Susan Gal, "Between Speech and Silence: The Problematics of Research on Language and Gender," in *Toward a New Anthropology of Gender,* ed. Michaela di Leonardo (Berkeley: University of California Press, 1991).

20. Gayatri Spivak, "Can the Subaltern Speak?" in *Marxism and the Interpretation of Culture,* ed. C. Nelson and L. Greenberg (Urbana: University of Illinois Press, 1988), 296.

21. Pierre Bourdieu, *Outline of a Theory of Practice* (Cambridge: Cambridge University Press, 1977), 170.

22. "Congress Report on the Punjab Disorder" (1920), 170. See also Kamala Visweswaran, "Family Subjects: An Ethnography of the 'Woman Question' in Indian Nationalism" (Ph.D. thesis, Stanford University, 1990).

23. Partha Chatterjee, "The Nationalist Resolution of the Women's Question," in *Recasting Women,* ed. KumKum Sangari and Sudesh Vaid (Delhi: Kali for Women, 1989), 235.

24. I wish to thank Sampath Kannan for this observation.

25. Uma Chakravarti, "The World of the Bhaktin in South Indian Traditions and Beyond," *Manushi,* Special Issue on Women Bhakta Poets (Delhi, January-June 1989).

4. Refusing the Subject

I thank Judith Stacey for her comments on an earlier version of this essay.

1. See also Sara Suleri's strategic denial of the category of "women," *Meatless Days* (Chicago: University of Chicago Press, 1989), 20.

2. Denise Riley, *Am I That Name?* (Minneapolis: University of Minnesota Press, 1988), 20.

3. Dreyfus and Rabinow also affirm that "there are two meanings to the word subject: subject to someone else by control and dependence, and tied to his [sic] own identity by a conscience or self-knowledge. Both meanings suggest a form of power which subjugates." Hubert L. Dreyfus and Paul Rabinow, *Michel Foucault: Beyond Structuralism and Hermeneutics* (Chicago: University of Chicago Press, 1982), 220.

4. See Carlo Ginzburg, "Checking the Evidence: The Judge and the Historian," *Critical Inquiry* 18 (Autumn 1991).
5. Catherine Belsey, *Critical Practice* (London: Methuen, 1980), 106.
6. Ibid., 70.
7. Ibid., 90. See also Norma Alarcón's essay "Cognitive Desires" for a stimulating discussion of what she terms "the subject in process." In *New Essays in Feminist Criticism,* ed. S. F. Fishkin and Elaine Hedges (London: Oxford University Press, 1993).
8. Ibid., 91.
9. Oscar Lewis, *Five Families* (New York: Basic, 1969).
10. Here, of course, I refer to Ruth Benedict, and not to the meticulous Benedictine monks.
11. Pierre Nora, "Between Memory and History: Les Lieux de Mémoire," *Representations* 26 (Spring 1989): 15.
12. Nathalie Davis and Randolph Starn, "Introduction: Memory and Counter-Memory," *Representations* 26 (Spring 1989): 4.
13. Paul Thompson, introduction to *Our Common History,* ed. P. Thompson (Humanities, 1982), 16.
14. C. V. Subbarao cited in KumKum Sangari, "Politics of the Possible," *Cultural Critique* (Fall 1987): 169, 178.
15. Homi Bhabha, "DissemiNation: Time, Narrative, and the Margins of the Modern Nation," in *Nation and Narration,* ed. Homi Bhabha (New York: Routledge, 1991), 295.
16. Ibid., 292.
17. These formulations broach the argument that nationalism reified particular kinds of women. See Uma Chakravarti, "Whatever Happened to the Vedic *Dasi*? Orientalism, Nationalism, and a Script for the Past," and also Partha Chatterjee, "The Nationalist Resolution of the Women's Question," both in *Recasting Women,* ed. KumKum Sangari and Sudesh Vaid (New Delhi: Kali for Women, 1989). I thank Max Prat for the reference to Michelet. See also Jenny Sharpe, *Allegories of Empire* (Minneapolis: University of Minnesota Press, 1993), for a discussion of the Rani of Jhansi in Indian history.
18. Judith Butler, "Contingent Foundations: Feminism and the Question of Postmodernism," in *Feminists Theorize the Political,* ed. Judith Butler and Joan Scott (New York: Routledge, 1992), 9.
19. Ibid., 8.
20. Passerini, *Fascism in Popular Memory* (Cambridge: Cambridge University Press, 1987), 19.
21. Nora, "Between Memory and History," 18; Susan Sontag, "The Anthropologist as Hero," *Against Interpretation* (1966; reprint, Anchor Books Doubleday, 1986, 1990), 18.
22. Bhabha, *Nation and Narration,* 309.
23. Ibid., 229.
24. Nora, "Between Memory and History," 8.
25. Ibid., 9.
26. Ibid., 10.
27. Ibid., 11.
28. Ibid., 15–16.
29. Ibid., 16.
30. Bhabha, *Nation and Narration,* 310.
31. Ibid.

32. Richard Terdiman, "The Mnemonics of Musset's *Confession,"* in *Representations* (Berkeley: University of California Press, 1989), 26.
33. James Chandler, Arnold I. Davidson, and Harry Harootunian, "Editor's Introduction: Question of Evidence," *Critical Inquiry* (Autumn 1991).
34. Nathalie Davis, *Fiction in the Archives* (Stanford, Calif.: Stanford University Press, 1987), 5.
35. See Ginzburg, "Checking the Evidence."
36. Ibid., 85.
37. Ibid., 86–87.
38. Ibid., 90. See also Sudipto Kaviraj, "Imaginary History," Nehru Memorial Museum and Library Occasional Papers on History and Society, second series, no. VII (New Delhi, 1988), 6.
39. Victor Turner, *The Anthropology of Performance* (New York: Performing Arts Journal Publications, 1986), 105.
40. See Kaviraj, "Imaginary History."
41. Ginzburg, "Checking the Evidence."
42. Davis, *Fiction in the Archives,* 114.

5. Feminist Reflections on Deconstructive Ethnography

I thank Ruth Behar for suggesting that I write some reflections on "Betrayal," and for giving me the opportunity to present them at a conference she organized entitled "Woman Writing Culture: Anthropology and Its Other Voices," University of Michigan, October 25–26, 1991. I am indebted to Gyan Prakash's reading of this essay which was helpful in framing some of the arguments I present here.

1. Sigmund Freud and Josef Breuer, *Studies on Hysteria,* cited in Reuben Fine, *The Development of Freud's Thought* (New York: Aronson, 1973), 18.
2. Gananath Obeyesekere, *The Work of Culture* (Chicago: University of Chicago Press, 1990), 231.
3. Gayatri Spivak, "The Political Economy of Women as Seen by a Literary Critic," in *Coming to Terms,* ed. E. Weed (New York: Routledge, 1989).
4. Cited in Gyan Prakash, "Postcolonial Criticism and Indian Historiography," *Social Text* 32, no. 32 (1992): 11.
5. See Stephen A. Tyler, "Post-Modern Ethnography: From Document of the Occult to Occult Document," in *Writing Culture,* ed. James Clifford and George Marcus (Berkeley: University of California Press, 1986).
6. See, for example, Teresa de Lauretis, "Eccentric Subjects: Feminist Theory and Historical Consciousness," *Feminist Studies* 16, no. 1 (Spring 1990): 115–50, and Judith Butler, *Gender Trouble* (New York: Routledge, 1990).
7. Norma Alarcón, "The Theoretical Subjects of *This Bridge Called My Back,"* in *Haciendo Caras,* ed. Gloria Anzaldúa (San Francisco: Kitchen Table, 1991).
8. See Drucilla Cornell, *Beyond Accommodation: Ethical Feminism, Deconstruction, and the Law* (New York: Routledge, 1991).
9. Gayatri Spivak, "Can the Subaltern Speak?" in *Marxism and the Interpretation of Culture,* ed. C. Nelson and L. Greenberg (Urbana: University of Illinois Press, 1988), 188–89.
10. Victor Turner, *The Anthropology of Performance* (New York: Performing Arts Journal Publications, 1986), 75–76.
11. However, for an analysis of Turner's earlier writings, see Stephen W. Foster, "Symbolism and the Problematics of Postmodern Representation," in *Victor Turner*

and the *Construction of Cultural Criticism,* ed. Kathleen M. Ashley (Bloomington: Indiana University Press, 1990).

12. Turner, *The Anthropology of Performance,* 77.
13. Ibid.
14. Catherine Belsey, *Critical Practice* (London: Methuen, 1980), 91.
15. Turner, *The Anthropology of Performance,* 80.
16. Marilyn Strathern, "Out of Context: The Persuasive Fictions of Anthropology," *Current Anthropology* 28, no. 3 (June 1987): 265.
17. Laura Bohannon (a.k.a. Elenore Smith Bowen), "Shakespeare in the Bush," *Natural History Magazine* (August/September, 1966).
18. Phyllis Gorfain, "Play and the Problem of Knowing in *Hamlet:* An Excursion into Interpretive Anthropology," in *The Anthropology of Experience,* ed. Victor Turner and E. Bruner (Urbana: University of Illinois Press, 1986), 207.
19. Ibid., 208.
20. Ibid., 209.
21. Ibid., 210, 226.
22. Ibid., 216, 217.
23. Ibid., 222.
24. Foster, "Symbolism and the Problematics of Postmodern Representation," 125.
25. Tyler, "Post-Modern Ethnography."
26. Steven Sangren, "Rhetoric and the Authority of Ethnography," *Current Anthropology* 29, no. 3 (1988). See also Nicole Polier and William Roseberry, "Tristes Tropes: Post-Modern Anthropologists Encounter the Other and Discover Themselves," *Economy and Society* 18, no. 2 (May 1989).
27. Sangren, "Rhetoric and the Authority of Ethnography," 407.
28. R. Radhakrishnan, "Transnationalism: Questions of Perspective," in *Theory and Postcoloniality: Neither One nor Other* (London: Blackwell, forthcoming), 5.
29. Gayatri Spivak, "Can the Subaltern Speak?" 279.
30. Jean-Paul Dumont, *The Headman and I* (Austin: University of Texas Press, 1978), 12. See also Robert Thornton, "The Rhetoric of Ethnographic Holism," in *Rereading Cultural Anthropology,* ed. George Marcus (Durham, N.C.: Duke University Press, 1993).
31. Spivak, "Can the Subaltern Speak?" 280.
32. Butler, "Contingent Foundations," 15.
33. See, for example, Nancy Hartsock, "Rethinking Modernism: Minority vs. Majority Theories," *Cultural Critique* 7 (Fall 1987): 187–207, and Frances Mascia-Lees et al., "The Postmodern Turn in Anthropology," *Signs* (1989).
34. Anthony Appiah, "The Postcolonial and the Postmodern," in *In My Father's House* (Oxford: Oxford University Press, 1992), 143.
35. KumKum Sangari, "Politics of the Possible," *Cultural Critique* 7 (Fall 1987): 178.
36. Oscar Lewis, *Five Families* (New York: Basic, 1959), 5.
37. George E. Marcus and Dick Cushman, "Ethnographies as Texts," *Annual Review of Anthropology* 11 (1982): 29.
38. Belsey, *Critical Practice,* 46–47.
39. Ibid., 51.
40. Marcus and Cushman, "Ethnographies as Texts," 32.
41. Belsey, *Critical Practice,* 68.
42. See Rey Chow, "Postmodern Automatons," in *Feminists Theorize the Political,* ed. Judith Butler and Joan Scott (New York: Routledge, 1992), 102.
43. Marcus and Cushman, "Ethnographies as Texts," 25.
44. George E. Marcus and Stephen Tyler, comments on "Out of Context: The Persuasive Fictions of Anthropology" by Marilyn Strathern, *Current Anthropology* 28, no.

3 (1987), 277, and George E. Marcus and Michael Fischer, *Anthropology as Cultural Critique* (Chicago: University of Chicago Press, 1986).

45. Marc Manganaro, "Textual Play, Power, and Cultural Critique: An Orientation to Modernist Anthropology," in *Modernist Anthropology: From Fieldwork to Text*, ed. Marc Manganaro (Princeton, N.J.: Princeton University Press, 1990).

46. Edwin Ardener, "Social Anthropology and the Decline of Modernism," in *Reason and Morality*, ed. J. Overing (London: Tavistock, 1985).

47. Strathern, "Out of Context," 259.

48. Ibid. G. W. Stocking, "The Ethnographer's Magic: Fieldwork in British Anthropology from Tylor to Malinowski," *Observers Observed*, ed. G. W. Stocking (Madison: University of Wisconsin Press, 1983). See also Thornton, "Rhetoric of Ethnographic Holism."

49. Strathern, "Out of Context," 259.

50. James Clifford, *The Predicament of Culture* (Cambridge, Mass.: Harvard University Press, 1988), 121.

51. Strathern, "Out of Context."

52. Clifford, "On Ethnographic Surrealism," in *The Predicament of Culture*.

53. See George W. Stocking, "The Ethnographic Sensibility of the 1920's," in *Romantic Motives*, ed. G. W. Stocking (Madison: University of Wisconsin Press, 1989).

54. Strathern, "Out of Context," 260.

55. Clifford, *The Predicament of Culture*, 93.

56. Richard Handler, "Ruth Benedict and the Modernist Sensibility," in *Modernist Anthropology*, ed. Marc Manganaro (Princeton, N.J.: Princeton University Press, 1990).

57. See Stocking, "The Ethnographer's Magic," 112, and "The Ethnographic Sensibility of the 1920's."

58. The formulation is Kathleen Gough's in "Anthropology and Imperialism," *Monthly Review* (1968): 12.

59. Marshall Berman, *All That Is Solid Melts into Air* (New York: Simon and Schuster, 1982).

60. Geetha Kapur, "The Center-Periphery Model; or, How Are We Placed?" *Third Text* 16, no. 17 (Autumn-Winter 1991).

61. Dipesh Chakrabarty, "Who Speaks for Indian Pasts?" *Representations* 37 (Winter 1992): 22.

62. Geetha Kapur, "The Place of the Modern in Indian Cultural Practice," *Economic and Political Weekly* (December 7, 1991), 2085.

63. Ibid. See also Kapur, "The Center-Periphery Model," 14.

64. Fredric Jameson, "Modernism and Imperialism," in Terry Eagleton, Fredric Jameson, and Edward W. Said, *Nationalism, Colonialism, and Literature* (Minneapolis: University of Minnesota Press, 1990), 64.

65. Chakrabarty, "Who Speaks for Indian Pasts?" 19.

66. See Partha Chatterjee, *Nationalist Thought in the Colonial World* (London: Zed, 1986).

67. Chow, "Postmodern Automatons," 101.

68. See Milton Singer, *When a Great Tradition Modernizes* (New York: Praeger, 1972); also, Lloyd and Suzane Rudolph, *The Modernity of Tradition* (Chicago: University of Chicago Press, 1967).

69. Kapur, "The Center-Periphery Model," 10. See also her "Contemporary Cultural Practice: Some Polemical Categories," *Third Text* 11 (Summer 1990): 113.

70. Kapur, "The Center-Periphery Model," 13.

71. Ibid., 15.

72. Ibid., 13.

73. Sangari, "Politics of the Possible," 161.
74. Ibid., 185.
75. Ibid., 181.
76. Ibid., 161.
77. Ibid.
78. Appiah, *In My Father's House,* 152.
79. Ibid., 155.
80. Ibid
81. Ibid.
82. Ibid., 157.
83. Nellie Richard, "Postmodernism and Periphery," *Third Text* 2 (Winter 1987–1988).
84. Linda Nicholson, introduction to *Feminism/Postmodernism,* ed. Linda Nicholson (New York: Routledge, 1990), 4.
85. Kapur, "Contemporary Cultural Practice: Some Polemical Practices."
86. See Alarcón, "Cognitive Desires," in *New Essays in Feminist Criticism,* ed. S. F. Fishkin and Elaine Hedges (London: Oxford University Press, 1993).
87. Chow, "Postmodern Automatons," 103.
88. Richard, "Postmodernism and Periphery," 7.
89. Chela Sandoval, "U.S. Third World Feminism: The Theory and Method of Oppositional Consciousness in the Third World," *Gender* 10 (Spring 1991): 22. Such an understanding is in marked contrast to what Aiwha Ong observes as a marginalizing theoretical move made by some western feminists: "Although a common past may be claimed by feminists, third world women are often represented as mired in it, ever arriving at modernity when western feminists are already adrift in postmodernism." Aiwha Ong, "Colonialism and Modernity: Feminist Re-Presentations of Women in Non-Western Societies," *Inscriptions* 3, no. 4 (1988): 87.
90. Appiah, *In My Father's House,* 141.
91. Kapur, "The Center-Periphery Model," 10.
92. Kapur, "The Place of the Modern in Indian Cultural Practice," 2803, 2805.
93. Chow, "Postmodern Automatons," 113–14.
94. Ibid., 114.
95. Ibid.
96. Alarcón, "The Theoretical Subjects of *This Bridge Called My Back,* " 356.
97. Ibid.
98. Ibid., 366. See also the extension of multiply positioned subjects into what she calls "subjects in process" in "Cognitive Desires."
99. Prakash, "Postcolonial Criticism and Indian Historiography," 15.
100. See KumKum Sangari and Sudesh Vaid, introduction to *Recasting Women* (New Brunswick, N.J.: Rutgers University Press, 1989).
101. Chandra Talpade Mohanty, introduction to *Third World Women and the Politics of Feminism,* ed. Chandra Mohanty, A. Russo, and L. Torres (Bloomington: Indiana University Press, 1991), 14.
102. Chow, "Postmodern Automatons," 111.
103. Ibid., 112. See also Spivak, "The Political Economy of Women," 220.

6. Feminist Ethnography as Failure

I would like to thank Charlie Hale and Judith Stacey for their comments on an earlier version of this essay, as well as the organizers of the conference "Feminist Dilemmas in Fieldwork," held at UC Davis on March 7, 1992, for providing me with the opportunity to develop the questions in this essay. I am thankful to the departments of anthropology and history at UC Davis for making my visit possible. Finally I would like to thank students in my spring 1992 seminar on feminist ethnography for challenging and engaging my ideas on "failure," in particular, Lara Angel, Saloni Mathur, and Cathy O'Leary. I am grateful to Lara for permission to quote from a classroom journal she kept during the fall of 1991.

1. Gayatri Spivak, "Reading *The Satanic Verses,*" Public Culture 2, no. 1 (Fall 1989): 82.
2. M. G. Ramachandran (popularly known as MGR), formerly chief minister of Tamil Nadu, was the regional equivalent of a Ronald Reagan, only a slightly better actor.
3. Philip De Vita, *The Naked Anthropologist* (Belmont, Calif.: Wadsworth, 1992).
4. Kathryn Anderson and Dana Jack, "Learning to Listen: Interview Techniques and Analysis," in *Women's Words,* ed. Sherna Gluck and Daphne Patai (New York: Routledge, 1991), 24.
5. Kristina Minister, "A Feminist Frame for the Oral History Interview," in *Women's Words* (New York: Routledge, 1991), 36–37.
6. An example of this optimism is to be found in the chapter titled "Feminist Ethnography," in Shulamit Reinharz's book *Feminist Methods in Social Research* (Oxford: Oxford University Press, 1992).
7. Gayatri Spivak, "Subaltern Studies: Deconstructing Historiography," in *In Other Worlds* (London: Methuen, 1987).
8. Kobena Mercer, "1968: Periodizing Post-Modern Politics and Identity," in *Cultural Studies,* ed. L. Grossberg et al. (New York: Routledge, 1992).
9. Ruth Frankenberg and Lata Mani note four tendencies within contemporary feminism that describe the situation. They first identify a "white feminist rearguard that continues to argue for the primacy of gender domination, as well as a second, so to speak, 'neo-rearguard' tendency, again especially by white feminists, to reabsorb notions of multiply determined subjectivity under the single 'mistress' narrative of gender domination." Next they describe other feminists, often but not exclusively women of color, who insist on the "simultaneity of the workings of axes of domination." Finally there is a fourth tendency, an outgrowth of the third, which complicates the ideas of "simultaneity" and "multiplicity" by examining how "oppression may be experienced in specifiably complex and shifting relationships to different axes of domination." See Ruth Frankenberg and Lata Mani, "Crosscurrents, Crosstalk: Race, 'Postcoloniality,' and the Politics of Location," *Cultural Studies* 7, no. 2 (May 1993), 305.
10. See, for example, Dipesh Chakrabarty, "Who Speaks for Indian Pasts?" *Representations* 37 (Winter 1992).
11. Clifford Geertz, *Works and Lives* (Stanford, Calif.: Stanford University Press, 1988), 143.
12. Ibid., 135.
13. See, for example, Vizenor's notion of "trickster theory" in Gerald Vizenor, *The Trickster of Liberty: Tribal Heirs to a Wild Baronage* (Minneapolis: University of Minnesota Press, 1988) and "Trickster Discourse: Comic Holotropes and Language Games," in *Narrative Chance: Postmodern Essays on Native American Literature* (Albuquerque, N.Mex.: University of New Mexico Press, 1989).
14. Emphasis mine. See Vincent Crapanzano, "Hermes' Dilemma: The Masking of Subversion in Ethnographic Description," in *Writing Culture,* ed. James Clifford and George Marcus (Berkeley: University of California Press, 1986).
15. Geertz, *Works and Lives,* 23.
16. See Gayatri Spivak, *The Post-Colonial Critic* (New York: Routledge, 1990).
17. Spivak, "Deconstructing Historiography," 200.
18. Ibid.

19. Dell Hymes, *Reinventing Anthropology* (New York: Vintage, 1974); Talal Asad, *Anthropology and the Colonial Encounter* (London: Ithaca, 1973); Richard Fox, introduction to *Recapturing Anthropology*, ed. Richard Fox (Santa Fe, N. Mex.: School of American Research, 1991); Michaela di Leonardo, *Gender at the Cross-roads of Knowledge* (Berkeley: University of California Press, 1991); Faye Harrison, *Decolonizing Anthropology* (Washington, D.C.: AAA Monograph, 1991); Michelle Rosaldo and Louise Lamphere, *Woman, Culture, and Society* (Stanford, Calif.: Stanford University Press, 1974); and Rayna Rapp, *Toward an Anthropology of Women* (New York: Monthly Review, 1975).

20. Eleanor Leacock and Mona Etienne, *Women and Colonialism* (New York: Monthly Review, 1980), and Maria Mies, ed., *Women: The Last Colony* (London: Zed, 1989). The reasons for this are too intricate to detail here, but I believe they are related to the form second-wave feminism took in the United States and the tendency, at this historical moment, to argue the primacy of race or class or sex as single determinants of oppression, rather than as simultaneous or multiple axes of oppression.

21. Marnia Lazreg, "Feminism and Difference: The Perils of Writing as a Woman on Women in Algeria," *Feminist Studies* 14, no. 1 (Spring 1988): 96.

22. In a particularly unfortunate move, some feminists have taken simplistic exception to Paul Rabinow's contention that we "study up" rather than attempting the problematic project of "giving voice" to dominant or marginal groups. They argue that "an exclusive focus on the elite, eschewing the dominated or marginal, is a dangerous if comfortable, correction." I am of the opinion that "studying up" continues to be a valuable yet underemphasized practice in anthropology. See Paul Rabinow, "Representations Are Social Facts," in *Writing Culture,* ed. James Clifford and George Marcus. See also Frances Mascia-Lees et al., "The Post-Modern Turn in Anthropology," *Signs* (1989).

23. James Clifford, "Traveling Cultures," in *Cultural Studies,* ed. L. Grossberg et al.

24. Ibid., 100.

25. See Deborah d'Amico-Samuel, "Undoing Fieldwork: Personal, Political, Theoretical, and Methodological Implications," in *Decolonizing Anthropology,* ed. F. Harrison (1991). See also Akhil Gupta and James Ferguson, "Beyond 'Culture': Space, Identity, and the Politics of Difference," *Cultural Anthropology* 7 (1992): 6–23.

26. David Scott, "Locating the Anthropological Subject: Post-colonial Anthropologists in Other Places," *Inscriptions* 5 (1989).

27. Ibid., 27.

28. Ibid., 79.

29. Mary John, "Postcolonial Feminists in the Western Intellectual Field: Anthropologists and Native Informants?" *Inscriptions* 5 (1989): 55.

30. Ibid., 62.

31. Ibid., 50.

32. Ibid.

33. Arjun Appadurai, "Introduction: Place and Voice in Anthropological Theory," *Cultural Anthropology* 3, no. 1.

34. However, see Sherry Ortner, "Reading America: Preliminary Notes on Class and Culture," in *Recapturing Anthropology*.

35. Biddy Martin and Chandra Talpade Mohanty, "Feminist Politics: What's Home Got to Do with It?" in *Feminist Studies/Critical Studies,* ed. Teresa de Lauretis (Bloomington: Indiana University Press, 1986), 196.

36. Ibid., 208.

37. Claude Lévi-Strauss, *Tristes Tropiques* (1955; reprint, New York: Atheneum, 1975).

38. See Paul Rabinow, *Reflections on Fieldwork in Morocco* (Berkeley: University of California Press, 1977), 2.
39. Laura Nader, *Reinventing Anthropology* (New York: Vintage, 1974), 303.
40. Rabinow, *Reflections on Fieldwork in Morocco*, 1.
41. Caren Kaplan, "Reconfigurations of Geography and Narrative: A Review Essay," *Public Culture* 3, no. 1 (1990): 25.
42. Clifford, "Traveling Cultures," 100.
43. Angie Chabram, "Chicana/o Studies as Oppositional Ethnography," *Cultural Studies* 4, no. 3 (1990): 234.
44. Ibid., 230.
45. Harry Middleton Hyatt, *The Millers of Millersburg, Kentucky* (n.d.)
46. Harry Middleton Hyatt, *Descendants of John Walton of Baltimore, Md. and Harrison Co., Kentucky*, 12.
47. I am reminded here of the very different effects knowledge of a slave-owning grandfather had on Patricia Williams's sense of self and identity. See her "Gilded Lilies and Liberal Guilt" and "On Being the Object of Property," in *The Alchemy of Race and Rights* (Cambridge, Mass.: Harvard University Press, 1991).
48. Ursula Le Guin, *The Dispossessed* (New York: Avon, 1974), 44.
49. Arjun Appadurai, "Global Ethnoscapes: Notes and Queries for a Transnational Anthropology," in *Recapturing Anthropology*, 196.
50. Ibid.
51. Ibid., 202.
52. Ibid., 208.
53. Aurora Levins Morales and Rosario Morales, *Getting Home Alive* (Ithaca, N.Y.: Firebrand Books, 1986), 26.
54. See Gupta and Ferguson, "Beyond 'Culture.'"
55. Emphasis mine. Gilles Deleuze and Félix Guattari, "What Is a Minor Literature?" reprinted in *Out There: Marginalization and Contemporary Cultures* (1986; reprint, New York: New American Museum, 1986), 60.
56. Appadurai, "Global Ethnoscapes," 192.
57. Caren Kaplan, "Deterritorializations: The Rewriting of Home and Exile in Western Feminist Discourse," *Cultural Critique* 6 (1987): 191.
58. Ibid.
59. R. Radhakrishnan, "Transnationalism: Questions of Perspective," in *Theory and Postcoloniality: Neither One nor Other* (London: Blackwell, 1993), 1–2.
60. Ibid., 3.
61. Appadurai, "Global Ethnoscapes," 194.
62. Ibid., 202
63. See Rabinow, "Representations are Social Facts," in *Writing Culture*, ed. Clifford and Marcus.
64. Bruce Robbins, "Comparative Cosmopolitanism," *Social Text* 31, no. 32 (1992): 181.
65. Ibid., 173.
66. Richard Fox, introduction to *Recapturing Anthropology*, 5.
67. Gupta and Ferguson, "Beyond 'Culture.'"
68. KumKum Bhavnani and Margaret Coulson, "Transforming Socialist-Feminism: The Challenge of Racism," *Feminist Review* 23 (June 1986).
69. Marilyn Strathern, *Partial Connections* (London: Rowman and Littlefield, 1991), 22. See also Aijaz Ahmad's bold assertion that cosmopolitan location refers explicitly to the desire of postcolonial intellectuals to be located in the West. Aijaz Ahmad, "Orientalism and After: Ambivalence and Cosmopolitan Location in the Work of Edward Said," *Economic and Political Weekly* (Bombay) (July 25, 1992).

70. bell hooks, "Homeplace: A Site of Resistance," in *Yearning: Race, Gender, and Cultural Politics* (Boston: South End, 1990), 42.
71. Ibid.
72. Ibid., 46.
73. Kaplan, "Deterritorializations," 191.
74. Strathern, *Partial Connections,* 21.

7. Identifying Ethnography

I would like to thank Kirin Narayan, Renato Rosaldo, and especially Rina Benmayor for comments on versions of this essay. I thank also Chandra Mohanty for inviting me to speak on the panel "Theorizing Asia: The Pedagogy and Practice of Asian Studies in the U.S. Academy," Hamilton College, October 17, 1991, where I first had a chance to elaborate some of the ideas expressed here, and Una Choudhuri for including me in a panel discussion of Indu Krishnan's film *Knowing Her Place* for the NYU Performance Studies Intercultural Symposia, March 24, 1992.

1. See, for example, Gayatri Spivak, *The Post-Colonial Critic* (New York: Routledge, 1990), 65, 91.
2. Gauri Bhat, "Tending the Flame: Thoughts on Being Indian-American," *COSAW Bulletin* 7, nos.3–4) (1992): 1–2.
3. Ibid., 2.
4. Ibid., 4.
5. See also José Limon, "The Folk Performance of Chicano and the Cultural Limits of Political Ideology," in *Social Process and Cultural Image in Texas Folklore,* ed. R. Bauman and R. D. Abrahams (Austin: University of Texas Press, 1981), for discussion of the terms *Chicano* versus *Mexican-American,* and Rosa Linda Fregoso and Angie Chabram, "Chicana/o Cultural Representations: Reframing Alternative Critical Discourse," *Cultural Studies* 4, no. 3 (1990): 3–12. Rina Benmayor, A. Juarbe, C. Alvarez, and Blanca Vazquez, "Responses to Poverty among Puerto Rican Women," *Report to Joint Committee for Public Policy Research on Contemporary Hispanic Issues of the Inter-University Program for Latino Research* (New York: Hunter College, 1992). Rosa Torruellas, Rina Benmayor, A. Goris, and A. Juarbe, "Affirming Cultural Citizenship in the Puerto Rican Community: Critical Literacy and the El Barrio Popular Education Program," *Centro Cultural Studies Task Force, Language and Education Task Force* (New York: Hunter College, CUNY, 1991).
6. See Stuart Hall, "Cultural Identity and Cinematic Representation," *Framework* 36 (1989): 68–81, and Paul Gilroy, "It Ain't Where You're from, It's Where You're At," *Third Text* no. 13 (1990).
7. This is not a unique phenomenon for second- or third-generation groups. ABC, for example, is also slang for "American Born Chinese."
8. Salman Rushdie, *The Satanic Verses* (Consortium, 1988), 54.
9. Bhat, "Tending the Flame," 4.
10. Bharati Mukherjee, "The 400-Year-Old Woman," *San Francisco Review of Books* 16, no. 3 (1991). See also Nita Kumar, *Friends, Brothers, and Informants* (Berkeley: University of California Press, 1992).
11. Meena Alexander, "Language and Shame: Reflections on My Life in Letters," *Ikon* 12, no. 13 (1992): 20.
12. Ibid., 21.
13. Ibid., 23.
14. Nasser Hussein, "Hyphenated Identity: Nationality Discourse, History, and the Anxiety of Criticism in Salman Rushdie's *Shame*," in *Qui Parle?* (Summer 1990): 8.

15. Cited in ibid., 11.
16. Ibid., 10
17. Ibid.
18. Trinh T. Minh-ha, *When the Moon Waxes Red* (New York: Routledge, 1991), 157.
19. Ibid., 159.
20. As Chandra Mohanty writes, "women of color" "often used interchangeably with third world women ... is a term which designates a political constituency, not a biological or even a sociological one. It is a sociopolitical designation for people of African, Caribbean, Asian and Latin American descent, and native people of the U.S. What seems to constitute 'women of color' or 'third world women' as a viable oppositional alliance is a common context of struggle, rather than color or racial identification." See her "Cartographies of Struggle," in *Third World Women and the Politics of Feminism,* ed. Chandra Mohanty et al. (Bloomington: Indiana University Press, 1991).
21. Mukherjee, "The 400-Year-Old Woman," 7.
22. Spivak, *The Post-Colonial Critic,* 62.
23. The place of the "Aryan" in the construction of South Asian identities has a long and complicated history that cannot be fully discussed here. In 1923, for example, the U.S. Supreme Court disallowed the claim of a Punjabi Sikh to be considered a member of the Caucasian race. See Baida Nath Varma, "Indians as New Ethnics," in *The New Ethnics,* ed. Saran and Eames (New York: Praeger, 1980), 29.
24. Sunita Sorabhji, "Indians Win Minority Status," *The Indian-American* (September 1991).
25. See Karen Leonard, "Pioneer Voices from California: Reflections on Race, Religion, and Ethnicity," in *The Sikh Diaspora,* ed. N. Gerald Barrier and V. Dusenberry (Columbia, Mo.: South Asia Books, 1989), and her book *Making Ethnic Choices* (Philadelphia, Pa.: Temple University Press, 1991).
26. See Marcelle Williams, "Ladies on the Line: Punjabi Cannery Workers in Central California," in *Making Waves: An Anthology of Writings by and about Asian American Women* (Boston: Beacon, 1989).
27. "One can say that the earlier Indian immigrants, living mainly in the Fresno Valley of California ... maintain their cultural identity ... but have not quite access to the primary group network of power holders in American society. Their position is lower-middle-class.... As compared to them, the newer immigrants of the 1960's and 1970's are in the upper-middle to upper-class structure of the occupational ladder." In Varma, "Indians as New Ethnics," in *The New Ethnics,* ed. Saran and Eames, 38.
28. Mukherjee, "The 400-Year-Old Woman," 7.
29. Ibid., 56.
30. Kalpana Vrudhula, " 'Rentike cheddah revadi, Nenu ikkada unnanu' (*'Do Not Belong to This or That, but I Am Here'*)," *COSAW Bulletin* 7, nos. 3–4 (1992): 10–13.
31. Ibid.
32. Bhat, "Tending the Flame," 3.
33. Ibid.
34. Leonard, "Pioneer Voices from California," 134.
35. Ibid., 121.
36. Kartar Dhillon, "Parrot's Beak," in *Making Waves: Asian Women United of California* (Boston: Beacon, 1989), 214–15.
37. Mukherjee, "The 400-Year-Old Woman," 56. See also Nita Kumar, *Friends, Brothers, and Informants,* 13.
38. Indira Ganesan, *The Journey* (New York: Knopf, 1990), 44–45.

39. "Indians can be classified as new ethnics because their migration to the U.S. started first as a trickle in 1895 and reached its peak of 5,000 immigrants in San Francisco in 1910.... In 1922 there were 2,600 Indians in the U.S. but in 1940 only 2,400 were counted. Of the more than 3,000 Indians in 1950, the student population was 1,500. In 1946 rigid immigration laws gave India an annual quota of 100, which was not changed until the Immigration Act of 1965. Then started the second wave of immigration." Varma, "Indians as New Ethnics," in *The New Ethnics,* ed. Saran and Eames, 29.

40. Spivak, *The Post-Colonial Critic,* 83.

41. See Smadar Lavie and Ted Swedenburg, introduction to *Displacement, Diaspora, and Geographies of Identity* (Durham, N.C.: Duke University Press, forthcoming 1993).

42. Dorinne Kondo, *Crafting Selves: Power, Gender, and Discourses of Identity in a Japanese Workplace* (Chicago: University of Chicago Press, 1990), 300.

43. Renato Rosaldo, *Culture and Truth* (Boston: Beacon, 1989), xi.

44. Lata Mani, "Multiple Mediations: Feminist Scholarship in the Age of Multinational Reception," *Feminist Review* no. 35 (Summer 1990): 24-41.

45. Kirin Narayan, *Storytellers, Saints, and Scoundrels* (Delhi: Motilal Banarsidass, 1992), ix.

46. Ibid.

47. Ibid., x.

48. Ibid., 8.

49. Lila Abu-Lughod, "Writing against Culture," in *Recapturing Anthropology,* ed. Richard Fox (Santa Fe, N. Mex.: SAR Press, 1991), 140.

50. Ibid., 143.

51. Ibid., 142.

52. Amitav Ghosh, *In an Antique Land* (Delhi: Ravi Dayal Press, 1992). See also his "The Iman and the Indian," *Granta* 20 (Winter 1986).

53. Narayan, *Storytellers, Saints, and Scoundrels,* 7.

54. Kirin Narayan, "How Native Is a Native Anthropologist?" *American Anthropologist* (forthcoming 1993).

55. Rosaldo, *Culture and Truth,* 180.

56. E. Valentine Daniel, *Fluid Signs: Being a Person in the Tamil Way* (Berkeley: University of California Press, 1984), 56.

57. Gilles Deleuze and Félix Guattari, "What Is a Minor Literature?" in *Out There: Marginalization and Contemporary Cultures* (1986; reprint, New York: New American Museum, 1990).

58. Paula Gunn Allen, *The Woman Who Owned the Shadows* (New York: Strawberry, 1983).

59. Gloria Anzaldúa, "Speaking in Tongues: A Letter to Third World Women," in *This Bridge Called My Back* (Persephone Press, 1981), 165.

60. Gloria Anzaldúa, Borderlands/La Frontera (San Francisco: Spinster's, 1987), 59. See also Norma Alarcón's essay "Anzaldúa's Frontera: Inscribing Gynetics," in *Displacement, Diaspora, and Geographies of Identity,* ed. Smadar Lavie, and T. Swedenburg (Durham, N.C.: Duke University Press, 1993).

61. James Clifford, *The Predicament of Culture* (Cambridge, Mass.: Harvard University Press, 1988), 271.

62. Ibid., 275.

63. Ibid., 269.

64. Kondo, *Crafting Selves,* 302.

65. Ibid.

66. Dorinne Kondo, "M. Butterfly: Orientalism, Gender, and a Critique of Essentialist Identity," *Cultural Critique* (Fall 1990): 14.
67. Spivak, *The Post-Colonial Critic,* 66.
68. Rosaldo, *Culture and Truth,* 180.
69. Kondo, *Crafting Selves,* 300.
70. Ibid., 304.
71. See, for example, bell hooks, "Culture to Culture: Ethnography and Cultural Studies as Critical Intervention," in *Yearning: Race, Gender, and Cultural Politics* (Boston: South End, 1990).
72. Angie Chabram, "Chicana/o Studies as Oppositional Ethnography," *Cultural Studies* 4, no. 3 (1990): 238.
73. Ibid., 235.
74. Ibid., 238–39.
75. Ibid., 237.
76. Linda Alcoff, "The Problem of Speaking for Others," *Cultural Critique* (Winter 1991): 5–32. Joan Scott, "The Evidence of Experience," *Critical Inquiry* 17, no. 4 (Summer 1991): 777.
77. Scott, "The Evidence of Experience."
78. Ibid., 779.
79. Chabram, "Chicana/o Studies," 242.
80. Geertz, *Works and Lives,* 89–90.
81. Toni Morrison, "The Site of Memory," in *Out There: Marginalization and Contemporary Cultures* (New York: New American Museum, 1990), 299.
82. Hall, "Cultural Identity and Cinematic Representation," 68.
83. Janet Varner Gunn, *Autobiography: Toward a Poetics of Experience* (Philadelphia: University of Pennsylvania Press, 1982), 141.
84. For some fine instigatory autobiography see Patricia J. Williams, *The Alchemy of Race and Rights* (Cambridge, Mass.: Harvard University Press, 1991).
85. Rina Benmayor, Ana Juarbe, Celia Alvarez, and Blanca Vázquez, "Stories to Live By: Continuity and Change in Three Generations of Puerto Rican Women," in *Centro Working Paper Series. Oral History Task Force* (New York: Hunter College, CUNY, 1987), 2.
86. Ibid., 3.
87. Rosa Torruellas, Rina Benmayor, Anneris Goris, and Ana Juarbe, "Affirming Cultural Citizenship." Also Rina Benmayor, Ana Juarbe, Celia Alvarez, and Blanca Vázquez, "Responses to Poverty among Puerto Rican Women," 4.
88. Benmayor, Juarbe, Alvarez, and Vázquez, "Responses to Poverty," 72.
89. Ibid., 58.
90. Hall, "Cultural Identity and Cinematic Representation."
91. My own view is that such identities are context dependent. When I am reluctant to claim membership in the latter two coalitions, it is because I am concerned my bases of privilege would work against the political efficacy of the coalitions, not for lack of felt affinity with them.
92. Kumar, *Friends, Brothers, and Informants,* 5.
93. Laura Angel, "Interviewing the Self," senior thesis, Lang Undergraduate College, BA/MA anthropology program, New School for Social Research. May 1993.

8. Introductions to a Diary

I would like to thank Pankajam and Mythili Sivaraman for sharing with me some of their own stories, as well as their stories about Subbalakshmi. I am grateful to them for their kind patience and faith in this enterprise. I hope the effort has been worth the long wait. I also thank S. Anandhi for introducing me to the Sivaraman family.

1. While I have many difficulties with Ashis Nandy's argument, I refer here to his understanding of a secularism founded on mutual respect for all religions. See "The Tolerance of Secularism and the Recovery of Religious Tolerance," in *Mirrors of Violence,* ed. Veena Das (Delhi: Oxford University Press, 1990).

2. See Pierre Bourdieu, *Outline of a Theory of Practice* (Cambridge: Cambridge University Press, 1977).

3. See, for example, Dipesh Chakravarty, "The Difference-Deferral of (a) Colonial Modernity: Public Debates and Domesticity in British Bengal," *Subaltern Studies* 8 (1993), for a discussion of the emerging nationalist regime of domesticity.

4. Leila Ahmed, "Between Two Worlds: The Formation of a Turn-of-the-Century Egyptian Feminist," in *Life/Lines,* ed. Bella Brodzki and Celeste Schenck (Ithaca, N.Y.: Cornell University Press, 1988).

5. Sumit Sarkar, *Modern India: 1885–1947* (Delhi: Macmillan, 1983), 217. According to Sarkar, "The suppression of this revolt left 2,337 rebels killed, 1,652 wounded, and no less than 45,404 prisoners."

6. Dipesh Chakrabarty, "Who Speaks for Indian Pasts?" *Representations* 37 (Winter 1992), 9.

7. Ibid.

8. Ibid., 25.

Index

Index

Index

Kamala Visweswaran received her Ph.D. from Stanford University in 1990 and now teaches anthropology at the graduate faculty of the New School for Social Research in New York. She has worked in India since 1987 and is currently completing a manuscript on women and Indian nationalism.

Pushpamala N. (artist of *The Voyage,* reproduced on the cover) lives and works in Bombay, India. She studied sculpture at the M.S. University, Baroda, India, and has worked with a variety of media, juxtaposing folk and popular sources with contemporary images.